D1474126

# From Strategy to Execution

Daniel Pantaleo · Nirmal Pal
Editors

# From Strategy
# to Execution

Turning Accelerated Global Change
into Opportunity

 Springer

*Editors*

Dr. Daniel Pantaleo
SAP AG
Global Communications
3999 West Chester Pike
Newton Square, PA 19073
USA
daniel.pantaleo@sap.com

Nirmal Pal
4 Gettysburg Rd
Southbury, CT 06488
USA
nirmalpal@psu.edu

ISBN 978-3-540-71879-6          e-ISBN 978-3-540-71880-2

DOI 10.1007/978-3-540-71880-2

Library of Congress Control Number: 2008920729

*Production:* le-tex Jelonek, Schmidt & Vöckler GbR, Leipzig
*Cover design:* WMX Design GmbH, Heidelberg

Printed on acid-free paper

9 8 7 6 5 4 3 2 1

springer.com

*To my wife, Judy, and all my daughters, Elizabeth, Sarah, Schotland, and Briannon, for their love and sustaining encouragement.*

*– Daniel C Pantaleo*


*To my wife, Mitra, my daughters Neela and Nupur, and my grand children Nina, Nikhil and Sophia Malini for their sustaining love and support.*

*– Nirmal Pal*

# FOREWORD

By Clayton M. Christensen
*Robert & Jane Cizik Professor of Business Administration*
*Harvard Business School*

Innovation sure seems hard, at least as evidenced by the track record of those seeking to innovate. Every time venture capitalists put money into a company they think it will be successful – and yet on average, only two out of ten companies that they invest in become commercially successful. Every time corporate executives invest to develop a new product, they think it will succeed. And yet most product development projects get cancelled before the projects reach completion. And of those that are completed and launched into their markets, 75% fail commercially. That's right. After those responsible for those new products do their market research, and after they test-market the products, still 75% fail. Innovation sure seems hard.

I remember when I was first taught the principles of quality management in manufacturing 30 years ago; that I was taught that manufacturing quality was random. We learned how to plot Statistical Process Control (SPC) charts, in which we'd make a part for a product, and then measure its critical dimensions or performance parameters. There was a center line on the chart – the target that we hoped we'd hit – and there were upper and lower control limits. The spread between these limits was the tolerance that the product's engineers decided was allowable. As we'd plot our production on this chart, dot by dot, there was a maddening scatter around the center line – it just seemed impossible to get it exactly right, every time. I remember being taught at that time that the reason for the scatter plot was that there was just an element of randomness in our manufacturing process. Believing in that randomness, we were therefore taught methods for coping with that randomness. We were taught sophisticated sampling algorithms for inspection, so we could reject bad lots before they were shipped to the customer – and customers were warned that we could not guarantee that every part met spec. So the customers often inspected *every* part – all to cope with the alleged randomness of manufacturing.

Of course, we have subsequently discovered that manufacturing isn't random. Whenever we get a deviation from the result we expect, it has a cause. It just appears to be random because we haven't known what caused it. The quality movement, and Toyota in particular, have subsequently given us tools to learn the right lessons from our mistakes – to figure out one by one the factors that caused our failure to produce a perfect product; and then to learn how to control those factors. So today, manufacturing in most industries seems to be more a predictable science than an art whose outcomes are intrinsically inconsistent. But it was not always so.

I believe that our understanding of the processes of innovation until very recently has been where the manufacturing quality movement was 30 years ago. Most managers and students of the problem assert that we cannot predict in advance which new ideas, products and businesses will become commercially successful innovation because innovation at its core is a random process. Believing this, they then recommend how to better cope with this unpredictability – just like the leaders of the quality movement advised 30 years ago. Recommendations include "letting a thousand flowers bloom;" "bringing Silicon Valley inside," and "failing fast" all reflect the "inspection" mentality that pervaded manufacturing in the prior generation. The entire venture capital industry, in fact, has been structured around the belief that even the best investors just can't pick the winners ahead of time – so they've structured the industry to hedge their bets against the alleged randomness of innovation. If you want two significant commercial successes, you've got to try ten – and you put them on a short leash so that you won't keep pouring good money after bad. It's akin to our practice of inspecting parts at early points in the manufacturing process so we wouldn't keep adding value to products that were going to be rejected anyway.

I believe that successful innovation is nearly as unpredictable as historically has seemed the case. Rather, the unpredictability stems from sloppy scholarship on the part of many academics and consultants who have studied the problem; of the pervasive tendency to seek simple answers to a complex, systemic challenge; and of our pervasive proclivity to learn the wrong lessons from our experience. We accept at face value the "best practices of successful companies," rather than seeking to learn, as Toyota has taught us, to seek the root cause of our failures. Nobody has distilled innovation into a cookbook yet – a set of formulae which, if followed, will guarantee a masterpiece every time. But I think it is a lot more predictable than we have thought – provided, of course, that we use valid theories to guide our decisions, and don't apply a good formula in an inappropriate situation.

I have expunged the unmodified term "innovation" from my vocabulary – because innovation isn't innovation. There are important distinctions in the types of innovation – and the methods that yield success in one type of innovation often cause failures with others. In developing new products, some innovations simply entail improving the individual components from which the product is assembled. Others entail re-conceptualizing the fundamental architecture of the products – dividing, combining or eliminating components, or re-defining the role that each plays in the performance of the product. Other innovations relate to processes rather than products – but process innovation also can be divided into improvements within individual steps, vs. defining fundamentally different process architectures. These types need to be managed very differently.

Many product and process innovations fail because their commercial success required them to be embedded within a business model innovation – and the managers involved sought false economies by trying to leverage an inappropriate business model. It turns out that this is a very common cause of failure.

Here's a way to visualize what happens. Imagine that you were a member of Congress, and you come up with a great idea for a governmental program that will address an important societal need. So you draft a bill, and introduce it into the legislative process. Not long after you introduce it, you get a letter from a powerful labor union asserting that they will block it, unless you modify certain provisions so that it solves problems they perceive in the program. Then a short time later you get a call from a powerful senator from Texas who chairs the committee that must approve your legislation in order for it to be considered by the full body. He informs you that unless you add provisions that help Texas, he'll line up his friends to defeat it. Then the Minority Whip calls with the same message – she doesn't think she can assure the required votes unless you make a host of additional changes, to make it attractive to, or overcome objections raised by, powerful legislators whose support will be critical to passage. By the time your bill finally is enacted into law, you've had to morph and modify your original idea into something that is scarcely recognizable – but you have to do it, in order to win the support of the powerful people whose votes are necessary for your proposal to be enacted at all.

A very similar process occurs in the funding of innovation. Never does an innovative idea pop out of a person's head as a fully fleshed-out business plan. It always emerges in half-baked condition, and it needs to get shaped into a business plan that can get funding from the corporate treasury. So you draft a plan and circulate it to the powerful people whose support will be required. Within a short time you get a call from the sales manager – who announces that he won't support it unless you change your value proposition to appeal to the company's best customers, with whom the sales force has great relationships. Then the engineering manager sends you a note, insisting that you re-use several component designs that already are in the library, rather than doing everything from scratch. Then the CFO calls and says she'll just block your plan, unless you change the pricing and margin structure so that it fits the company's economic model better – and so on. The business plan that comes out of this process is a very different one than went in – but it had to happen this way, in order for the innovation to win approval for funding from the powerful people and entities whose support is essential. This process is at work in every company, all of the time. But its effect is to morph and modify the original idea *into a product and business plan that fits the business model of the company,* rather than the market where the need was originally identified. In the circumstance that we've called *sustaining innovation*, this "legislative" process of resource allocation is a *good* process. But in disruptive circumstances, the process will cause the innovation to fail.

Discerning managers need to understand what *causes* customers to buy a product – not what customer characteristics are correlated with a propensity to purchase, but what *job* arises in the life of a customer that would *cause* him or her to "hire," or purchase the product. This insight, and only this insight, can enable the innovator to define a value proposition that will connect with this causal mechanism. Then these managers need to assess that sort of team structure needs to be employed, given the nature of the product or process innovation. And she needs to think through the sort of business model that will be required to take the value proposition to the targeted customers in the appropriate way. In the cases of established markets, a viable strategic plan can be formulated in advance, and then implemented. In cases where the market does not exist, the project needs to be managed so that a viable strategy can evolve. The financial metrics that are appropriate measures of value for one type of innovation will yield grossly inaccurate measures of value for others. And so on.

Innovating successfully certainly isn't simple. But it's not random. Recent research has significantly clarified for discerning managers how the winning formula must differ, depending on the different circumstances in which they might find themselves, as typified in the paragraph above.

I hope that those who read this volume will read it with this type of discerning eye. Don't look for blanket best practices of successful innovators. There are none. Don't comb through these chapters for simple silver-bullet solutions. There are none. Rather, each of these authors has picked a dimension of the problem – and hopefully, each gives you enough for you to satisfactorily answer the question you always must ask as a discerning reader: what's the sort of circumstance when this will work, and when won't it?

My hope is that because the editors who have architected this volume and many of those who have written its chapters have tried to help us understand the circumstance-contingent complexity of innovation, this will be an important contribution to what we know about this crucial challenge.

*The Harvard University Graduate School of Business Administration*
*Boston, Massachusetts*
*November, 2007*

# ACKNOWLEDGMENTS

In the first decade of the new millennium we are witnessing an ever increasing pace of change in all spheres of business and in all geographies, which impact both large and small enterprises. Globalization is shifting the centers of value creating activities as collaboration and coordination across national and enterprise boundaries are becoming the essence of competitive advantage. Successful enterprises are beginning to respond rapidly to these changes with innovations not only in business processes, product, and services, but also with innovations in fundamental business models and profit models, and the application of technology to support these innovations. These innovations provide sustainable competitive power with longer term success depending on the ability to connect thought and action, theory and practice, and business and technology from strategy formulation to tactical execution.

To fully understand the pervasive implications of these innovations in all spheres of business and to develop new business priorities require a wider collaboration among technologies, human competencies, policies, cultures and business models. That is precisely why we invited recognized thought leaders representing each of these segments from academia, industry, and think tanks, to share their experiences and insights on the opportunities and challenges associated with getting corporate innovations from strategy to execution. We are deeply grateful to our contributing authors for finding time from their busy schedules to prepare their contributions and for their patience in dealing with numerous editorial changes. In the end we are proud for the orderly collection of their thoughts and insights which, we hope, will make this book a must read for all business executives and managers.

We also thank our publisher, Springer, and specially Dr. Werner A. Mueller, Vice President, Business/Economics and Statistics, for recognizing the potential of this book and encouraging us to complete the manuscript with speed.

We thank Annette M Woods for helping us with copy editing the manuscript, Ray Liddick of Open Door Visions for helping us with typesetting and Cali Buckley for Index preparation.

Daniel C Pantaleo and Nirmal Pal,
Newtown Square, Pennsylvania, November, 2007

# TABLE OF CONTENTS

# SECTION 1:

# THE ACCELERATING PACE OF CHANGE

## 1.1

# GLOBAL IMPERATIVES – THE ACCELERATING PACE OF CHANGE

**Daniel Pantaleo**, *VP, SAP Global Communications*
**Nirmal Pal**, *Executive Director Emeritus, SMEAL College of Business, Pennsylvania State University*

## INTRODUCTION

The 21st century has brought with it an increase in the already rapid pace of change in all spheres of life and business. Successful enterprises have begun to respond to these changes by constantly evaluating and adjusting their business processes, business strategies, operations structure, financial models, and the speed of execution of their businesses. This process of constant evaluation and adjustment is the survival trait of companies within the hyper-competitive marketplace of the global, digital economy. Organizations that are able to respond to opportunities by rapidly and constantly updating their business practices will maintain competitive advantage and sustain leadership in their markets.

## GLOBAL IMPERATIVES

In Figure 1 we have identified seven key management imperatives resulting from the accelerating pace of change based on research and documentation developed by the SAP Corporate Strategy Group[1] and the January 2006

*Figure 1: Global Imperatives*

McKinsey Quarterly[2]. These imperatives both individually and collectively present significant challenges and opportunities to the business leaders of today and are described below in more detail.

## 1. Globalization - The centers of gravity of economic value-creating activities are going through a profound change around the world.

The world is experiencing a rapid shift in the location of economic value-creating activities driven by an environment that has seen significant advances in global communications, technology innovations on many different fronts, market liberalizations in many geographies around the world and the availability of large pools of skilled labor in developing countries. The US, Europe and Japan will no longer be the exclusive and predominant geographies with at least four other emerging geographies, Brazil, Russia, India and China (the so-called BRIC countries), soon or already accomplishing parity. Other Asian countries will closely track behind them joined by East European, South American and other developing economies. Another key point to note is that value creation is not just shifting to these geographies. The process of how economic value is created is itself going through a profound change. The front office in the USA is already supported by a back office in India, the assembly line in Europe is supported by supply lines in China, and the design center in Japan is a virtual collaboration of teams in various parts of the connected world. Welcome to this multi-polar world! Thomas Friedman, in his celebrated book, the "World is Flat", talked about how communities, countries, and companies can and must adapt to leverage these profound changes for their own survival and success.

## 2. Innovation - There is an emerging focus on business model innovation.

Beyond product and process innovation, the innovation of business models is a major focus of corporate leadership. Companies are increasingly capable of continuously analyzing and adapting their value chains to assure the strategic application of resources. They are also able to define their markets and their ecosystems of suppliers, producers, and partners with increasing clarity. This holistic perspective has introduced opportunities to capitalize on dynamic co-innovation in the ecosystem. Based, moreover, on the painful lessons of many corporate Goliaths felled by upstart Davids, corporate leaders have also become far more alert to potential disruptions to their established market presence. This environment demands agility and constant attention but creates the opportunity for far more advantageous but risk-intensive innovation of business models. Business model innovation is increasingly identified by "C" level officers as both an always-present concern and an always-present opportunity. This is borne out by the results of both the benchmark SAP Business 2010 global study with the Economist Intelligence Unit as well as the IBM 2006 annual CEO survey in which corporate leaders cite business model innovation as a top-of-mind issue. As the core businesses of established corporations shrink, incremental growth and the growth from new customers will not sustain stable profit growth nor will it sustain the interest of investors or stockholders. The resulting 'growth gap' is increasingly being bridged by the introduction of innovative business models. Often self-disrupting and in turn disrupting the markets of competitors, these innovations lead to new businesses outside of the established market. Such actions limit the cannibalization of the core business while introducing new and significant revenue streams, usually through separate business operating structures and processes. To be successful, the introduction of such an innovative business model needs to dynamically balance the customer value proposition, the flexible assignment of resources and imaginative profit models. Ongoing studies by IBM and SAP are finding that the value return for investment made in business model innovation exceeds the gains from product or process innovation.

### 3. Corporate Strategy Management - Management of corporate strategy is increasingly being pursued analytically.

The technology enabled explosion of information can work against the focused execution of strategy. Senior managers responsible for the execution of corporate strategy and seeking to analytically manage that practice can easily be blinded into delayed action by the over abundance of information. As clearly addressed in their book, "Competing on Analytics – The New Science of Winning" Tom Davenport and Jeanne Harris offer several key insights into this situation. They explain that analytics can mean "… the extensive use of data, statistical and quantitative analysis, … predictive models, and fact-based management to drive decisions…"[3] They continue by pointing out that the results of analytics can drive both human decisions or fully automated decisions. Hence, with the increased sophistication and presentation of information, the same technological tools that created data overload are becoming more useful for isolating and identifying the key success elements for executing corporate strategy. Therefore I/T (hardware and software platforms) purchase decisions become corporate strategy decisions. CFOs and COOs are increasingly involved in the technology buy decisions because the I/T infrastructure must support the corporate business model, must allow for agility in the innovation of that model, and must be able to identify and present those key performance metrics of corporate strategy execution against that model. Analytics provides a lens for differentiating the elements for the successful management of corporate strategy. Clearly defining and monitoring business processes, being alert to potential disruptions, leveraging compliance and governance issues as execution advantages, and attracting, retaining, and developing talent are each attention points in the effective execution of corporate strategy. Analytics has a role in each of these.

### 4. Beyond Corporate Governance and Compliance - The corporate perception in society is increasingly important requiring that corporate citizenship and social responsibility need careful planning as well as strategic placement and management.

Increasing oil prices, global warming, the publicly incomprehensible size of CEO packages, and cases of corporate malfeasance are only a few of the examples causing the distrust of corporations in the public's view. As a result, the societal cost of doing business is increasing dramatically. It is becoming as important to convince the buying public that your corporation is a good corporate citizen as it is to demonstrate value and quality in your products, services, and corporate governance. The immediacy of the ripple effect in the global market means that Sarbanes-Oxley has mandated standards and practices even for companies beyond the United States' borders. Good practice in corporate governance and compliance are now just table stakes as corporate reputation is defined well beyond business practices and products. The journey into the uncertain domains of corporate social responsibility and corporate citizenship requires a clear vision and the same level of strategic execution as any business plan. In fact, corporate social responsibility and corporate citizenship are strategic components of a complete business model. The topical area where you chose to support a publicly visible corporate presence in the citizenship and social responsibility domain must make sense, be legitimate, and be believable. Positioning Lord Brown of BP as the spokesperson of a green-concerned company promoting the development of alternative energy sources created a substantial and positive public impact. What happens to that campaign with his unanticipated and early departure is yet to be seen. With the pervading SAP presence in the oil and gas industry, its support for the Extractive Industries Transparency Initiative makes sense and is believable. The EITI initiative seeks to overcome the "resource curse" and marries the enablement of economic diversification with better resource management. Since SAP has traditionally been a strong player in the effective management of corporate resources this support represents a legitimate corporate social responsibility stance. It is also important to be internally aware of the differences between corporate philanthropy, disaster response, corporate citizenship in local and regional community initiatives, and true corporate social responsibility. Clearly articulating the relationship and the differentiation among these options will assure the appropriate balance of people and fiscal support among them. Corporate social responsibility remains the longer-term, publicly visible reputation lever.

## 5. Expanding Knowledge Access - Creativity and value can result from understanding the new nature of work and how information and knowledge workers approach their work.

Search engines, engaging interfaces, ubiquitous corporate information and reporting systems, and even personalized portals customized to the key metrics the user needs on the job can do more than increase access to information. There is an increased focus on the Information Worker that has resulted in responses ranging from new systems supporting what are perceived as their unique needs to conferences, workshops and how-to articles for those who manage these workers. In truth, a new dimension has been added to the definition of the information worker as even individuals who we would not normally consider information workers access information sources and interpret such content on the job. Over the last five years there has been a sharp increase in the recognition by corporate leaders of the imperative to attract and retain talented employees - increasingly those employees are knowledge workers. According to John Seely Brown, "For the knowledge worker life is less linear; inputs and outputs are less well defined; and information is less 'targeted'. These are, rather, areas where making sense, interpreting, and understanding are both problematic and highly valued – areas where, above all, meaning and knowledge are at a premium."[4] In his book, "Thinking for a Living", Tom Davenport says, "Knowledge workers can either find knowledge, create it, package it, distribute it, or apply it."[4] Because the natural tendencies of knowledge workers to, for example, work alone and not readily share knowledge are counter to what a company needs in the dynamics of an agile workforce, it is important to know how to lead, inspire, and encourage these workers and create a productive knowledge work culture. Successful and high performing knowledge workers leverage the knowledge of others quickly to capitalize on new opportunities or solve tough problems. Knowledge workers also check ideas and perspectives with others from widely dispersed networks from which they gain career benefits, construct their sense of professional self, and ensure sound thinking. Such successful knowledge workers also understand that to get knowledge one often needs to give knowledge. Recognizing these characteristics and consciously structuring a knowledge work environment can help to assure the retention of successful knowledge workers and create an environment that attracts talented people.

## 6. Resurgence of Business and I/T Alignment – There is growing demand from business end-users and executives for real time, responsive and flexible I/T solutions.

The business user will continue to gain influence as a decision maker within the corporation relative to the chief information officer (CIO). The largely untapped business user community, including information and knowledge workers, will be a focus area for growth going forward. While winning the "heart" of the business end user with quality solutions is of strategic importance, understanding the needs of the chief financial officer (CFO), chief operating officer (COO) and other C level executives (CXO) who require and expect their I/T platforms and solutions to support their existing and changing business models and strategies is perhaps central. Business users and executives will demand that I/T solutions be central to the business strategy and serve as a competitive weapon to drive internal changes and cope with external changes. They will require that I/T solutions help them understand the changing needs and wants of their customers, and will demand more flexibility, openness, collaboration and speed from I/T solutions.[5] Business and I/T alignment will take on a new meaning with business demanding more on-demand synchronization of their I/T solutions with the realities of the business world. The growing body of knowledge addressing emerging platform strategies and the link between customized solutions and agile corporate strategy is evidence of the renewed interest in the alignment of I/T and corporate strategy.

## 7. The Rise of the Small-Medium Enterprise (SME) - Small-medium sized enterprises offer the opportunity for growth only for the knowledgeable.

The SME market remains relatively under-penetrated and will drive solid industry growth in the coming years across industry verticals. SMEs will enable innovation through ecosystem collaboration and co-innovation. Ubiquitous access to information and the World Wide Web give a small local company a global perspective and the ability to participate in the global value chain. Within the industry ecosystems, a few large enterprises will be supported by a increasing number of smaller and nimbler companies worldwide.

Large corporations who have been successful in winning at the high end of the market and who are alert to potential disruption from "good enough" solutions in the lower end of the market can look to the small and mid-sized space for growth if they proceed with care. To be successful in this new space, it is imperative that large corporations demonstrate an astute knowledge of the companies in this space and the special needs of SMEs. For example, service and product models must be different, go-to-market strategies must be reinvented, licensing agreements must break established molds, and new organizational structures must tolerate risk and not be forced to fit existing operational paradigms.

In addition, there is another massive yet quiet change that is taking place within developed economies, especially in USA; the shift to services-based businesses from both manufacturing- and agriculture-based businesses. As can be seen in the chart of US GDP analysis, services-based businesses in 2007 accounted for roughly 75 percent of US GDP and are projected to continue to grow rapidly in the near future. Service-based businesses are defined by co-creation of value by the provider and the consumer while the ability to leverage knowledge remains the essence of success. The emerging importance of knowledge work and the knowledge worker will continue to increase because of this shift. Of the total services-based businesses, Prof. Uday Karmarkar of UCLA estimates the Information Services businesses to be about 53 percent of the total and growing. The significance of this observation will be seen later in this chapter when we examine the intensity of change.

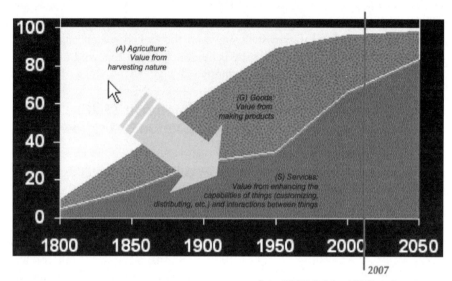

Source: US GDP Analysis and IBM Research

***Figure 2:*** *A Growing and Massive Shift to Services - Based Business*

## DIMENSIONS OF ACCELERATED CHANGE

*"The world is changing very fast. Big will not beat small any more. It will be fast beating the slow"*
*– Rupert Murdoch, Chairman and CEO, News Corporation.*

In a fast changing world it is your ability to anticipate and respond to change that is the formula for success and sustained performance. Bill Ford, the chairman of Ford Motor Company, recently said, "The business model that sustained us for decades is no longer sufficient to sustain profitability". In fact, just two days after Bill Ford made the above statement, he decided to resign as CEO at Ford, bringing in Alan Mulally from Boeing as the new CEO. The prevailing wisdom is that when fundamental and deep changes are required it is better to bring in a change agent from outside the industry. IBM took similar action in 1993, when Lou Gerstner was brought in to transform and run the ailing company.

The conclusion of the Global CEO study[6] conducted by IBM in 2006 is that "Worldwide, CEO's are not bracing for change; instead, they are embracing it." This study was conducted in spring, 2006 and included responses from 765 CEO's and business leaders from 20 different industries and 11 geographic regions from around the world. IBM executives conducted face to face interviews with 80 percent of these business leaders from companies large and small, some public and some privately held. A key insight from the survey suggests that, "surrounded by change on so many fronts, CEO's do not seem intimidated or content simply to cope. Instead they are embracing change." In fact, two out every three of the 765 CEO's surveyed worldwide said that they will have to make fundamental changes in their businesses over the next two years. In a similar study conducted by SAP and the Economist Intelligence Unit in 2004[7], an overwhelming majority of senior business leaders across the world identified continuous changes in market forces to have the greatest impact on their businesses in next three to five years.

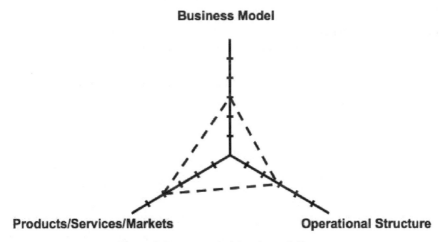

**Business Model**

**Products/Services/Markets**                **Operational Structure**

*Figure 3: Dimensions of Accelerated Change*

These fundamental changes will occur across three major dimensions of change, as seen in the figure above:

1. Business Model – Rethinking the value proposition of your business, rethinking the way you develop and deliver value to your most profitable customers, rethinking the financial model and the profit formula, and then making appropriate changes to the core resources of your organization.
2. Products/Services/Markets – Anticipating and sensing the changing needs and wants of your customers, and responding by making appropriate changes to your products/services and your go-to-market strategies.

3. Operational Structure – Reconfiguring your core resources, including key business processes, technology infrastructure and human capital, to correspond to the changes in business model and products/services/ markets as described in 1 and 2 above.

## Change Impacts on Business Models

*"In order to identify more aggressive growth platforms, many companies are being forced to challenge the traditional definitions of their business, and are motivated to redefine their business"*
*– John Hagel, Business Consultant and Author*

We define business model innovation as the ability to implement changes in your key resources and processes of the organization, in the customer value proposition, and in the profit formula of your business in order to substantially change the way you create value for your customers and business partners and other stakeholders of your business. An in-depth look at clearly defining business model innovation as well as the issues driving and determining the innovation of business models is considered in greater detail in Chapter 2.1.2.

Kimberly-Clark was primarily in the paper business for over 70 years, when Darwin Smith, then the chief executive, decided to sell all their paper mills and paper related businesses to focus on consumer goods like Kleenex and Huggies. Their success in competing with the best of the major consumer products companies is legendary and taught in business schools as an exemplar of business model change.

Consider the actions taken by computer hardware manufacturers like IBM, HP, and Dell. Their main focus was manufacturing, where a lot their assets were invested. As the competitive cost of outsourcing became impossible to ignore without any sacrifice of quality these companies outsourced manufacturing to their business partners and focused on research, design and development. IBM now claims to be in "business performance transformation" business for their customers. The recent sale of their personal computer division to Lenovo of China continues this focus on the profitable segments of their business while also supporting the development of a comprehensive China strategy and open source strategy. Unisys Corporation similarly divested their personal computer and other hardware manufacturing to focus on solutions and services, from which they derive over 70% of their present revenue.

During late 2006, INTEL suddenly announced that they will layoff ten thousand employees, about ten percent of their worldwide work force, in an effort to restructure the company. They had taken their eyes off of AMD, a fierce competitor and fast follower, who not only caught up with INTEL, but also exceeded INTEL in some areas. INTEL had successfully transformed their business in the past from memory chips to microprocessors, but was caught off guard by AMD and now has to take swift action to survive.

All of the above represent constant rethinking of the value proposition of the business model. In the words of Prof. Jay Conger of the London Business School, "The challenge for leaders is to build agile, perceptive organizations...Leaders must discipline themselves to continually reexamine their business models, engaging the entire organization to ask: Does our value proposition still make sense? What in our business model needs to be reinvented? Where are our non-customers going and why?"

If you fail to heed this advice, someone with a disruptive business model will soon eat your lunch.

## Change Impacts on Products and Services and Markets

*"Any new product has a competitive life cycle of about 12 months maximum. It's pretty clear that technology life cycles are shortening, and that new technologies and new products can be copied fairly quickly around the world"*
*– A.G. Lafley, President and CEO,*
*Proctor and Gamble Company.[8]*

Much has been written already on the subject of products and services innovation, but it takes on a new and important perspective in the world of perpetual and speedy change.

Figure 4 shows a simple way to analyze your products and services with regards to their life cycle and development times. Let us take an example from the automobile industry again. In the early 90's Ford Motor Company built a family sedan called the Taurus. It was the most successful family sedan of its time. Ford was very customer centric and each year made innovative changes to the design of this vehicle that made it a best seller for a number of years. But as their attention shifted to more profitable SUV's, Ford lost focus on continuous product innovation on the Taurus, and started to lose market share to the likes of the Honda Accord and the Toyota Camry. Ultimately, as we all know, in late 2006, Ford stopped producing the Taurus altogether; a sad commentary on Ford, but a good example of what happens if you do not continuously update products with short life cycles.

It would also be wrong to assume that product positioning on the matrix is fixed, as it will surely change with time as the needs and wants of the

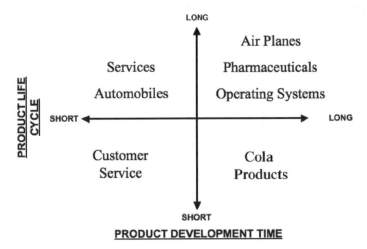

*Figure 4: Products and Services Innovation*

consumers change. In the last decade we have seen a rapid shortening of product life cycles combined with a faster increase in product development time and cost; a trend that is expected to continue in the near future.

Now let us look at go-to-market strategies and how someone with a disruptive strategy can upset the applecart. Dell comes to mind right away. Right from the beginning, Dell did not employ direct sales staff or sell through store fronts, but rather required their customers to come to them with phone first and with phone or Internet later. Until recently Dell was the worldwide market leader in the PC business, driving a 40 billion dollars business with great success.

Starbucks is another good example. Before Starbucks, coffee was a commodity selling for around one dollar. But with the creation of the Starbucks experience, people lined up for coffee and were happy to pay four times as much. Both Starbucks and Dell provide very good examples of disruptive strategies that went against the established norms, and became successful against competition by an order of magnitude.

## Change Impacts on Operational Structure

How you configure your key resources of worldwide human capital, business processes and infrastructure, along with the flexibility of this configuration will determine your success in this rapidly changing world. In the following sections we discuss the change impacts on these resources in more detail.

## Change Impacts on Key Business Processes and Human Capital

*"Most change initiatives that end up going nowhere don't fail because they lack grand visions and noble intentions. They fail because people can't see the reality they face"*
                                                                  *– Senge, et all (2004)*

Business processes are the underpinning of how value is designed, developed and delivered. Typically, business processes can be deconstructed into sub-processes and further to the lowest level process modules. These process modules then can be examined from the customer's perspective of value. If a process module is not adding value in today's environment it is adding cost and must be discarded. Alternatively, if the process module can be performed by your business partner more efficiently, then outsourcing can be a viable option. Effectiveness and efficiency will come from an organizations' ability to quickly combine or recombine a process from these modules as needed.

Business process changes are driven initially by implementing best of breed processes and then automating these processes with the latest proven technology. However, in a rapidly changing environment current best of breed must soon give way to next in breed. To maintain competitive advantage, it is necessary to invest in business process life cycle management, and continuously research next generation process automation software that will allow implementation of next practices at an economically acceptable cost level.

Simultaneous with the changes to your key business processes and the supporting technology infrastructure, you have to decide what human capital you need in terms of talent and skills, and where you need them in your geographically dispersed organization. This will require continuous retraining of your current employees and those of your business partners and hiring of new talent. As is well known, automobile manufacturing companies routinely outsource component modules to their suppliers and business partners to manufacture. Toyota, which is one of the most agile competitors in this industry, sends their engineers on assignments to their suppliers, sometimes for as long as two years, for training on the latest processes and technologies.

To stay with the automobile example, only a few years ago, companies like GM, Ford, and Chrysler used to take 50 plus labor hours to manufacture a car. Today, they can routinely produce a Ford Edge or a Buick Regal out of their assembly lines in 20 plus labor hours demonstrating remarkable agility of their manufacturing processes. However, Toyota or Honda can do the same in 17 labor hours, and more over, Toyota can produce different models of cars on their multi-platform assembly line. Thus Toyota has taken their process and operational flexibility far beyond the competition. While, as these top-end market contenders drive upscale, Tata motors seeks to serve today's non-consumers by developing a car for India for the equivalent of about $2,200 USD. This disruption expands the market by creating new consumers and provides an alternative to customers who do not value the benefits of high-end vehicles.

## Change Impacts on Infrastructure

> *"The Internet is the infrastructure through which organizations, both Old and New economy, will thrive. The reduction of friction and transaction costs facilitates collaboration on a worldwide basis – with customers, suppliers and partners. This collaboration and the efficiencies associated with it, creates competitive advantages that can't be ignored by any company that wishes to survive in the market place."* – Michael Dell, Chairman, Dell Inc.

Formalized services are the language and building blocks of efficient change management as they will provide a built-in mechanism for an enterprise to continuously sense customer reaction to the value proposition offered by the enterprise. These formalized services could be both product-based and services-based, and could be either internal or external to an organization.

Formalized services also form the basis of composing and recomposing process modules in a systematic way so as to ensure the overall value proposition of the recombined process. Agility will come from the ability to do this quickly on an as needed basis using the latest technology. This capability is referred to as the *service oriented architecture* (SOA) in the technology press.

A good example of using such service oriented architecture to build on-demand process automation can be seen in pricing applications at Amazon. com. Amazon, as we all know, sells not only books, but almost anything that their business partners make. So when you sign up on Amazon and make a pricing inquiry, Amazon's pricing module reaches out to the price postings of their partners on a real time basis and gives you the price, which may vary from time to time. This way, Amazon does not have to store pricing information or update it whenever anything changes and is able to respond to your query quickly and efficiently.

Earlier we talked about the rise of SME's, many of whom will act as the business partners of a large organization.. SOA solutions will allow for interaction and seamless communications between the complex systems of the larger organization and the simpler solutions of the SME's.

# HOW TO MEASURE THE INTENSITY OF CHANGE

What tools and methodologies are available for responding in a systematic way to the accelerating changes occurring in all spheres of business? We offer the following change-intensity framework for examining your business segment and making appropriate management decisions about change impacts.

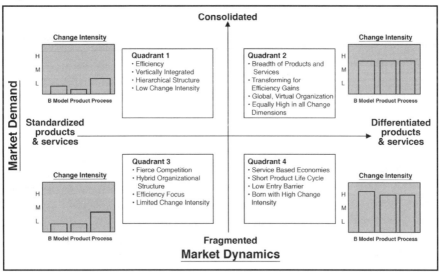

***Figure 5**: The Intensity of Change within Market Demand and Dynamics*

We have divided the market into four quadrants based on market demand and market dynamics. Market demand indicates the level of standardized products and services versus differentiated products and services with the space between containing a gradual mix and levels of customization. Market dynamics indicate whether a market is consolidated, dominated by few large players, or fragmented, where there are many competitors.

Change intensity will depend on where in the four quadrants your business segment belongs and how far away from the center point your segment is located. If you are lucky enough to have your business segment in quadrant one, then you don't really need to worry about change intensity although you are a target for disruptive innovation of products and services from the low end of the market. Companies like IBM, GE, GM, Ford, US Steel, PANAM, TWA, Boeing, and many others were once in quadrant one until they were disrupted by "good enough" products and services that eroded their market share. Today the companies that belong to quadrant one are perhaps only the big oil companies and few others in related industries like gas and electricity.

Quadrant one companies would periodically examine their processes and supporting technology infrastructure for efficiency gains but not worry too much about changing their business models, products and services or go-to-market strategies. Changing models among competitors and changes in customer value, however, make constant reevaluation of the business model necessary for continued growth.

There are not many companies in quadrant three. Some of your business segments may fall within this quadrant as a transition to market consolidation, which will bring it north in this framework. If you find yourself in quadrant three, competition will force you to put more focus on your business process changes than you would as a quadrant one company. If you have a business segment in quadrant three you don't really have to worry about changing your business models, products and services or marketing strategies.

Now if you find your business segment to be in quadrant four, you are diametrically opposite to quadrant one. Companies in quadrant four have constant change in mind. In fact, many well-known companies of today were born in quadrant four with their disruptive technologies and disruptive business models. To name a few the following come to mind right away, eBay, Amazon, Google, Starbucks. These are good examples of disruptive business models and disruptive technologies. In addition, quadrant four companies are primarily in the services business, specifically in the information services business. From our earlier discussion you will remember that the services business in the US is estimated to be 75 percent plus of GDP and the information services business to be 53 percent plus of GDP with both growing in a steep curve. These statistics suggest that your business may be on the right hand side of the framework or move to the right hand side soon.

In quadrant four, the ability to change business models is of utmost importance as new competitors with more agility and new technologies will quickly disrupt the established norms. Let us take the information technology and services industry as an example. After the dot-com bust and the disruptions caused by 9/11, many I/T companies closed business in the

Silicon Valley. Although the Indian I/T companies were doomed to similar failure, companies like Infosys, Wipro and others were able to change their business models quickly, moving rapidly into business process outsourcing and quadrupling their revenue in the last five years. They could not have moved so swiftly into these new businesses without the ability to sense the market conditions and change their business models, processes, and products and services very quickly and efficiently.

Many companies in quadrant four have found themselves in quadrant two after a series of mergers and acquisitions that allowed for consolidation of some segments of this quadrant. For example, you can not open the newspaper today without finding companies like Wipro or Infosys acquiring a company somewhere in the world and thus moving into quadrant two from quadrant four. In addition, companies like IBM and HP are moving into quadrant two from quadrant one, thus becoming direct competitors of companies whom they regarded as business partners only a few years ago. Certainly, coopetition is becoming more the norm than the exception.

Earlier, we talked about the emergence of SME's within the industry ecosystems, where there are a few large corporations supported by many small enterprises. This would mean a combination of quadrant two and quadrant four companies operating within an industry ecosystem. As we made a prediction earlier in this chapter, we foresee such a combination becoming more prevalent as ecosystems become incorporated into corporate strategies.

Let's take a few more examples. Remember WINTEL? Microsoft's Windows operating system ran in INTEL microprocessors all over the world making both companies kings in their areas of business and positioning them solidly in quadrant one. I wonder if today they will consider themselves in quadrant one, as Microsoft office products are facing competition from others like Google, and we already talked about INTEL's competition with AMD. Are these two companies moving to quadrant two? Let's talk about Google. Web search is the most prolific on line activity, and Google is the most sought-after search engine, making Google a darling of the Wall Street. However, with Microsoft and others entering this lucrative field and market consolidation taking place, Google will also soon be moving into quadrant two.

So, as you can see, you will have a moving target. In today's analysis your business segment could be in one quadrant, but move to another as a result of the changes in the environment. The change intensity framework provides a lens so that you can be systematic in analyzing the positioning of your business segment today and the trajectory your business is following relative to the changes in the market forces.

## UNDERSTANDING FUNDAMENTAL ECONOMIC TRENDS OF CHANGE

As we have seen, business today is undergoing faster and more profound change than ever before. Evidence of this change is most readily perceived in the context of six fundamental economic trends detailed below. Each trend presents challenges and opportunities. Business leaders who seize the opportunities and alter their practices to capture new competitive advantages, will sustain a winning trajectory in the global marketplace. Conversely, executives who treat the challenges as threats are destined to become market victims, followers who have ceded leadership to competitors.

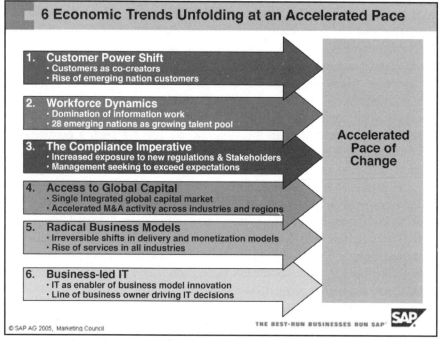

*Figure 6:* Six Economic Trends Unfolding at an Accelerated Pace

**1. Customer power shift.** Entry of new customers in the global market and increased market transparency enabled by enhanced access to information has triggered a tectonic shift of power to the customer. First, customers, both consumers and businesses, are increasingly influencing design and delivery of products and services, as well as business models. Second, developing nations are emerging as the main drivers of growth in global GDP. Savvy multi-nationals are localizing product and services to gain market share.

- Multi-national companies will shift their efforts away from OECD (Organization for Economic Cooperation and Development) nations and will increase revenue earned in emerging nations from 21% to 34% by 2015.[9]
- Consumer and special interest groups are driving co-creation in both digital-based (e.g., media companies are migrating from producer to facilitator of content) and physical goods industries (e.g., consumer packaged goods customers are defining new products).[10]

2. **Workforce dynamics.**  Tacit and transactional work has eclipsed transformation (e.g., manufacturing, agricultural) as the primary lever for value creation. This shift in economic activity towards information-oriented work will create a shortage of 10 million information workers in developed nations.[11] As a result, global recruitment is targeting 33 million college educated professionals in 28 emerging nations that have invested in a qualified, accessible information worker talent pool.[12]

- Services as a percentage of worldwide GDP has grown from less than 50% of GDP to over 66% (from 1970s to 1995). Examples are US (85%), Germany (75%), Russia (66%), and India (59%).[13]
- Information worker employment will continue to add more jobs than both agriculture and manufacturing. Even emerging industrial giants such as China, will see 1.3% service sector employment growth versus .9% for agriculture and manufacturing combined in the next decade.[14]
- Emerging nations have 4x the amount of qualified young professionals as the top eight developed nations. The number of emerging nation college graduates will grow at 5x the developed nation rate.[15]

3. **The compliance imperative.**  Businesses have come under increasing public scrutiny due to cross-border operations and the advent of stringent regulations in the wake of 9/11, Enron, Parmalat, trade disputes, environmental issues and other catalyzing events. Regardless of size, enterprises participating in the global economy will face the same challenges as they grapple with new and often inconsistent regulations. Additionally, activist stakeholders are aggressively challenging management on issues as varied as social responsibility, ethical leadership, and privacy. Facing multiple, constantly changing requirements, executives are choosing to turn compliance and broader social responsibility into a competitive advantage by exceeding the global expectations of government.

- The coupling of increased international operations with the lack of global regulatory harmonization has left only 65% of executives confident that their firms are compliant with foreign regulations.[16]
- Total settlements in shareholder lawsuits against American companies increased from $145M in 1997 to $5.5B in 2004.[17]

4. **Access to global capital.** The world is rapidly moving to a single globally integrated network of financial markets. This integration is ushering in an era of plentiful capital with emerging markets serving as both recipients and providers of capital, and record levels of M&A activity transforming industries by creating efficient global giants focused on leveraging their advantages and outsourcing all other functions. However, this integrated global financial market has changed faster than regulations and has created challenges as 24 by 7 markets compress time, making rapid reaction paramount. SMEs (Small - Medium Enterprises) are at the tip of this global capital paradox. With access to capital, they are increasingly pursuing both low-end and specialty niche market opportunities, but simultaneously face the challenge of becoming dependent on global giants consolidating their markets.

- BRIC (Brazil, Russia, India, China) nations comprise 4 of the top 5 Foreign Direct Investment (FDI) recipients. Concurrently, emerging market giants will remain acquisitive – having already raised the acquisition rate from 15 to 59 companies (2000-2005).[18]
- The World Bank reports that most investment promotion agencies (83%), FDI experts (57%), and multi-nationals (65%) expect FDI to grow in the mid-term (2007-2008).[19]
- Merger & acquisition activity has accelerated with acquired assets growing by over 35% in 2005 and a predicted record of over $3.3 trillion in acquired assets for 2006.[20]
- 60% of midsize enterprises believe there is at least medium risk that they will become overly dependent on a few large customers due to market consolidation.[21]

5. **Radical business models.** For the first time in history, almost every industry is simultaneously developing new radical delivery and monetization models. For industries such as media & entertainment, digitization is leading to an irreversible shift in monetization methods after decades of stability. Further, to counter rapid commoditization triggered by intense competition, product companies are not only creating high-value

services for enhanced revenue and profit growth, but are also wrapping these services into entirely new business models (e.g., charging for cubic-feet of cooled air rather than for an air conditioner and maintenance).

- 30% of innovation efforts will revolve around business models, with market outperformers focusing twice as much on business model innovation than underperformers.[22]
- Services revenue as a percentage of overall revenue grew from 12% in 1998 to 22% in 2004 for the $500 billion consumer durable goods market.[23]
- The global market for outsourced I/T service and business processes is forecast to grow from $30 billion in 2005 to $110 billion 2010.[24]

6. **Business-led I/T.** Increasingly the technology priorities of CEOs are driven more by creating innovative business differentiation than by lowering costs through efficient, automated processes. This migration of preference from information technology to business technology will be led by a new generation of tech-savvy general managers who introduce new applications into their workplace. Strategic use of I/T will not be restricted to just large enterprises but will also extend to small and medium business.

- 35% of CIOs have spent more than half of their career outside of I/T. That percentage is likely to grow as 79% of CIOs would promote subordinates for business aptitude rather than I/T skill and knowledge.[25]
- 63% of all enterprises have 5 or more rogue applications on their network with a forecast of 93% of all employees using at least one rogue application.[26]
- 68% of executives at midsize enterprises view I/T as critical to their ability to grow, with 63% of CEOs and managing directors taking direct responsibility for major I/T decisions.[27]

# NEW BUSINESS PRIORITIES IN A WORLD OF ACCELERATED CHANGE

To excel under these conditions of global accelerated change, CEOs are renewing their commitments and approach to four perennial priorities. First, in an increasingly competitive world, executives must foster sustained, differentiated **accelerated innovation** on products, processes, and business

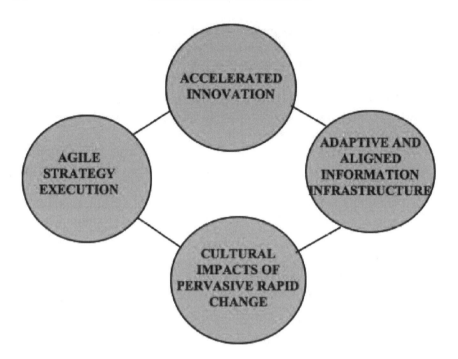

*Figure 7: New Business Priorities in a World of Accelerated Change*

models. Second, in an era of accelerated competition, **agile strategy execution** will be the most important success factor for any innovation. Accelerated innovation and agile strategy executions will only be possible if executives understand the **cultural impacts of pervasive, rapid change** and promote appropriate initiatives. Finally, **an adaptive and aligned information infrastructure** is imperative as  continuous, current and global access to knowledge is the key to sustained competitive advantage.

1. **Accelerated innovation.** Shifting customer power, industry transformation, radical business models, and globalization of capital have significantly reduced the half-life of innovations, while simultaneously and dramatically increasing the need for it. Sustained leadership demands quicker, more "open" innovation on products, services, processes, and business models. In the pursuit of differentiated innovation, companies are focusing on:

   • Treating innovation as a core business process
   • Co-innovating with business partners and customers
   • Embracing rapid experimentation to test new markets

- Broadening innovation to business processes and models
- Capturing value from new monetization models

2. **Agile strategy execution.** The business environment has become more unforgiving than ever before. The consequences of a single misstep or delay in rolling out a strategy can be severe. Executives must be alert to emerging threats or opportunities and swiftly adapt their strategies to new conditions in a non-stop cycle of strategy development, execution, measurement and refinement. In such an environment, smaller, more agile companies can have a distinct advantage. Challenged by the velocity of business change, CEOs must invest in speeding global execution by:

- Minimizing latency between business strategy and execution
- Ensuring frictionless process change
- Increasing speed of value from innovation
- Collaborating in a borderless ecosystem with enterprises of all sizes
- Institutionalizing a discipline of predictable performance

3. **Cultural impacts of pervasive, rapid change.** Shifting customer power, workforce dynamics, radical business models and industry transformations are forcing companies to change at an accelerated pace and adopt a mindset embracing change as an opportunity for improved performance and market leadership. To capture the opportunities inherent in these changes, organizations must create a workplace that can accommodate a greater global presence, a stronger focus on information-related work, and a highly-educated, tech-savvy generation of employees.

Globally integrated capital markets and rising fiduciary expectations exert more governance and compliance pressure on companies. Similarly, workforce, customer, and stakeholder globalization raises the bar as executives must ensure business integrity at all levels, for all operations, in all locations. Facing this complex environment, many companies are embracing corporate stewardship as a means of not only meeting expectations, but also creating differentiation.

Successful corporations will gain advantage by:

- Leveraging a global talent market and workforce
- Valuing global cultural diversity
- Gaining competitive advantage from compliance, governance, and risk management

- Exceeding expectations of new, energized, global stakeholders
- Protecting reputation in an era of instant transparency
- Maintaining business and individual integrity during change
- Grooming next generation leaders for planned succession

4. **Adaptive and aligned information infrastructure.** Amidst all the changes described above, the information technology infrastructure, in terms of global availability and access to timely and meaningful information and knowledge, must remain flexible and aligned to the rapidly changing business environment. Infrastructure investment decisions are exceedingly being made by tech-savvy business leaders to ensure the continuity and currency of underlying technology solutions. Companies can align I/T strategy by:

- Gaining competitive advantage from an adaptive information architecture
- Aligning the information technology innovations to those of the business model innovations
- Making information management investment decisions based on recommendations of tech-savvy business executives
- Improving information worker productivity and global collaboration
- Maintaining the currency, consistency and integrity of global information and knowledge during rapid and pervasive change
- Grooming next generation knowledge workers by expanding access to real-time and relevant knowledge

# CONCLUSIONS

*"Corporate titans make mistakes, new competitors emerge, new technologies and consumer habits disrupt established patterns in unforeseen ways. All of these forces require businesses big and small to make changes and mid-course corrections, and usually the sooner, the better"*
    *– Wall Street Journal Editorial, September 7, 2006*

The above quote is an example of what business leaders and analysts are saying about change and its impact. The future and fortunes of many of the best known companies of today will rise or fall depending on how good they are in anticipating, sensing and responding to what is shaping out to be a period of perpetual, rapid and pervasive change. Continuously examining your business model, organization, and practices to respond to accelerated change is the management imperative of the successful organizations of tomorrow, and the tomorrow is here today.

# ENDNOTES

1   SAP Corporate Strategy Group.
2   Ian Davis, Elizabeth Stephenson, The McKinsey Quarterly, January 2006.
3   Competing on Analytics – The New Science of Winning", Thomas H. Davenport and Jeanne G. Harris, Harvard Business School Press, 2007.
4   Tom Davenport, "Thinking for a Living".
5   Business 2010 an SAP and EIU Study, 2006.
6   Expanding the Innovation Horizon, The Global CEO Study, IBM, 2006.
7   Business 2010 an SAP and EIU Study, 2006.
8   Ashby, Meredith and Miles Stephen, Leaders Talk Leadership, Oxford, 2002.
9   "Organizing for Global Advantage in China, India and other Rapidly Developing Economies" The Boston Consulting Group, March 2006h.
10  "It Takes a Web Village." BusinessWeek, September 4, 2006.
11  Nebolsky, Charles and Wan, Dadong. "Where Have All the Gurus Gone?" Accenture Outlook, 2005.
12  Farrell, Diana, et. al. "Sizing the Emerging Global Labor Market." McKinsey Quarterly, 2005.
13  Beardsley, Scott, et. al. "Competitive Advantage from Better Interactions." McKinsey Quarterly, 2006 Number 2.
14  World Bank.
15  Farrell, Diana, et. al. "Sizing the Emerging Global Labor Market." McKinsey Quarterly, 2005.
16  DiPiazza, Samuel. "8th Annual Global Survey: Bold Ambitions, Careful Choices." PriceWaterhouseCoopers. 2005.
17  The Economist.
18  Aguiar, Marcos; et al. "The New Global Challengers: How 100 Top Companies from Rapidly Developing Economies Are Changing the World." Boston Consulting Group. May 2006.
19  Prospects for Foreign Direct Investment and the Strategies of Transnational Corporations, 2005-2009. United Nations Conference on Trade and Development, 2005.
20  Pash, Shaheen. "Outlook Rosy for 2006 M&A Activity." CNNMoney.com, December 2005.
21  The Economist Intelligence Unit, Thinking big: Midsize companies and the challenges of growth, 2006.
22  "IBM Global CEO Study 2006 – Expanding the Innovation Horizon." IBM, 2006.
23  Auguste, Byron; Hammon, Eric; Pundit, Vivek. "The Right Service Strategies for Product Companies." McKinsey Quarterly Number 1, 2006.

24    Chakrabary, Sujit, et. al. "The Untapped Market for Offshore Services." McKinsey Quarterly, 2006 Number 2.
25    CIO Insight, 2006. Online.
26    FaceTime Greynets Research Study, August 2005.
27    The Economist Intelligence Unit, Thinking big: Midsize companies and the challenges of growth, 2006.

# 1.2

# ECONOMIC TRENDS OF CHANGE

**John M. Jordan,** *Executive Director, Center for Digital Transformation, Pennsylvania State University*

Six fundamental forces underlie the need for business change. These forces are each integrated in the later chapters of this book. Taking a broad-brush approach, we can see the reach and impact of these six forces, each of which interacts with others to multiply both the effect and complexity of any given trend.

## 1. WORKFORCE DYNAMICS

At base, every business relies on people, and several large-scale shifts are currently underway. Past trading empires, such as England's, relied on capital for ships, docks, and credit. During the Industrial Revolution capital was used to build factories, while the giant German chemical and dyestuffs firms of the late 19th century (the predecessors of today's pharmaceutical and petrochemical sectors) grew still more reliant on infrastructure. The twentieth century saw the rise of mass consumption, in part driven by the invention of self service, and later the first phases of an information economy.

Today's economy includes both capital infrastructure and intangible assets such as brand and brainpower. Many of today's most powerful economic entities are knowledge-driven, whether by deal-making, patents and other intellectual property, or entertainment. While technology can automate some aspects of this kind of work, there is no counterpart to Henry Ford's assembly line for hedge funds, search engines, or brand campaigns. As many managers of such businesses say, "Our market capitalization walks out the door every night."

## Education

As knowledge becomes more important in everything from branding to engineering to intellectual property, education systems assume new importance, transcending the role of geography and natural resources. At the same time that students from virtually every nation migrate, at least temporarily, to study in the United States' institutions of higher learning, leaders across the world struggle to reinvent education through both formal and workplace mechanisms. Engineering, medicine, and science draw particular attention because of their obvious economic impact, but the role of humanities and social sciences in helping increasingly diverse populations understand and govern themselves should not be underestimated.

Global population flows illustrate this trend. Emerging nations have four times the number of qualified young professionals as the top eight developed nations. The number of emerging nation college graduates will grow at five times the developed nation rate. Many of these graduates will continue to study in the U.S. and Europe before returning home, accelerating the trend still further.[1]

## Aging

The demographics of aging are already established: to take two examples among developed and developing countries in 2025, India will be far better positioned than the United Kingdom in that a relatively broad base of working-age adults will support a smaller number of retirees (see graph). The UK, in contrast, projects to have an inverted age pyramid, with a large number of retirees supported by a smaller number of their offspring's generation. Of course, 15 years is a long time in a dynamic world, and either disease (such as avian flu) or immigration/emigration could change the picture dramatically. In addition, the sheer scale of India's population introduces its own issues that the UK will not confront. Finally, continuing advances in medical care could increase the lifespan across both countries, making the UK's demographic future even more problematic.

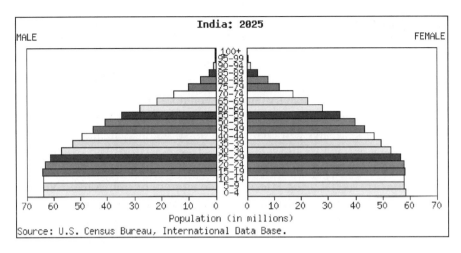

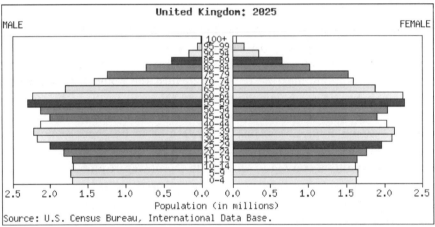

*Figure 1: Projected Population Distribution by Age in India and the UK*

## Human Migration

Immigration and emigration will continue to be emotional, political, and economic "hot buttons" across the world. France, for example, has seen the rise of both a nativist, albeit minority, presidential candidate and a new president who is both a) himself not French-born and b) deeply opposed to Turkey's joining the EU. The immigration debate in the U.S. could well determine the winner of the 2008 presidential election. By contrast, Australia's success in attracting immigrants has fueled its success – not to mention its very existence. Maintaining both momentum and manageability on this front will be a key to the future.

## Job Migration

What economist Alan Blinder has called "the next Industrial Revolution" – offshoring – means that, information work can migrate anywhere. Radiologists can read U.S. x-rays across the world, overnight during India's or Australia's daylight. Equity analysis, credit scoring, and, of course, customer-service and help-desk call centers are moving to low-wage, high-brainpower markets, and will continue to do so while switching costs and barriers to exit are and should remain low. The impact on class structure in the developed world will be fascinating: unlike displaced factory workers, information-work offshoring affects a wide stratum of individuals. Nurses and truck drivers are not vulnerable, but paralegals, software engineers, and mortgage bankers are.[2]

## Politics

Workers are citizens, and the political changes afoot in UAE, Venezuela, Russia, and South Africa, for starters, present significant managerial challenges and opportunities. At the same time that classic dynamics of rising expectations must be balanced against the realities of available resources, improved communications (driven primarily by the mobile phone outside the EU and North America) fuel both heightened expectations and person-to-person connections. Just as Howard Dean was both empowered and later undone by the dilemma of politics in the Internet era, so are developing countries coming to terms with the power of global media and communications.

## Multiculturalism

The impact of value systems in global trade is reinforced almost daily. WalMart's international expansion hit major speed bumps in Germany, in large part because of cultural issues: customers were unaccustomed to store workers bagging purchases for them, and employees resisted singing the Bentonville company songs. Offshoring customer service to India remains controversial in the U.S. Ikea has successfully transcended its Swedish origins and made its designs globally relevant.

# 2. POWER SHIFTS TO CUSTOMERS

At both the business-to-business and business-to-consumer levels, sellers are having to react to exacting and particular buyers. At base, this situation results from basic laws of supply and demand. As material goods have become generally plentiful in the developed world, scarcity has moved from the supply side to the demand side of the transaction: if there are too many goods to buy, buyers become scarce. Secondly, in the midst of an information deluge, attention becomes scarce, and therefore valuable. The effects of these two transitions on advertising, marketing, pricing, and service have been dramatic.

On the business-to-business side, greater availability of information and the development of more forms of standardization have led to a change in the role of account representatives and a sharp decline in the utility of conferences and tradeshows. Customers can get full product details, updated catalogs, $3^{rd}$-party assessments, and product comparisons at any time, without having to invoke a representative. Switching costs for many categories of transactions have also declined, meaning that sellers are being forced to innovate new ways to win and hold customers.

In general terms, the power shift to the customer has increased the complexity of suppliers' activities. Customers demand – and get – specialized kitting and packaging, deliveries on stringent timetables, and of course competitive pricing. Even capital investment is made at the customer's behest, as when a packaging company builds a facility on or next to the site of a beverage bottler, or when vendor-managed inventory ties up the supplier's working capital rather than the retailer's.

The power shift varies widely across industries: for every "WalMart effect" in consumer packaged goods, there's a pharmaceutical sector that still retains pricing, distribution, and other forms of control over hospitals. Regulatory restrictions have some part in these disparities, but other factors are also at work. The maturity and robustness of a particular industry's supply chain, for example, influences the degree of customer power: if a shipment cannot even be located, it can hardly be expedited. Product development and use cycles also matter: the cellular industry enforces service contracts in some countries, but paradoxically, churn rates are lower in countries where customers are free to switch carriers at their discretion.

However, the "customer power" theme should not be taken to an extreme: improved communications can improve the performance of markets, and sellers can in fact benefit. A classic case is the use of cell phones in transportation-poor markets. Calling ahead to find out the best price for cotton or corn helps sellers get the current price for their crop. As markets function better, benefits are shared. In a study of sardine fisherman in India, Robert Jensen of Harvard found that the use of cell phones helped fishermen avoid oversupplied (and low-priced) docks. The phones paid for themselves in two months as fishermen's profits rose 8% on average while consumer prices dropped by an average of 4%, in part because less of the catch was wasted.[3]

Another expression of customer power can be seen in the movement toward "servicization," that is, the shift from capitalized investment in infrastructure to subscription-driven payments for functionality. For example, both military and civil aviation operators are moving away from owning jet engines and are instead paying for thrust-hours or other similar units of work. Once again, customers benefit both by shifting assets off their balance sheets and by allowing those who know a process best – the builders of a product used across an industry – to assume responsibility for maintenance, parts inventories, and other complex processes.

In the consumer sector, reduced information asymmetry can be seen in such major transactions as home-buying and car shopping, where previously the pricing of these large expenditures was done out of sight of the buyer using inside knowledge. Primarily for customers' benefit, a large variety of websites – Zillow for houses and Edmunds, Yahoo, and MSN for cars – is now exposing pricing inputs to the customer. The role of both real estate agents and car salespeople has been transformed in under a decade. In other sectors, such as travel, the rise of self-service has driven many agents out of business or into specialized niches: as customers do more of the work and the process is opened up, airlines no longer pay the intermediary for the work of printing tickets on ARC (Airlines Reporting Corporation) stock.

In a time when prices for many products are dropping, when middle-class wage growth is extremely slow or even negative, and when selection is increasing, retailers have been able to find some extremely profitable ways to serve demanding consumers. Jim Gilmore, a consultant at Strategic Horizons, asserts that people don't want infinite selection, they want what they want. His example was of a 75-item list of bottled beers in a restaurant, in contrast to the customer's desire for a draft Budweiser.

Some sellers have succeeded in navigating between the burden of consumer bewilderment – exhibited in most big-box chains – and the desire for "what they want" rather than what the retailer wants to sell. Addressing the need for so-called "affordable luxury," brands such as Starbucks and Courvoisier have been able to gain market share among people who can't afford the best of everything but will treat themselves to a luxury item in an otherwise moderate budget. In the case of coffee, a key element of the experience is the customization: requests that would be frowned upon at McDonalds are encouraged or even required by the elaborate language and culture of a Starbucks outlet.

Because things and experiences can be customized in one domain, demand will spill over into adjacent markets. Like Starbucks, Amazon.com encourages consumer individualism, presenting a customized storefront and personalized recommendations that anticipate desires and dramatically whittle down the vast inventory. People who don't want infinite selection but want exactly what they want, even if they don't know it yet, would appear to be a problematic user base, yet Amazon's powerful technologies enable consumers to use self-service to get the benefits of personalization and competitive pricing.

As customers experience the power of scarcity of demand, they exercise it elsewhere. As more fast-food vendors including Panera Bread and Subway prepare food to order, McDonald's industrial model has had to adapt. Even Burger King, which told customers to "have it your way," found that it couldn't really cope with nonstandard orders and dropped the campaign. Among customers in their 20s, the default assumption is often of a customizable offering, such as cellphones, whose limitless ringtone options generate enormous profit for the carriers. This insight led Toyota's Scion brand to design and market automobiles with multiple modes of personalization outside the factory: this is not your father's options list. Likewise, after Dell pioneered the build-to-order concept for computers, HP followed suit.

In addition to being met by customization, this consumer pressure on the seller is being successfully addressed with the power of design – witness the iPod, Ikea, and Dyson vacuums – and of course brand. Both business and consumer channels are being faced with the shift from push (broadcast) to pull (including search), and with multi-media customers. If advertising is delivered via cellphone, radio, billboard, and word of mouth to the same driver simultaneously, whose message will get through? What does it mean for advertisers that clickthroughs directly report customer behavior in response to web-based ads even as Super Bowl TV spots cannot be tracked for efficacy except at a macro level? The rise of customer power, and of the information environment that largely makes it possible, will continue to have unexpected consequences for businesses in virtually every sector.

# 3. CAPITAL GOES GLOBAL

*"Money goes where it is wanted and stays where it is well treated."*

*-Walter Wriston*

As the scale of institutional capital accumulation grows, the scope of activity can no longer be considered on the local or national basis. Just to give some sense of the magnitude of these investments, the Robeco Group of the Netherlands holds nearly $150 billion under management, while the California Public Employees Retirement System (CalPERS) manages about $250 billion. Barclay's Global Investors led the way among mutual fund firms in 2005, with $1.4 trillion under management.[4] To operate investments at this scale, private money managers have in the past half-century usurped the role formerly held by national treasuries, and markets have supplemented the role of central bankers.

Money is increasingly behaving as information, moving instantaneously to opportunity. No longer bound by the time scales of paper, information moves in more and more instances to near-real-time, lowering risk and exposing opportunities sooner. Consider that only 20 years ago it took the London Stock Exchange *weeks* to settle a trade. The acceleration of speed and concomitant gains in market liquidity made possible by automation and greater information transparency have clearly contributed to today's borderless state of finance.

Markets beget markets, trying to make capital feel "well treated." When Brazil opened its BOVESPA stock exchange to foreign investment, trading volume increased ten fold.[5] More and more countries are opening secondary markets, particularly in futures and options, but also in derivatives. The creation of complex yet liquid markets for risk encourages still more capital formation as an increasing number of external forces – weather, political upheaval, currency swings – can be hedged.

Governments across the world have contributed significantly to the globalization of capital flows. Moves toward regulatory standardization (the European Union being the most visible – but far from the only – such effort), improved transparency and accountability in more and more countries, regulatory approval for larger deals, and taxation policies all encourage investment. A powerful force in economic development has been privatization of often under-funded State resources, which has allowed private capital to invest in national infrastructure. This trend can lead to some counterintuitive arrangements: the Indiana toll road is now operated by a Spanish-Australian concern while DP World, a Dubai company, operates ports on six continents. Between 1989 and 1994, capital flows to the emerging world jumped from $80 billion to $200 billion with the growth accounted for exclusively by private capital.

The case of Chrysler helps illustrate the magnitude and speed of the shift to government involvement. In 1979, the U.S. automaker had stumbled badly as its cars lacked the gas mileage and quality of Japanese imports. Operating on the logic that Chrysler was "too big to fail" without resulting in dire economic consequences, labor unions made wage concessions, the government maintained high trade barriers to Japanese vehicles (particularly trucks), and Congress approved a $1.5 billion loan guarantee. It was perhaps the high-water mark in government intervention in micro-economic policy. In 2007, Chrysler's market share and profits had grown similarly shaky, but not only was there no mention of a government-led bailout, the company was sold to a single private equity firm, which was in essence paid to take the asset off Daimler's hands.

The Chrysler deal also illustrates another important point: in some ways the globalization of capital is a cat chasing its tail. As bigger mergers and acquisitions are allowed (and become feasible), bigger capital pools are required. As these larger capital pools form, opportunities need substantial scale to be interesting. 2006 was the busiest year ever for M&A activity, with deals totaling over $3.4 trillion including the acquisition by an Indian group of a multinational steelmaker headquartered in Luxembourg. In addition, L'Oreal, the largest beauty-products company in the world, reached across the English Channel to buy the Body Shop. Every major sector is represented, from healthcare to metals, banking to telecom, and retail to pharmaceuticals. Cross-border and even cross-continent deals have become commonplace.

Global visibility results in economic opportunity at all levels of scale. One of the most powerful innovations of the past 20 years has been the microfinancing for which Muhammad Yunus won a Nobel Prize in 2006. At the same time, the giant capital projects (such as dams and ports) in which the World Bank specialized have become controversial and often less attractive. Small and medium enterprises, NGOs, and other forms of organization have realigned in light of the reality of global capital.

# 4. BUSINESS MODELS EVOLVE

Driven by a variety of forces, companies are finding new ways to create and harvest value. We have already spoken about globalization: competition is less and less often defined locally, so the wide reach for both threats and opportunities is a key factor in business model change. As information about stuff proves often to be more valuable than the physical items themselves and information networks multiply, information-intensive business models multiply, as we will see. Finally, the speed of change is accelerating, spurred by everything from governmental relaxation of trade barriers to increased consumer surplus.

## Servicization

The shift from products to services (and product-service hybrids) has taken hold in many industry verticals. Culture is often a critical barrier to change in this regard: despite the high margins earned by its financial services arm, GM sold off a controlling interest in GMAC (to the same private equity firm that bought Chrysler) in order to focus on the pure manufacturing piece of the business. Industrial processes, such as the cleaning of heat exchangers in power plants, are now sold as services, in large measure because the cleaning-supply firms realized that they hold considerable process knowledge for which a procurement manager seldom compensated them. Now that the customer is a line-of-business manager, prices are less likely to be commoditized.

## Economic Complexity

In an agricultural or industrial economy, exchanges of money for products are relatively straightforward. With the rise of a service economy – more people worldwide now work in services than they do in agriculture – such notions as assets, ownership, and value evolve. Physical infrastructure is frequently seen as a drag on performance; joint ventures, futures contracts, and other financial arrangements muddy the waters of ownership; and value is frequently a function of customer perception rather than the cost of physical inputs. Other lines are blurring as well: is ethanol agriculture or energy? Are genetically modified seeds intellectual property, biotech, or agriculture? A cell phone or smart phone is a physical device, but relies on network service to actually deliver value. These changes in core analytic categories helps spur business model disruption and innovation.

## Technology Platforms

- Information technology helps break down barriers to entry in a variety of ways. Borrowing models that CEO Vern Raburn learned in the personal computer industry, the Eclipse very light jet is built more like a PC than a Cessna. Standardized components are used wherever possible inside a modular, rather than hard-wired, architecture. The cost drops commensurately, innovation in any given component can be accommodated, and the aircraft can be serviced more readily.
- Compared to the capital-intensiveness of AT&T in the 1980s, today's phone companies can be lightweight to the point of invisibility: Skype, which uses PCs to allow people to speak to each

other anywhere on the Internet for free, is a telephone company without a network, owned oddly enough by the not-really-a-retailer eBay. In addition to competing with phone companies,eBay is also a bank of sorts after its PayPal acquisition.

- Virgin Mobile pioneered the MVNO model, which in the industry stands for Mobile Virtual Network Operator. Like Skype, it is a phone company without a network, focusing on branding and customer service while renting network service from Sprint.
- The Tesla roadster, an electric car selling for about $100,000 that can move from 0-60 mph in about 4 seconds, uses batteries designed for laptops. Tellingly, Tesla's co-founder also helped launch PayPal; he is no stranger to business model innovation.

## Transparency

As we have seen previously, transparency can be a significant driver of business model change. When decades-old trade secrets and pricing models are exposed to competition, surplus often flows to the customer. An extreme example is the music industry, which formerly sold entire albums and later compact disks rather than individual songs. As digital music files allowed people to hear music before they bought it, and to buy or burn individual tracks conveniently at whatever level of resolution they chose, the music industry was slow to change its business model, choosing instead to attempt to legislate and litigate the outdated business model into law. More promising are the trajectories of the diamond and financial services industries.

---

### DeBeers

Until only a few years ago, DeBeers held a monopoly position in the world's diamond market. The practice of buying back inventory (ultimately $5 billion worth) exposed DeBeers to antitrust litigation and hampered cash flows: DeBeers was banned from doing business in the United States, and failed to turn a profit for the decade beginning the year after its 100th anniversary and ending in 1999. Beginning in 1999, the company radically revised its operations, releasing its stranglehold on the supply side to become a marketing-driven entity targeted at increasing global demand. The company used its reach and unsurpassed industry knowledge to track stones from origination to sales floor to guarantee that they are "conflict free" (to counter charges raised in the movie *Blood Diamond* and elsewhere) and produced without any child labor. Indeed, the ability to address the human rights charges so decisively has turned out to be a competitive advantage for the company which reported net earnings of $730 million in 2006. Now privately held, DeBeers also increased its investment in the health and well-being of the people in its producer nations, including Botswana, Namibia, South Africa and Tanzania. It is also working with those nations to increase the amount of finished jewelry produced near origin to increase employment and harvest more value from the ultimate diamond buyer.[6]

## Entrepreneurship

Many entrepreneurs and innovators are focusing more on the business rather than on the invention or the brand. That is, instead of building a "better mousetrap" innovators like Michael Dell, eBay's Pierre Omidyar, and Virgin's Richard Branson have successfully reinvented the value chain and business model of their respective industries. Microfinancing serves as another powerful business model story, as does Google, which to date has successfully walked the fine line between maintaining an engineering-driven culture and multiplying cash flows.

# 5. COMPLIANCE BECOMES IMPERATIVE

Several of the above forces have heightened the importance of clean execution of regulatory and compliance processes. While compliance is high on the managerial list of priorities, it is more of a second-order effect, an outcome of globalization, consumer surplus, and information-intensiveness than a driver of them. Nevertheless, the consequences of insufficient focus on managing compliance can be devastating.

As we have observed, the globalization of capital requires leveling various national playing fields. To make money "feel welcome," governments around the world have recognized the importance of integrity, transparency, and predictability. Doing business in the European Union, for example, can largely be accomplished by mastering one set of rules rather than 27. The trend continues: according to the World Trade Organization, roughly 300 bilateral trade agreements are now in place. Many of these agreements allow companies access to new markets, albeit at the cost of meeting local requirements. Given the competitiveness of the economic climate, compliance has become a core competency for many firms. Without it, a firm effectively cedes a market to a competitor.

Factors other than globalization are contributing to the rise of state intervention. In the U.S., the federal government alone constitutes over 20% of GDP, making it a major component of the services sector. Regulation is both a natural activity in which governments engage and a phenomenon that feeds itself. Technological advancement means that standards, externalities, and intellectual property issues transcend national boundaries. The increase in health-related and ecological awareness in the past 50 years has also spurred many regulations. Most every country is facing longer life expectancies and therefore increasing numbers of retirees (including many living on investments) as well as rising health care costs. In addition, education as a factor in global competitiveness is high on local, state, and national agendas, as are a wide variety of immigration issues. All of these macro-scale issues open the door for state intervention.

As the manufacturing economy recedes in importance relative to services, new assets such as brand and talent require new reporting and regulatory frameworks. Workplace safety for white-collar workers, or airline flight crews, or school teachers can vary dramatically from the expectations of factory workers. Accounting for both taxation authorities and financial markets has become ever more complex, with significant debates still unresolved, particularly over the components of goodwill and other intangibles such as brand. The entire concept of a balance sheet can be difficult to reconcile with assets such as reputation and brainpower.

At base, regulation is another consequence of material surplus. Abundance confers a need for reliable, consistent quality metrics, especially in cross-border markets. Personal verification of oil, or beef, or creditworthiness is frequently impossible in global markets with multiple layers: the rancher buys feed on credit and sells on a futures contract, which is then repackaged into still more complex derivatives, all of which are a long way from the feedlot. Due to the rise of grading standards and enforceable contracts, commodities like corn or wheat have become almost perfectly fungible. As more products assume the characteristics of commodities, the need for yardsticks increases. Government and standards bodies thus can lubricate commerce, making compliance essential.

Finally, many business and government leaders have realized that trust is a key component of economic well-being. If faith in money, or the rule of law, or even a brand is weakened, customers will flee to safer havens. The Tyco, Enron, Adelphia, Parmalat, and other scandals exacted a huge cost, making regulators active and executives wary. Oil companies, despite their recent financial performance, operate under the microscope of environmental, economic, and political concerns (see sidebar). Recently there has been a realization on the part of the U.S. Congress that some stipulations of the

Sarbanes-Oxley Act were excessively burdensome. Even so, the overall trend appears to be toward more risk exposure – to litigation, regulatory sanctions, and privacy concerns – rather than less.

---

**BP**

As of 2001, BP stood as one of the world's most admired companies as well as an apparent success story of privatization, given that it had been at least partially state-owned until 1987. In the following five years BP suffered a series of blows due to sloppy safety standards, questionable financial practices, and poor execution of basic maintenance of its refineries and pipelines.

- An inquiry into a refinery explosion in Texas in 2005 blamed policies, procedures, and incentives that combined to create "a corporate blind spot" to safety. 15 people died in the accident which, significantly, was not blamed on "operator error." $1.6 billion has been set aside to compensate the victims' families.
- In 2006 BP had to shut down its Prudhoe Bay oil field in Alaska because a pipeline, which had not been cleaned or internally inspected for 14 years, began to leak.
- BP faces civil litigation over regulatory complaints that it manipulated the propane market in 2004. BP may also be charged with manipulating unleaded gasoline futures in 2002.

In light of these and other missteps, many of which relate directly to regulatory and compliance issues, BP's board of directors fired Lord John Browne, who was named as Britain's most-admired executive three different years.

---

# 6. BUSINESS IS LEADING THE USE OF INFORMATION TECHNOLOGY

In addition to automating manual processes, information technology has proven that it can create marketplace differentiation. At many leading companies, Chief Information Officers are recognized for their roles in the stewardship of information and knowledge, two key components in today's economy. Data has gone from being a record of a transaction to become a source of competitive advantage. Enterprise hardware, software, and business processes are being managed accordingly.

In the 1950s and 60s, government led the introduction of computing, while in the 1980s and 90s, individuals and hobbyists helped drive corporate adoption of the personal computer and the Internet. Today's picture is more complicated. In areas such as RFID and data mining, enterprises are now clearly leading both government and hobbyists. However, as personal computing becomes more mobile and the line between work and personal time blurs, technologies such as blogs, webmail, and Blackberries are coevolving as both personal and enterprise tools. Although this blurring challenges the IS organization with permeable boundaries, fluid processes, and part-time connectivity, many creative solutions are emerging as a result.

In part this creativity results from the standardization of the enterprise computing platform made possible by the adoption of Internet technologies. Standards-based computing is becoming more and more the rule rather than the exception, and vendors are innovating along axes that tend more toward the open than the proprietary: interoperability is clearly a market mandate. This trend allows CIOs to become information facilitators rather than system managers, as the rise of outsourcing attests.

Another signal of the rise of information is the career trajectory of people in corporate CIO roles and their relationship to CEOs. Current-generation CIOs tend to have line of business experience, and often rotate through the IS organization en route to high-visibility positions. The responsibilities of the job more often include the management of organizational change, large projects and programs, and customer expectations as opposed to technical tasks such as coding or architecture. In a 2006 survey, 35% of CIOs reported that they have spent more than half of their career outside of I/T. That percentage is likely to grow as 79% of all CIOs surveyed said they would promote subordinates for business rather than I/T skill and knowledge.[7]

Microsoft's COO Kevin Turner has perhaps the highest profile of the executives with CIO stints, but HP's CIO, Randy Mott (formerly at WalMart and Dell), is another leader helping to shape a business rather than running a function. In an even more visible sign of top management involvement in IT, JP Morgan Chase CEO Jamie Dimon cancelled a $5 billion outsourcing contract upon taking office. In organizations without such strong IT leadership, the COO and CFO often provide oversight and can help shape the direction of the information environment. For every FedEx or WalMart, there are dozens of companies where IT is counted as an overhead expense to be minimized. Whether they are a cause, a symptom, or a victim of an information-poor mindset, these executives often feel marginalized.

To be a source of advantage, data needs to inform decisions. As a result, data-handling and decision processes are co-evolving at such leaders as CapitalOne, Goldman Sachs, and GE. These processes can change in several ways, whether at the point of sale or service, in front of a dedicated analyst, or, increasingly, in the flow of core business processes. If a customer service representative knows the caller on the line is a platinum customer who hasn't had a transaction in over three months, she can offer incentives in the course of the call's normal resolution. Lines of credit can be routinely extended after a natural disaster hits a known range of ZIP codes. Weather, demographics, geospatial, and traffic data routinely inform decisions on new retail, manufacturing, or distribution sites. Embedded sensors in industrial applications feed the new-product development process with field data.

There is also downside. As data becomes valuable, IT risk is business risk, as the cost of recent data breaches at TJX, the Veterans Administration, and elsewhere illustrate. CIOs now need to be concerned with not only project risk, whether in custom development or package implementation, but regulatory risk (particularly across jurisdictions with differing rules for privacy, for example) and litigation risk as customer data is being treated with increasing sensitivity in both the EU and other markets.

---

## TJX

The Massachusetts-based retailer, parent to T.J. Maxx, Marshalls, and Home Goods, disclosed in 2007 that it had set an unenviable record as it exposed at least 45.7 million credit- and debit-card numbers to an outside ring of hackers.[8] One estimate ranged as high as 200 million records, but the precise number may never be known. Drivers-license data was also compromised, which could lead to identity theft.

The breach was traced to a Marshalls discount clothing store in Minnesota, where an in-store wireless network was compromised. From that opening, which was exploited from a car in the parking lot, outsiders with suspected ties to Russian organized crime groups gained access to TJX's core database in Framingham, Massachusetts. There they set up personal accounts into which they copied credit-card records, which then could be downloaded from any computer on the Internet. Auditors found multiple lapses in security, from the wireless encryption to firewall configuration and uninstalled security software.

Banks are expected to spend over $300 million to issue replacement cards, and at least one group of bankers is suing TJX. Industry analysts vary in their estimates of the company's current exposure, but a total of over $1 billion is quite plausible. Current laws require credit-card issuers to assume liability for stolen cards, but given the scale of the TJX breach, legislation may be introduced that would require the party responsible for maintaining credit-card security to share in the exposure.

The future promises still more potential for business value. As computing moves from applications on a processor to services on a network, assets and resources become more flexible. Three different facets of the underlying dynamic are leaving labs to enter practical deployment:

- Cloud computing refers to the availability of computing resources within the Internet. The physical location of a server or an instance of software is immaterial to the user, but Google, Yahoo, Microsoft, and other vendors are building enormous data centers, often located near cheap hydroelectric power plants, to deliver functionality over the network.
- Virtualization refers to resources more typically within an enterprise that can play multiple roles and/or seem to be multiple places. A Virtual Private Network, for example, allows someone physically outside an enterprise network to access resources inside the firewall. Server virtualization, meanwhile, allows a given machine to run multiple operating systems, support different business process, and increase its cost-effectiveness by becoming a fungible rather than dedicated piece of infrastructure.
- Services-oriented architectures are another way for enterprises to reduce maintenance costs and increase flexibility. Applications talk to each other and share data in standards-based ways, allowing new functionality to be assembled from existing resources in a much more modular fashion than traditional development would allow.

# CONCLUSION

Given the breadth, depth, and momentum of these large-scale changes, it is no surprise that business leaders are having to reconsider many fundamental assumptions and change both their own and their organizations' behavior.

The chapters that follow analyze many of these reconsiderations and innovations in closer detail, giving executives a rich palette of options for consideration.

# ENDNOTES

1   Farrell, Diana, et. al. "Sizing the Emerging Global Labor Market." *McKinsey Quarterly,* 2005.
2   Alan S. Blinder. "Offshoring: The Next Industrial Revolution?" *Foreign Affairs*, March/April 2006.
3   "The Digital Provide: Information (technology), market performance and welfare in the South Indian fisheries sector," *Quarterly Journal of Economics*, August 2007.
4   If Barclays were a country and ranked by GDP, it would be the eighth largest economy in the world, trailing France and ahead of Canada.
5   "The Globalization of Capital Markets," paper delivered at Second Interregional United Nations Training Workshop on International Taxation and Steering Committee of the ad hoc Group of Experts on International Cooperation on Tax Matters, 23-27 April 2001.
6    For more on DeBeers, see "How to Succeed in the Multi-faceted Diamond Business: The Gospel According to De Beers," published April 18, 2007 in Knowledge@ Wharton, available at http://knowledge.wharton.upenn.edu/.
7   CIO Insight August 2006 Survey: http://www.cioinsight.com/article2/0,1397,2012823,00.asp.
8   Joseph Periera, "Breaking the Code: How Credit-Card Data Went Out Wireless Door" *Wall Street Journal*, May 4, 2007.

# SECTION 2:

# NEW BUSINESS PRIORITIES IN A WORLD OF ACCELERATING CHANGE

# 2.1

# ACCELERATING INNOVATION

**Mark Johnson,** *Co-Founder and Chairman, Innosight*
**Josh Suskewicz,** *Associate, Innosight*

Innovation – and accelerated, continuous innovation at that – is now more of a competitive imperative than ever before. The associated phenomena of globalization and commoditization exert a leveling force that rapidly and ruthlessly erodes competitive advantage. As a result, hard-earned differentiation is fleeting, and, simultaneously, the race to keep up with an ever multiplying set of competitors is pitched. The only antidote is to innovate.

This chapter will detail strategies that help enterprises jumpstart their innovation efforts. First, let us address the two ways companies can accelerate innovation independently, as each has different implications and requirements. Broadly, the two forms of acceleration are:

- Accelerate time to launch
- Accelerate time to mainstream market penetration

Mark Johnson and Josh Suskewicz

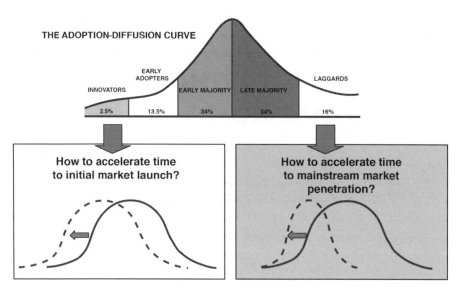

*Figure 1: Accelerating Innovation: The effect of the two forms of accelerated innovation on the distribution of Everett Rogers' adoption-diffusion curve over time; the chart on the left represents starting the adoption-diffusion process earlier by getting to market faster, and the chart on the right represents the more rapid diffusion of an innovation that is able to penetrate the mainstream faster.*[1]

The first form of acceleration involves speeding up the development and commercialization cycle that takes a business idea out into the market – rapidly forming and releasing product and service offerings, so as to, in some cases, set the pace and grab first mover advantage, and in others, to follow fast and blunt the deleterious effect of your competitor's innovation efforts. We will look to global silicone provider Dow Corning's surprisingly dexterous creation of Xiameter, a new business unit that operates on a fundamentally different business model than its parent, to illustrate key principles of what it takes to get to market fast.

The second form of acceleration is aimed at rapidly hitting a market sweet spot, thereby increasing the pace of consumer acceptance once your new product or service innovation hits the market so as to quickly attain scale and stay ahead of your competitive set. The development of retail health pioneer MinuteClinic, which is currently leading a furious race to scale, demonstrates the critical mechanisms needed to drive mainstream acceptance.

To be truly sustainable, these acceleration efforts must not be isolated efforts, but rather part of a company's ingrained innovation capability.

Therefore we will look at key underlying elements of the innovation process that catalyze rapid product development and allow companies to consistently and predictably evolve along with – and at the head of – their markets.

# ACCELERATING TIME TO LAUNCH

## Structure: Setting Teams up for Success

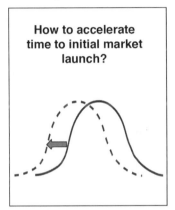

You have identified a pressing strategic need. It may be an emerging disruptive threat that could redefine competition in your market, or it may be a fantastic opportunity that has to be seized immediately, before your competitors spot it and close the gap. What can you do to ensure that your company executes as quickly as possible?

The best way to rapidly develop a product or service offering and get it out into the market is to set up a heavyweight team, grant it operational autonomy, and task it with complete responsibility for the project. The team should have decision making power, and should take it upon itself to break down and reconstruct processes so that they match the project's needs. The team should be led by an authorized project champion with enough power within the company to get things done. Team members should be co-located to avoid communications complexities and should be freed from other responsibilities so that they can focus on one project at a time. In addition, team leaders should have the ability to staff up and down as needed.

The heavyweight team should be backed by explicit senior management support recognized throughout the organization, so that corporate antibodies do not interfere. Senior management can – and must – play an active role in accelerating innovation, especially at the early stages (see graphic).

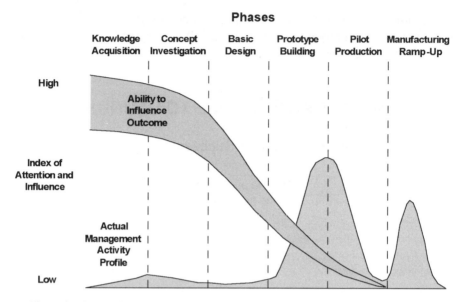

*Figure 2:* *Phases of Innovation: The degree of senior management involvement in new growth projects and the ability of senior management to influence outcomes is all too often off-phase. We advocate that senior managers become more involved in early stages of the process in order to shepherd innovative ideas that might otherwise be squelched by business-as-usual processes.*[2]

Additionally, the heavyweight team should have the power to break through corporate orthodoxies – within limits, of course – that might otherwise constrain it. Business-as-usual processes and corporate priorities can stagnate innovation efforts, if not stifle them entirely. Successful companies are set up to perform in a certain way: to execute upon their business model. To that end they are methodical and incredibly skilled; our research has made it clear that incumbents will almost always win battles of sustaining innovation. Yet, at the same time, these companies are big, lumbering, and, by nature, conservative. Therefore, they have trouble innovating at speed, especially if the innovation opportunity is potentially disruptive to their core business model. They tend to struggle in situations that require nimbleness and flexibility.

In order to avoid this dilemma, teams focused on new development should be kept at arms length from the standard processes that drive the core business. This is an organizational issue, requiring senior management mandate, corporate autonomy, customized processes and allocations. However, the issue is also cultural. The team must be given the freedom to "write its own rules": to build its own team culture in order to rapidly seize an opportunity space. Note that the most insidious rules are often unstated –

the mid-manager dismissing an innovation idea by saying, "oh, we don't do that," or the momentarily inspired employee realizing, "but this will never pass spec." These latent negative forces must be short-circuited.

The final point we'd like to make here about team structure is that teams should be staffed with employees with the proper "schools of experience."[3] If someone's job is seen as a school, then the experiences encountered while doing that job are the curriculum, or courses, that have been completed while performing the job. The most effective employees in any given situation are most likely to be the ones who have wrestled with – and learned from and succeeded at – similar situations in the past. The skills and intuition needed to succeed in a fast-paced environment of accelerated innovation are most reliably learned from experience, from attending the right "schools." Instead of looking for people with "the right stuff" who have done well in your core business, focus on recruiting people who have faced – and succeeded at – similar challenges to those that can be reasonably expected to present themselves to the team.

In sum, an autonomous, focused, empowered, and appropriately experienced team will give you the best shot at first mover advantage.

---

When attempting to accelerate innovation efforts, watch out for these common inhibiting factors:

- Lack of direction and focus leading to waste
- Inadequate - or too much - resources in the right areas
- Internal red tape and intra-team communication complexity
- Over-engineering the perfect product
- Failure to address potential bottlenecks
- Lack of competition leading to complacency

---

## Funding Motivation: "just enough" Targeted Resources

The flipside of staffing a heavyweight team is funding it appropriately. We advocate an approach by which companies grant new ventures "just enough" targeted resources – enough to be able to make progress and test key assumptions, but just enough so that teams are under pressure to develop a viable business model quickly. Companies must be willing to make the investment in innovation, but should not be doling out blank checks. In essence, companies should consider themselves venture capitalists, parceling out targeted amounts of money based on results. Necessity, after all, is the mother of invention. Scarcity and the pressure to earn the right to move forward will motivate creativity, force low-cost business model development, and, of course, kill underperforming projects before they become malingering black holes.

But when doling out money in a stage gate process, companies must make sure to use the appropriate benchmarks to review progress. The product development funnel that works for a core business may well suffocate ideas that fall beyond the incumbent business model. Just as teams pursuing innovation require autonomy to thrive, the course by which ideas are developed into products and services must be independent of business-as-usual processes as well.

To that end, distinct metrics will support rather than shackle innovation efforts. Core valuation tools like net present value and return on investment work very well when evaluating existing markets and knowable, highly sustaining development efforts. However, markets that don't exist can't be measured; don't let ratios built for core businesses restrain innovation efforts due to the misleading readings they are likely to produce. Instead, companies should focus on progress-tracking metrics like knowledge-to-assumption ratios, which are reflective of the development of the business idea as well as both directional and actionable. Indeed, this sort of "plan to learn" approach[4] in which teams focus on identifying and rapidly addressing risks and assumptions should guide strategic efforts (we will develop this further in our discussion on developing a core competence in innovation in Strategy: Plan to Learn on p. 62).

## Case study: Accelerating Innovation at Dow Corning[5]

These principles are best illustrated by Dow Corning's rapid creation of its Xiameter business unit in 2002. The company, which develops and sells silicon solutions to a wide range of industries across the world, is set up to deliver high technology solutions customized to its clients' needs. They have a world-class R&D operation and a large, well-trained sales force to deliver on their business model. Yet, as the 1990's wore on, Dow Corning began to face commoditizing pressures and was having trouble maintaining price premiums in certain market segments.

At the same time, Dow Corning was trying to figure out how to respond to the rise of the Internet and emerging e-commerce paradigms. The company had been historically configured to provide personalized, high-value added service throughout the sales process, and was therefore seemingly allergic to hands-off, automated sales processes. The Internet threatened their core business model, but, if played correctly, offered a way out of the increasingly apparent commoditization trap they found themselves in at the low end of the market.

In order to address this unique confluence of threat and opportunity, Dow Corning CEO Gary Anderson tasked a well-regarded executive, Don Sheets, to study the issue. Anderson promoted Sheets to peer level with the other business unit heads, and gave him an independent budget. Sheets set to work, and within six months had formulated an exciting but threatening business model: Dow Corning would set up an autonomous e-commerce unit that would sell bulk silicone products for 10-15% less than the prices established by the core business. Faced with disruptive pressures at the edges of its markets, Dow Corning would set up a new business model to disrupt itself.

Sheets was given his assignment in January 2001. He hit on the business model he wanted by June, and the new brand launched in January 2002, six months after it was conceived. Within three months Xiameter had paid back all the money invested in it, and within a few years had become a significant contributor to the company's suddenly much healthier bottom line. So how did the Xiameter team innovate so quickly and so well? Retrospectively, the people involved point to a few key elements of their strategy:

- Senior management commitment. Senior management let it be known throughout the organization that they personally sanctioned the Xiameter team to break rules. In addition, senior managers put their money where their mouth was by providing funding, opening up corporate ranks for staff selection, and letting the team utilize key Dow Corning resources (such as their state-of-the-art IT infrastructure) when necessary.
- Stake in the ground. Very early on, senior management decreed a launch date: Xiameter would be out the door by January 7th, 2002 no matter what. This deadline galvanized the team and forced focus and quick decision making. The deadline also underscored the seriousness of the effort, opening doors and paving the way for rapid action. Finally, it encouraged a "good enough" mentality; instead of wiling away at a particular aspect of the solution for weeks, Xiameter staff tackled problems collaboratively and moved on. There would be no waiting for unattainable perfection, no bottlenecks of diminishing marginal return.
- Autonomy. Being fully autonomous facilitated the types of counter-cultural decisions required to innovate at top speed. The team was completely removed from the normal Dow Corning system. They could remake any and all rules they needed to, and answered to no one but Sheets, who reported directly to Anderson, the CEO. This freedom to act was reinforced physically; the team was given their own floor in corporate headquarters to do with as they wished.

- New culture. Early on, the Xiameter team tore down the cubicles on their floor and arranged their desks in a circle with a fridge stocked with Coca-Cola in the middle. A stodgy old chemicals company was looking like a dot-com. The working environment they created was fun, fast-paced, and exciting, and it encouraged rapid progress.
- Selective hiring. An innovative team should be built according to aptitude for decision-making, ability to operate in uncertain conditions, and commitment to change. Xiameter specifically recruited team members who demonstrated abilities needed to succeed in the new division, not necessarily in the parent firm.

When it came to staffing, Sheets had his pick of Dow Corning employees from all over the world. Sheets looked for experienced but independent-minded people who would put in their all for the team. One of his colleagues remembers an internal note on a candidate that read: "Independent, doesn't follow rules, but very focused on what he does. Perfect for Xiameter."

After conducting personal interviews, Sheets had one final challenge for the people he liked: at the end of the interview, he told them on the spot that they could have the job, but would have to tell him yes or no immediately. Most of all, he wanted people who could make fast decisions and live with the consequences. Each employee Sheets targeted accepted. The caliber of the people that ended up on to the team enabled decentralized authority and on-the-fly decision making, greatly increasing Xiameter's flexibility and ability to execute quickly.

## Accelerating Mainstream Market Penetration

MinuteClinic, the pioneering retail health provider, is smack in the middle of a race to scale.[6] The company invented the retail health concept in 2000, and for the last seven years has been refining their concept and streamlining their execution. Now, scores of competitors are hot on their tail in the race to penetrate the mainstream market. After a half decade of slow, incremental growth, new clinics are popping up by the hundreds. How does a company pull the inflection point forward and win the race to scale?

First, nail the job. Jobs-to-be-done is a concept that we've written about extensively elsewhere[7], but in brief it is a methodology that forces companies to view markets from the perspective of the consumer, thereby orienting innovation efforts around solving fundamental problems in people's lives. The concept is based on Harvard Business School marketing professor Ted Levitt's famous formulation that people don't go to the hardware store to buy a drill, they go to buy a hole in the wall. Providing the solution to a

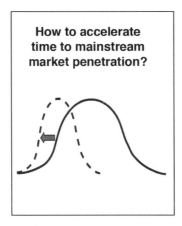

**How to accelerate time to mainstream market penetration?**

widespread and insufficiently satisfied customer job-to-be-done, then, is the best way to ensure mainstream penetration.

The MinuteClinic story is really about zeroing in on the right customer job. The founders of the company were pretty close from the start – they had the insight that the American medical system was over-engineered for simple procedures: it was way too difficult to receive straightforward care for common, easily treated ailments that could be more or less accurately self-diagnosed. They set up their business to solve the job of convenient care and got it nearly right.

The low-cost, cash-only, in-store clinics were immediately popular. People liked the fact that they could get their kid tested for strep throat in less than a half hour at the supermarket. They liked the clearly displayed and standardized lists of services and prices, and they liked the customer-focused care and service they got from the nurse practitioners who staffed the clinics. Even so, uptake was slow.

Why? Management eventually realized that even though their core value proposition was to provide convenience to customers, their early decision to work outside of the mainstream insurance networks – MinuteClinic was cash-only at first and did not accept insurance – needlessly complicated the purchasing decision of their customers. What had seemed like a simplifying maneuver – insurance is a complex headache for everyone – was in fact an inconvenience, as it forced the vast majority of consumers who already held health insurance to double pay for their healthcare. Once MinuteClinic made an effort to integrate within the healthcare system and accept insurance, it removed a significant barrier to consumption for its customers, making it that much easier to accomplish their core job-to-be-done – to attain rapid and convenient health care.

Before reaching an inflection point, MinuteClinic had to more deeply understand the job-to-be-done it was solving in people's lives. Companies should constantly evaluate the job-to-be-done of their target consumers, and adapt accordingly.

A frequent result of the adaptation process is simplifying the product offering. A clunky or overly complicated product will not be rapidly and widely accepted. In order to penetrate the mainstream, a product should either be modular and plug compatible, so people do not have to change their current infrastructure and behavior in order to use it, or be integrated and provide end-to-end value so consumers don't have to rely on other partners to get their job done.

*MinuteClinics are staffed by customer service-oriented certified nurse practitioners, and feature easy to read signage that helps customers know what to expect from their visit*

MinuteClinic features elements of these simplifying solutions. After early missteps, MinuteClinic has made itself plug compatible with the general healthcare system by working with the insurance companies to provide seamless coverage for patients and by situating its clinics in convenient retail locations – right next to pharmacies – in the path of the consumer. The convenient location enables customers to make just one stop for routine medical procedures – at a CVS pharmacy, where they can park near the front door, get service in 15 minutes or so, and pick up their prescription at the adjacent pharmacy counter.

MinuteClinic also integrated key functionalites in order to ensure seamless delivery of service. Nurse practitioners, for example, are trained to exact specifications, and clinics are run on a proprietary, home-grown IT system that creates and dispatches electronic medical records of patient visits. Instead of relying on existing infrastructure, MinuteClinic was able to develop these key elements of their system in-house in order to retain full control over sensitive variables.

Similarly important is the endorsement of key influencers. To quickly accept a new format, system, or product, consumers need to be reassured. They need to hear about the benefits of the new offering from figures they trust and view as authorities. It was essential for MinuteClinic to work with doctors and the broader medical system in order to obtain their stamp of approval and be seen as trustworthy and reliable. The company therefore chose to work with the medical community to co-develop appropriate clinical guidelines while demonstrating how they could work together to increase overall health and well-being.

Beyond signing up key influencers, companies hoping to accelerate their path to mainstream penetration must work to align their value networks so that powerful players are properly motivated to support them. Initially, MinuteClinic had positioned itself as a competitor to doctors and insurance companies; they saw themselves as an answer to a complex, clogged, and overly bureaucratic system. However, in order to gain traction, the company realized that it would need the support of established players to win popular and regulatory approval. Therefore, MinuteClinic changed course and began positioning itself as a complementary part of the medical system. It emphasizes its various beneficial effects in the value chain in corporate communications and lobbying efforts: its low prices save money for payers like insurance companies, employers, and government agencies, and its speedy alternative service helps unclog doctors offices, which all too often find themselves overrun by patients needing routine care. Furthermore, retail health clinics free highly-trained specialists to devote themselves to more complex and more lucrative treatments; instead of removing warts, they can focus on managing chronic diseases. MinuteClinic also sources new patients for local doctors. It assembles referral lists of local physicians, and when a patient comes into a branch without a medical home or with a condition that is beyond the treatment capability of the site, it refers them out to an affiliated physician.

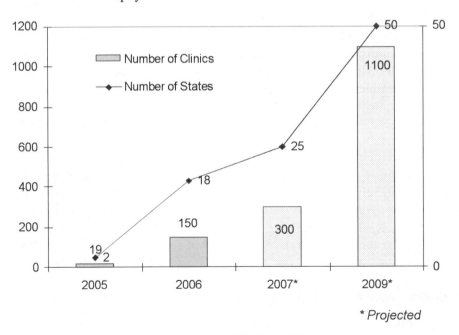

*Figure 3: Growth of US MinuteClinics*[8]

Ever since alighting on this new strategy in 2004, MinuteClinic has been off to the races. It has grown from 19 sites in two states in 2005 to 150 sites in 18 states in 2006, with plans for as many as 1100 sites across the country by 2009. The keys to this acceleration were nailing the job, providing a simple, plug-compatible and/or integrated solution, gaining the endorsement of key influencers, and aligning the value network.

---

When attempting to accelerate mainstream market penetration, watch out for these common inhibiting factors:

- Channel chokehold
- Over-engineered solution
- Competing and confusing standards
- Entrenched opposition
- Interdependent systems
- Regulatory barriers

---

## Making Accelerated Innovation a Core Competence

The principles and tactics laid out in the previous sections of this chapter provide guidance intended to help companies accelerate their innovation efforts. To be truly effective, we believe that companies need to support targeted innovation efforts with an effective innovation process. They must develop the skills, capabilities, and structures to make innovation repeatable and predictable. Without the right structures in place, organizations have an overwhelming tendency to fall into old habits. Existing processes can subtly influence even the best growth idea until it bears a striking resemblance to the company's old products and business model.

Innosight has written about these topics extensively elsewhere[9]; in this treatment we will focus on the elements of the innovation process that specifically encourage speed to market. Certain key elements of the acceleration process have been discussed already, such as senior management commitment and targeting resources. Here we will zero in on two remaining key points: tools and screens to rapidly surface and prioritize innovation opportunities, and the strategic mindset best suited to developing them.

### Surfacing Jobs-to-be-Done

One of the biggest keys to acceleration is to deeply understand the jobs-to-be done and tolerable tradeoffs of different consumer segments. In order to gain consistent access to these pressing jobs in the market, we recommend that companies establish jobs-to-be-done feedback channels through which they maintain consistent contact with key consumer groups.

To fuel the innovation process, companies need consistent mechanisms to constantly gather knowledge about the jobs that non-consumers and consumers are trying to do. This external input is critical for companies hoping to create new growth. At the most basic level, feedback can come from casual interactions. We have seen impressive results from acts as simple as inviting local target customers to an informal lunch, casually "interviewing" friends and family members at dinner, or intercepting potential customers in locations such as malls or playgrounds. Simply initiating conversations about the jobs individuals and businesses are trying to do can provide much insight into consumer needs.

Simple structures to make this feedback more systematic can include having outward-facing managers dedicate a fixed portion of their time to customer interactions and conducting regular focus groups with customers and non-customers to explore jobs. Even more systematic approaches include forming a dedicated group of consumers or businesses as standing test-beds for new ideas. This can allow companies to get quick feedback on whether new ideas actually meet the jobs of identified consumers. Finally, companies can consider solutions that are just beginning to emerge like vendor-hosted online communities that allow constant interaction with a group of current or potential customers.

Companies should consider creating mechanisms for unsolicited input as well. Opening channels for staff and consumers to share ideas can bring jobs insights from unexpected places.

Finally, celebrating good behavior helps to strengthen feedback mechanisms. One way to do this is to recognize staff members who use jobs concepts or undertake jobs research. Another key to success is encouraging senior management to model desired behaviors such as interviewing non-consumers. Procter & Gamble CEO A.G. Lafley is famous for visiting consumers in their homes and observing them using P&G's products.

These jobs-to-be-done feedback channels will help you maintain contact with the market, with consumers and non-consumers of your products.

---

Constrain innovation to speed it up by establishing "goals and bounds".[10]

Paradoxically, another key innovation structure is constraint. Clearly establish goals and bounds that outline the kinds of innovation that are desirable, discussable, and unthinkable for each

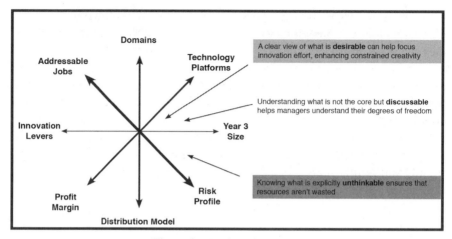

*Figure 4:* "*Goals and Bounds*"

of your business units. This will at once clarify strategic goals to the entire organization, focusing and streamlining efforts. It also may encourage the emergence of ideas that may have been assumed to be out of bounds if they at least fall into the discussable category. Of course, this framework will also discourage employees from wasting time on ideas that are simply unthinkable for your company, for whatever reason. What appears to be a constraint on creativity and imagination can actually be a catalyst for accelerating innovation.

## Strategy: Plan to Learn

The strategy driving accelerated innovation efforts should be geared towards addressing risks and assumptions as quickly as possible. It should be an emergent – rather than a deliberate – strategy.[11]

Generally, an emergent strategy is a bottom-up approach that entails evolving and adapting business plans based on signals solicited from the marketplace. This strategy focuses on running tests that get underneath key assumptions and risks in order to quickly figure out how to adjust strategies accordingly. Rather than picking a strategic course from the get-go, the emergent approach allows market feedback and smart analysis to guide the development of the strategy.

Innovation opportunities in particular are fraught with risks and unknowns. Assuming too much knowledge about market dynamics or previously unmet consumer needs can be very dangerous. The key is to

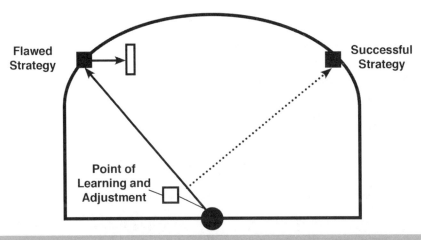

**Flawed Strategy**

**Successful Strategy**

**Point of Learning and Adjustment**

**More than 90% of successful new ventures start off following the wrong strategy[12]**

uncover and gain knowledge about these unknowns as quickly as possible, in order to enable rapid adaptation.

We therefore recommend that companies develop simple and inexpensive tests to quickly get valuable consumer feedback. They should "invest a little to learn a lot," as the mantra goes, in order to refine their understanding of true consumer jobs and performance tradeoff profiles. As assumptions are confirmed, risks dealt with, and knowledge unearthed, companies can move with greater confidence towards launch.

A key element of this approach is a "good enough" mentality. When developing solutions, look for the areas in which customers will be satisfied with "good enough" performance. Often, people are happy to trade off improvement and high performance in one aspect of a solution in favor of another, depending on the job they are trying to get done. Focusing on meeting a "good enough" threshold frees companies from the endless struggle for perfection and encourages them to get prototypes and test products out the door quickly and into the hands of customers where rapid and effective targeted improvements can be discerned.

One way to do this is to push for in-market work with innovators and early adopters to rapidly iterate towards a successful approach. This sort of testing, in "foothold markets", will provide input on product attributes, consumer performance thresholds, and business model considerations. Testing can also potentially identify "low hanging fruit" – easily picked early monetization opportunities that provide proof-of-concept transactional weight and help pay for the continuation of the project.

# CONCLUSION

As global competition heats up, companies in almost all industries are under increasing pressure to innovate at the pace and scale of the market. This imperative is challenging, no doubt, but we firmly believe that the study of innovation has begun to surface patterns and yield insights that make accelerated and sustainable new market growth increasingly achievable and repeatable.[13]

# ENDNOTES

1.   Adoption-diffusion curve adapted from Everett Rogers, "Diffusion of Innovations" (1995 4th cd).
2.   Gluck, Frederick W and Richard N. Foster, "Managing Technological Change" Harvard Business Review, September-October 1975.
3.   The "schools of experience" concept has been adapted from Morgan McCall's "High Flyers: Developing the Next Generation of Leaders," and is referenced in chapter seven of Clayton Christensen's "The Innovator's Solution".
4.   The "plan to learn" concept is adapted from Ian C. MacMillan and Rita Gunther McGrath's "Discovery-driven planning," Harvard Business Review, July 1, 1995.
5.   This case example is based on interviews the authors conducted with Dow Corning and Xiameter executives in the fall of 2006.
6.   This case example is based on interviews the authors conducted with MinuteClinic executives in December 2006.
7.   Our most recent thinking can be found in "Finding the Right Job for Your Product," MIT Sloan Management Review, Spring 2007.
8.   Data provided by MinuteClinic; Innosight analysis.
9.   A good summary of our recent thinking can be found in "Mapping Your Innovation Strategy," Harvard Business Review, May 2006.
10.  Innosight analysis.
11.  A good summary is provided in Innosight's "Mastering the Emergent Strategy Process," Strategy and Innovation, March-April 2006.
12.  Innosight analysis.
13.  We'd like to acknowledge the contributions of our colleagues Scott Anthony, Adeline Ng, and Natalie Painchaud to the development of this chapter.

## 2.2

# BUSINESS MODEL INNOVATION

**Stacy Comes,** *Director, Corporate Communications, SAP AG*
**Lilac Berniker,** *Manager, Innosight*

Companies of all sizes, in all countries and in all industries are facing accelerated change and corresponding opportunities and challenges. The market leaders of 2015 will be companies that embrace this as an opportunity, developing cultures that create change, drive it through the organization, and leverage the associated skills to innovate for execution excellence. Sustained leadership in this new business world demands quicker, more "open" innovation on product, services and business models.

Business model innovation is extremely valuable when done right, creating new markets or transforming existing ones and generating billions of dollars of market value. Knowing a company's business model provides more than insight into metrics and management levers. It can help illuminate an important, underutilized form of innovation that goes beyond product or process innovation.

There is little doubt that business model innovation can clearly impact the long-term success of a company. CEO surveys show that innovation in business models – how business is done – is rapidly becoming as or more important than product and service innovation as a driver of competitive advantage and growth. Companies are increasingly seeking to find new innovation levers beyond product innovation (adding a new blade to a razor) or process innovation (six sigma programs). True business model innovation – exemplified by clear triumphs such as Southwest Airlines, Apple iTunes and Wal-mart – has created astonishing growth. Business model innovations have reshaped entire industries and redistributed billions of dollars of value. They have caused powerful companies, operating according to traditional models, to fail while those that adopt new models – often entrants – achieve fantastic growth.

When Amazon.com emerged as a new entrant in the bookseller space, analysts cited its enormous inventory as a core advantage. Retail outlets, bound by the limits of floor space, could never compete with the millions of titles available through Amazon.com. The young technology behind online retailing was trumping years of careful market analysis and predictive stocking algorithms. The magic that has powered Amazon.com to an $11 billion market capitalization, however, was not just in the Internet. Dozens of online retailers failed, as unlimited inventory does not naturally result in a competitive advantage.

The true source of Amazon's success was in its business model innovation, leveraging the technology to profit not from the sales of books but from the timing of payments (see Figure 1). Amazon collects on its accounts receivable weeks before it pays its suppliers, and, taking a page from the financial services industry, creates profits from the float. Business model

## Amazon.com Operating Cycle

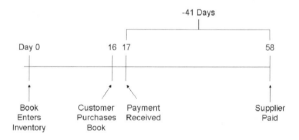

## Typical Book Retailer Operating Cycle

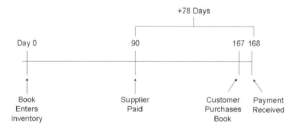

*Figure 1: Comparison of Operating Cycle and Cash Flow*

innovation, not technological innovation, created sustainable competitive advantage for the new entrant into a centuries-old business.

|                              | Land Based | Amazon.com |
|------------------------------|------------|------------|
| Superstores                  | 439        | 1          |
| Rent per square foot         | $20        | $8         |
| Occupancy costs (% of sales) | 12%        | <4%        |
| Sales per square foot        | $250       | $2,000     |
| Sales per operating employee | $100,000   | $300,000   |
| Inventory turnover           | 2-3X       | 50-60X     |

*Figure 2: Resource Comparison*

Although business model innovation has always existed, the term "business model" came to light most prominently in the late 1990s, when entrepreneurs flocked to Silicon Valley often with nothing more than an idea and a pocket full of funding from optimistic venture capitalists. Though there were more failures than successes in that era, the crew of dotcom entrepreneurs who managed to succeed did so by finding novel ways to sell their wares and ultimately creating an entirely new way of doing business.

Then why doesn't this immense promise and high-level attention translate to action? An analysis of major innovations in the last decade shows that few have been business-model related,[1] and a recent study determined that no more than 10% of innovation efforts at global companies are focused on business models.[2] All too often, it seems corporate innovation efforts are focused solely on developing new products or processes. That said, the term "business model" survived the dotcom bust and remains top of mind with executives today: In a 2005 survey by the Economist Intelligence Unit, 54% of executives said that between now and 2010, business model innovation will be even more important for success than product or service innovation.[3] CEOs echoed these results in the IBM CEO Study of 2006, in which nearly 30% of respondents cited business model innovation as a key focus area.[4]

## Follow the Money: Displacement in the Retail and Airline Industries

In retail, discounters that entered the market with innovative business models now account for 75% of the total valuation of their entire sector, having seized more than $300 billion of market value. Across a similar timeframe, low-fare U.S. regional airlines have grown from a blip on the radar screen to make up 55% of the market value of all carriers.[5] Despite all their talent, market power, and resources, incumbent companies rarely transition to new models. So what makes business model innovation so difficult, and why has it been relatively ignored, in practice, despite all of the attention it gets? A closer examination of these two industries highlights the opportunities that abound.

To start the discussion on the impact of business model innovation, let's take a look at one of the fundamental business model shifts that has shaken up the retailing industry. In the late part of the nineteenth and the early part of the twentieth centuries, the predominant mode of retailing in the United States and Europe was the full-service department store. First pioneered in Paris with Bon Marche and La Samaritaine, department stores were large, general merchandise establishments that brought together an assortment of goods previously available only from local merchants. By the 1880s, department store magnates like Marshall Field in Chicago had built stores on high-traffic corner lots in major cities where consumers streamed in to purchase everything from chocolates to couture.

While the level of personal customer service and attention was less than that found in small, specialty merchants, these department stores provided convenient luxuries that local merchants could not. Marshall Field's offered a full service restaurant, retiring lounges, gift wrapping services, and home delivery, and in its flagship Chicago store, featured a handcrafted, iridescent Tiffany glass ceiling.[6]

Department stores became successful because they were able to offer the same goods that specialty merchants offered, but more conveniently and at lower prices. These large retailers distributed an assortment of familiar products from a location frequented by a large volume of potential customers. Local merchants, who experienced less traffic, were victim to a high inventory, low turnover formula, which required them to charge high prices to achieve solid returns. In department stores, however, inventory turnover was much higher, enabling the large retailers to make attractive profits with lower markups. Department stores, to a certain extent, had trained consumers to expect an increased level of convenience at a lower price.

In the 1950s, department stores became vulnerable to the same forces that initially created their success. National brands had gained momentum, which caused consumers to be less reliant on the service or reputation of the retailer to make purchase decisions. Additionally, more consumers were driving automobiles, living outside city centers, and were willing to travel to suburbs to do their shopping[7], if it might save them money. Discounter pioneers like Marty Chase of Ann & Hope in Providence, Rhode Island, and Sol Price of Fed-Mart in Southern California, two of Wal-Mart founder Sam Walton's principal influences, figured out that by engineering their assortment around high-volume products and building warehouse-like self-service stores that minimized staffing and real estate costs while maximizing customer flow, they could make as much money annually as department stores while significantly undercutting them on price.[8] Effectively, discount retailers found a formula that traded a loss in markup for a rise in turnover, resulting in attractive profits in a very different business model.[9]

While the strategy may appear simple and inevitable in hindsight, department store managers were not unsophisticated. The problem was that they were likely comparing themselves to the wrong set of competitors— local merchants and other department stores—and were late to see the discounters as a credible threat to their business. Department stores failed to evolve with the changing needs of consumers. The new profit vehicle in retailing was built on a low-cost, low-price, high-turn business model, and by the turn of the century, the mammoth discount retailer Wal-Mart had taken over the industry.

Wal-Mart, which adopted the discount retailer profit model, is now the world's largest company, clearing all previous revenue records with $287 billion in 2005 and a market capitalization approaching $200B. Alternatively, Sears, which rose to prominence with the advent of department stores and catalog retailing, failed to adapt to changing consumer needs and emerging technologies. In 2005, the 120-year-old retailer was valued at just $11B and was forced to merge with discounter Kmart to reduce overhead costs and gain access to lower cost real estate.[10]

The same industry transformation developed in the airline industry later in the century, starting in the United States and soon moving overseas as the new model for conducting business proved fruitful. In 1978, the dominant airlines in the US were the major interstate carriers that catered to business travelers. Routes and prices were regulated by the federal government, affording the industry stability but encouraging inefficiency and inflating both prices and perks. At the time, Southwest Airlines was a Texas intra-state carrier operating short-haul flights not covered by federal regulations between Dallas, Houston, and San Antonio. Southwest capitalized on local business customers and dissatisfied leisure customers who were unhappy using interstate carriers like Braniff, which served these cities as an extension of flights from major out-of-state markets. With interstate carriers, flight delays were common, prices were high, and seats were allocated first to passengers continuing on more lucrative long-haul flights.[11]

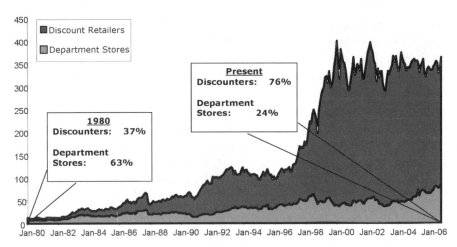

**Figure 3:** *Displacement in Retailing, Distribution of Market Valuation in the Retail Sector*
*Source: Datastream; Innosight analysis*

Southwest founder Rollin King, who had previously run an air taxi service, figured that if he could make short-haul flights timely, low cost, and profitable in their own right, he could steal share from the major carriers and increase demand for air travel. King pointed to a discussion he had with Andy Andrews, president of California regional carrier PSA, "Andy told us that the way you ought to figure your price was not how much you can get or what the other carriers are charging. He said, 'pick a price at which you can break even with a reasonable load factor.'"[12] The key to the model was reducing overhead, cutting out middlemen who claimed a share of the gross profits, and increasing utilization of planes. King shaved costs to the bone: selling direct to avoid travel agent commissions, picking airports with low fees, running a single-aircraft fleet, minimizing time on the tarmac between takeoffs and landings, and automating ticketing. Southwest set the price between Dallas and Houston at $20, a 25-30% discount compared to Braniff prices for the same routes.[13]

When deregulation opened new markets for expansion, Southwest chose to stick to its low cost model. Southwest already saw the benefit of operating a single type of aircraft that demonstrated low fixed costs per flight and fast turnaround potential and chose to expand its fleet with new jets from Boeing's 737 platform. In addition, the low-fare pricing structure that helped Southwest achieve market dominance on its Texas routes proved to be a winning strategy for entering and controlling new routes and airports. Recently, a host of new low fare carriers, including JetBlue and United's Ted in the United States and RyanAir and easyJet in Europe, have emerged, competing based on their own versions of business model innovation.

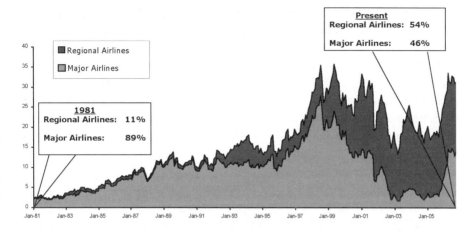

*Figure 4:* *Displacement in Airlines, Distribution of Market Valuation in the Airline Sector*
*Source: Datastream; Innosight analysis*

## Value Creation through Business Model Innovation

Business today is undergoing faster and more profound change than ever before. Business leaders who seize the opportunities and alter their practices to capture new competitive advantages will sustain a winning trajectory in the global marketplace. Business model innovation is often sparked by changes in underlying market conditions. These moments of disequilibrium can be threats or opportunities; companies that are slow to respond or incapable of transitioning will suffer, while those that spot shifts early and organize for business model innovation will succeed.

Understanding business model innovation will help companies of all sizes analyze their competitive positions and spot opportunities for growth. For those companies struggling in stagnant or rapidly evolving markets, however, business model innovation could be a matter of life and death. Adopting a new strategy can be viewed as a hedge against the potential negative outcomes in the marketplace and will enable a company to achieve new market growth, respond to competitor moves more quickly, and capitalize on disruptive innovations in the market.

Emerging trends and business model innovation can create tremendous growth opportunities for companies that adapt their strategy efficiently and execute business model innovation successfully. To derive value for an organization, senior executives must consider the following trends:

*Mature markets whose products are on the verge of becoming commodities:* the forces of globalization and increasing customer sophistication are pushing more and more products to commoditization. Going from a specialized, high-end business model to a mass-production, low-end model can be excruciating. Think of the troubles of PC makers such as Compaq and Dell, and consider how, in contrast, Apple transitioned to the iPod. Further, to counter rapid commoditization triggered by intense competition, product companies are not only creating high-value services for enhanced revenue and profit growth, but are also wrapping these services in entirely new business models (e.g. charging for cubic-feet of cooled air rather than for an air conditioner and maintenance).

*Democratizing or decentralizing products and services:* as globalization opens up new markets and advancing technology enables the consumption of formerly complex products by less sophisticated end-users, companies in industries as varied as software, defense, healthcare, and consumer packaged goods are coming under pressure to innovate their business models in order to tap into new growth segments. Enterprise software companies, for example, are targeting small businesses to find growth beyond the crowded corporate market, while retail health centers like those operated by MinuteClinic are moving basic care from doctor's offices into more consumer-friendly settings.

*Companies looking to leverage underutilized resources or capabilities:* many companies have excess capacity – be it technological, human, or manufacturing – that does not get optimized within a core business model. Simultaneously, tacit and transactional work has eclipsed transformation (e.g. manufacturing, agricultural) as the primary lever for value creation. Often, this can be exploited for cost-effective growth. Deutsche Postbank developed a successful transactions processing unit after realizing that their I/T systems and back office capabilities could be better leveraged to drive greater profits.

*Markets impacted by legal or regulatory change:* some of the most dramatic business model innovations have come in response to abrupt changes in business environments resulting from regulatory or legal changes that render existing business models obsolete, ineffective, or vulnerable. Regardless of size, enterprises participating in the global economy will face the same challenges as they grapple with new and often inconsistent regulations. Consider the effect of deregulation on the airline industry in the US; as major interstate airlines solidified their spoke-and-hub, multi-tiered pricing models, Southwest seized the opportunity to expand its low cost point-to-point approach.

*Companies considering or executing mergers and acquisitions of firms with different business models:* sometimes it is easier to buy a new business model than it is to create one from scratch, so long as a solid understanding of the need for individualized resources and processes informs integration efforts. Business model differences must be respected. Cisco has been very effective at buying and integrating companies; it purchased Linksys to enter the home router market and, by and large, left the company alone, enabling it to grow without the encumbrances entrenched in the Cisco bureaucracy.

*Companies looking to harness new technologies:* new technologies create opportunities that fundamentally change the way companies do business. Many companies fail to reap benefits from technological developments because they attempt to fit them into an existing business model. Oftentimes new technologies require entirely new models as digitization is leading to an irreversible shift in monetization strategies after decades of stability. For example, many print media companies have thus far failed to exploit the power of the Internet, and are struggling to replace revenue lost from the migration of consumers to the web.

## What is Business Model Innovation?

Product innovation is fairly well understood. The development of new capabilities or goods to sell to consumers and businesses is an art mastered by the likes of Microsoft and Proctor & Gamble. Process innovation is modestly more ephemeral, but students of Just-in-Time manufacturing can easily comprehend that re-engineering business processes in new ways could yield tremendous competitive advantage. However, while businesses large and small fall victim to the competitive onslaught of business model innovation, it has been left undefined – and almost unidentifiable except in hindsight.

Months of research conducted by SAP and Innosight to better define business model innovation and the opportunities created have yielded a framework for understanding the change associated with business model innovation. While the work continues to progress, it is clear to all involved that the scale of business model innovation is nothing short of a complete transformation of the firm. The core of business model innovation lies in new answers to the following two questions – the key answers that guide any business:

- What value is the company providing to its customers?
- How does providing this value profit the company?

By examining each question, and drawing upon case examples of companies who have executed successfully, we can tease out the power of business model innovation.

## What Value is the Company Providing to its Customers?

Discussions of the customer value proposition fill the meeting rooms of companies worldwide. The quality of the product, the role of the product in the customer's life or business, the support and service your firm provides, and the way you measure up against your competition overlay every business decision. However, these conversations are laden with assumptions about what the customer values, what "quality" means, what commands a premium price, and what drives purchase decisions. At the core of almost all innovative business models lay different conclusions about these and other assumptions about the customer, the competition, and the market.

With enviable foresight, the then-CEO of Dow Corning, Gary Anderson, recognized in 2002 that the assumptions his firm held regarding the needs of their customers were incomplete. The company, a specialty chemical manufacturer, is a premium supplier of silicone based products, providing high-end design services, personalized sales support and flexibility to its buyers around the globe. In its excellence, however, Dow Corning had begun to alienate a group of its own customers who had become experts in their own right about the silicone products they needed, and therefore began optimizing their buying habits on price alone.

This realization that Dow Corning's assumptions regarding customer value were valid only among a fraction of the total potential customer base led to the creation of a new business unit, dubbed Xiameter. The Xiameter team, led by Don Sheets, had a very different customer in mind. These were the customers who told the Dow Corning sales teams: "You don't get it. I just want a low price – I don't want value-added services."

Through an open-minded effort to better understand these customers, the Xiameter team came to paint a new portrait of their ideal customer: one that had no support needs, bought large quantities of standard product, and optimized for price. And, to mirror their target customer base, the Xiameter team shed the Dow Corning "premium-quality/specialized services/anything-for-our-customers" image and created a new image as a no-frills, efficient seller of large quantities of basic product, complete with a different brand name, new logo color, and low budget operations.

In the years since the inception of Xiameter, the division has grown to account for 30% of the total sales of Dow Corning. One of the most counterintuitive results of the effort, however, concerns the target customer base. It was assumed that Xiameter would pick off the most price-conscious customers of Dow Corning's main business. While that did occur, management was surprised to see many of the same customers frequenting both businesses regularly. The same customer had fundamentally distinct needs at different times. It was also assumed that this cannibalization of the core business would hurt Dow Corning's premium sales. On the contrary, the sales teams now feel they have greater leverage against discounting their product; for a real discount, they can encourage their customers to turn to Xiameter.

The founders of MinuteClinic conceived a fundamentally different view of the customer at the firm's inception. Driven to found the company after a profoundly unpleasant visit with his son to the urgent care clinic to eliminate the chance of Strep throat, Rick Krieger realized that this routine procedure required none of the ceremony and skill of a hospital. Rather, as a customer, he valued accuracy, convenience, and speed when seeking care for his son. He did not need on-call heart surgeons, oncology units, or even the capacity to set bones. All he needed was a competent nurse with a Strep test at his disposal, who was available during the off-hours to alleviate concern or prescribe antibiotics.

MinuteClinic provides its customers with just that: a nurse practitioner in a kiosk at a local drugstore who, for a set fee (or insurance co-payment), will address a relatively short list of medical concerns ranging from ear infections to wart removal. With the promise of a 15-minute-or-less wait-time and easy prescription filling at the pharmacy, MinuteClinic has the harried parent or concerned individual in mind. Referring the more complex cases to a physician, as appropriate, the company knows what value it provides – and does not provide – to its customers.

Recently, the CEO of MinuteClinic, Michael Howe, was asked whether the "MinuteClinic" brand somehow indicated weak quality, since most people seek thorough, thoughtful medical care. On the contrary, he replied, it encapsulated the exact value proposition for the customer – and indeed, there are times when thoughtful, thorough care is not required.

Who is your customer? Who isn't your customer? Of course, your firm stands for quality. The products are superior. The service you provide is extraordinary. But, is it possible that some part of the market simply does not value these measures of quality? If you continue to improve your product, year in year out, while your prices remain stable, could it be that these enhancements are not valued by the market? What assumptions does your firm make about its customers that continue to drive these enhancements – and is there a possibility that they are incorrect?

Two contrasting firms further exemplify this point. On one end of the spectrum lies IKEA: a company whose customers value price and innovative design over glorious furniture showrooms and even "ease of assembly." The company is extraordinarily successful because it realized that customers value the lower price, the pedestrian and quirky shopping experience, and the ability to go home with a hutch in the trunk of their car. The image of the customer in the mind of IKEA designers looks nothing like that of the Ethan Allen team, and every aspect of the products and services of both firms mirror those images. If Ethan Allen chose to alter its customer image, how drastically would the company's products and priorities change?

On the other side of the spectrum lies Nespresso, the high-end line of espresso machines and corresponding pods of coffee created by Nestlé. Requiring a sizable up-front investment in the machine and ongoing purchase of the pods directly from Nespresso or a select group of retailers, the Nespresso product targets customers who want a superior home coffee experience, far in excess of that of Nescafé or even traditional home espresso machines. Nespresso has isolated a market need for consistent, easy, high-quality espresso in the home and driven products and services directly at that need.

Whether high-end or low-end, efficient or full-service, companies have tremendous abilities to change their offerings to suit the needs of a variety of customers. However, more often than not, companies anchor upon a single vision of their customer – their "best" customer – that precludes investment in products and services that would serve the rest of the market. It is possible and sometimes necessary, however, to serve multiple types of customers because, if you don't, odds are good that someone else will.

## How Does Providing this Value Profit the Company?

The obvious objection that arises in the mind of any good manager is: how can I be profitable serving these other markets? A more appropriate question is: how could any firm be profitable serving these markets? Southwest was profitable on $20 flights. IKEA is profitable on $100 tables. Firms that successfully build new business models find a way to achieve profitability at the price point demanded by their market.

In one of the most challenging lending markets, Bangladesh, Grameen Bank made a profitable business out of microlending, the practice of making small, unsecured loans to would-be entrepreneurs, often women. Mohammad Yunus, an economics professor, founded Grameen Bank in 1983 to expand lending in order to break the cycle of poverty among the poorest segments in Bangladesh. To compensate for a lack of credit history or collateral, borrowers are required to form five-person groups. The first two members take out small loans from Grameen backed by the group's collective assets. Other members can begin to borrow as the first two members establish a repayment history. While average loan balances are just 5,500 taka (~US$90), Grameen remains profitable by limiting overhead and maintaining margins through high loan recovery rates. Screening, supervision, and collection services are carried out by "bicycle bankers" dispatched to villages. In addition, despite the lack of collateral, Grameen's loan recovery rate is an enviable 99% with many borrowers graduating up to larger loans as their businesses grow.

New companies must find profit in these markets, or they will flounder. Absent an anchor of 40% margins or complex overhead structure, companies are free to make organizational, pricing, and go-to-market choices that maintain profits. However, successful firms typically have demanding margin requirements, high overhead commitments, and years of entrenched processes, channels, partnerships, and sales models. These hard-earned assets, both physical and intangible, define competitive advantage, market power, and market valuation, but, they also bestow a rigidity upon the company which often must be broken in order to innovate the business model.

When embarking upon the research, we feared one conclusion would emerge: only start-ups can innovate on business models. Such a conclusion would have been devastating to incumbents. While the list of successful innovators is weighted heavily in favor of new ventures, there are shining stars among the incumbents as well.

If we turn back to the case of Xiameter, a division of Dow Corning, we see an example of a firm that generated profits at a lower market tier. Entering a more commoditized market, Dow Corning made an early decision to price their product at the spot rate of silicone, while securing supply through long term contracts. Armed with a strong margin opportunity – between cost and price – they were charged with the task of adjusting internal costs to maximize profitability. Recognizing that profitability would be impossible if the group were forced to accept the same overhead structure as its parent company, the management decision was made to allow Xiameter to operate independently, responsible for only the costs they incurred.

Freed from that burden, the Xiameter team had to manage its own operational costs. To minimize handling costs, products came in one quantity, shipping schedules were pre-set, and all orders were serviced strictly through a web interface. There had to be no human intervention in the delivery of an order. The team itself continues to be staffed entirely by fewer than 15 individuals, despite the growth in revenue. All special requests are transferred directly to the core business unit.

As it turned out, Xiameter could be quite profitable and deliver the customer value on these relatively low margins. But, the management of both Xiameter and Dow Corning had to accept that, while profitable, this business looked very different from the core business, both operationally and financially. Organizations that succeed in innovating business models recognize that they must be flexible with a new business, expecting profitability but also novelty and divergence from the core business.

New ventures are unencumbered by expectations of certain profit margins, market strategies, and cost structures by virtue of their nascent state. As large companies approach new markets with the intent of creating new business models, they must bestow these new efforts with the same flexibility of a start-up while maintaining the advantages of the larger firm. They will doubtlessly find themselves competing with these ventures, for whom that flexibility is a competitive advantage.

We were also concerned in our research that only privately-held incumbents were successful, and, while that does not appear to be the case, the challenges imposed by the financial markets are a formidable force in publicly-traded companies.

Financial market analysts add further rigidity to the structure of the income statements of publicly-traded firms. Margins are expected to increase, costs are expected to decrease, and any shift or stagnation in that progress is met with alarm. Companies, like Deutsche Postbank, who have transformed and enhanced their business models have expended significant efforts to explaining their new businesses to the financial markets. Beyond explanation, successful business models require analysts to re-value firms based on differing comparables and new lines of business. However, these formidable hurdles emerge as the growth of a new business model begins to impact the firm's success.

Before such investments yield fruit, news of a company's early ventures into business model innovation is often met with a skeptical eye and an earnings warning. Why would a firm that could theoretically grow margins opt to invest in a project with potentially lower margins? Consequently, most large firms seek to conceal these efforts until early stage success is met. More recently, larger firms like Amazon and Google have built a reputation and track record of investing in new business models and are thus given leniency by the financial markets. This leeway will hopefully, in time, transcend all publicly traded firms, as business model innovation becomes a more understood business strategy for growth.

Business model innovation is the convergence of both a new profit model and a new customer value proposition, unified to create an entirely new type of market player. The benefits of such innovation can fundamentally impact a firm's success, but the challenges of implementing business model innovation are great.

## Executing Business Model Innovation

Having spotted a new market opportunity and begun to outline the type of profit model that might support a venture, how does a company actually execute against this vision? It is rare indeed that a company is lacking good new business ideas. However, it is also rare that a company develops strong processes for executing against them.

Aside from the financial component of business model innovation, three elements of the company's strategy seem to challenge its ability to execute:

- The organizational structure required
- The channels to market
- The effective use of infrastructure, such as I/T

While elements of an execution strategy such as branding, marketing, and operations may naturally address the needs of the new business model, the above three areas require a wholly distinct approach. Organizational structure tends to be trivialized as a simple org-chart matter, channels to market tend to be exaggerated into an insurmountable hurdle, and the use of infrastructure can be an advantage, if approached appropriately. We shall handle each in turn.

## Organizational Structures and Business Model Innovation

The fundamental guiding principle of business model innovation is autonomy. New groups must be established to carry forward the new business model, and must not be bound by the pre-conceived notions of the parent firm. While this approach is often met with vigorous approval, drawing the appropriate lines is challenging.

Autonomy is difficult because while we recommend separateness, we do not mean complete detachment. Employees continue to be paid by the same payroll system, covered by the same health plans, and contribute to the same 401K. However, with those controls comes an overhead structure which may be financially burdensome to the new organization. Once invoked, however, the financial and budgeting process of the parent organization will often wend its way into the daily operations of the new group.

In one such organization, the group was expected to justify its budgetary numbers, as compared with its peer business units from the core business, on a quarterly basis. Like its peers, it was held to budgetary "challenges" every quarter in an effort to drive down costs. As a nascent organization, it was forced to justify its costs against a paltry revenue number and defend the ongoing corporate investment. This collective effort sapped at least 10% of the time of the group which kept its own investments both timid and short-term. The impact was disastrous, precluding the group from pursuing a new business model or even achieving success with the old one.

This example does not, of course, imply that the financial health of the new business unit should be ignored. Rather, it advocates for longer periods of evaluation against a very different set of metrics than are applied to the core. The underlying philosophy should be "patient for growth, but impatient for profits." Profitability is the mark of a sustainable business model. Growth will come with time.

Another resource often borrowed from the core business is product knowledge. Engineering skill, scientific strength, and product development acumen are among the key competitive advantages for an incumbent entering a new market. However, borrowing product platforms should be a careful process.

At Tata Motors in India, a group is eagerly constructing a new vehicle targeting a price point far below their current line or any other model available today. The Tata group that undertook this formidable effort, dubbed the 1 lakh car, initially looked to the other vehicle lines for inspiration, but soon recognized that to meet the aggressive price target the car would need to be built from the ground up. Certainly, engineering knowledge existed from prior experiences, but all efforts to mimic other lines would have been folly. Instead, they have re-designed every element of the car, and indeed, even the supply chains, partnerships, and distribution mechanisms, to achieve their goal.

Companies often approach the challenge of designing a low-end product by pruning an existing product. This is rarely successful. Not only does ruthless excising of functionality and features weigh heavily on the engineers who built them, but the organization is almost forced to adopt the perspective of "how can I make this product worse?" rather than "how can I make it serve a different customer better?"

In high-end markets, like that of Nespresso, the converse occurs. Nespresso's operating unit was given a great deal of operational independence, which enabled the group to make choices that optimized their product but ran counter to conventional strategy. Nestlé is among the largest buyers of coffee beans in the world for its Nescafé brand. With that buying power, there are tremendous economies of scale that could strongly influence the cost of producing the Nespresso products. However, Nespresso does not purchase its coffee through the same organizational buying channel as Nestlé. Different products serving vastly different markets required a different supply of coffee. It is a testament to Nestlé's understanding of the new business that this freedom was given to the new group.

Organizational separateness creates one final challenge: human resources. In some organizations, the new business groups are considered superior posts. In others, new business groups are risky ventures to be shunned. In both cases, a specific type of individual would be best chosen to participate in a new venture: one who is not wholly ingrained in the ways of the core business, one who thrives on the ambiguity of a new business, and one who is open-minded enough to suggest and pursue things in new ways. In some companies, a sea of willing hands is raised to this challenge, creating a divide between those selected and those rejected. In other companies a few rebels may exist, and recruiting must occur from the outside. Either way, it is important for the senior management to create a culture in which the groups are different but held in equal esteem. The present business would not thrive but for the continued efforts of the core employees, while the company rewards the risks taken but the new business group, whether successful or not.

The role of senior management extends beyond this cultural direction. In most cases of successful business model innovation, the senior management of the firm stood fully behind the new venture and actively participated in the strategic decisions of the group. If senior management holds the greatest experience and knowledge of the firm, who better to participate in shaping the future directions of the firm? Each such venture should be spearheaded by at least one member of senior management, infusing enthusiasm and leadership while, at the same time, encouraging the divergence of opinion and debate that marks creative endeavors.

The organizational challenges associated with creating and managing different business models under the same corporate umbrella should not be given short shrift when new groups are launched. Alignment on the limitations and freedoms, the recruiting, and the ongoing metrics of the new organization should be reached and agreed upon by senior management and the group's leadership very early. Absent alignment and consensus, the efforts of the group will be diverted towards these struggles instead of their true work.

## Channels to Market

The sales channel of the company typically raises the most predictable objections to business model innovation. Whether the company has a direct sales force, sells though channel partners, or some combination thereof, the existing structure is often among the most rigid of all corporate groups. It is entirely sensible that any efforts to change the form of revenues for the company could be seen as an immediate threat to their success.

Opposition typically takes the form of objections regarding resources or cannibalization. If resources are being diverted from their current sales efforts into the sale of new products, it is clear that the ability to execute against the current targets will be diminished. Further, because the current "best customers" are typically not those pursued by new business models, the daily experience of the sales and channel teams implies that there is little merit to this new business, and thus little hope that they will make up the lost numbers. Efforts to reduce the impact on current sales should be strongly considered when creating new businesses, as these concerns are valid. However, the resource concern should not stymie business model innovation efforts.

As the validity of the new business emerges, the cannibalization argument tends to overpower any resource concerns. If a similar product exists, why wouldn't some of the core customers switch? In all likelihood, some combination of the following may occur:

- The best core customers will not switch because the new offering does not meet their needs. In fact, the core offering continues to be tailored precisely to their needs.
- Some group will switch to the new offering, typically the ones that are not considered the "best" customers of the core product.
- Some customers will become customers of both.

All of these occurred at Xiameter, and they occur regularly in other businesses with multiple business models, products, and sales channels. Indeed, the low-end model proved empowering to the sales channels at Xiameter, enabling them to maintain the premium pricing of the core product.

Despite all calculations, predictions, and estimates, the concerns with cannibalization are real and valid. However, the alternative to launching a new business model is not maintaining the *status quo*, rather, it is inviting another company to launch that new business model by leaving the market opportunity on the table.

Experience has shown that failing to persuade the existing channels of the merits of pursuing the alternative product could end in disaster. Rather, the senior leadership must be clear in its choice to move forward, allaying the concerns of the current sales teams to the extent possible without constraining the new business group unduly. An uneasy tension will remain, as did at Xiameter, until a new equilibrium is reached and the benefits of the new business are well-understood.

## How I/T Changes the Game

Back in the days of the dotcom boom, unfamiliar e-commerce business models were springing up all over the web, promising to revolutionize the way the world bought books (Amazon), groceries (Webvan), and used goods (eBay). In 2007, six years after the dotcom bust, we are left with a puzzling situation. Some of those "revolutionary" companies have gone on to become major forces shaping commerce while others have gone down in the record books as some of the most spectacular flameouts in venture capital history. Despite those prominent failures, one thing is for certain: I/T has been key to enabling business around the globe.

This rise of the Internet, which enabled new ways of doing business, and the heady entrepreneurial and venture capital culture that came with it brought the business model to the front of the business pages. New technologies are often used to create new business models or adapt old models to new markets. Utilizing the Internet as the primary sales channel, giants such as eBay and iTunes leapfrogged the competition with their investments by reaching the consumer directly. Similarly, Amazon and Dell used both the Internet and in-house technology to create revolutionary supply chain processes to leverage their assets more effectively and create opportunities for interest income.

Success for the majority of companies aiming for business model innovation requires a focus on the speed of innovation and customer retention to create long-term value while adapting their strategies and the business model quickly to seize competitive advantage. Companies can leverage I/T for a multitude of purposes, from sales channel and back office process expedition, to enablement of customer research and product innovation.

Dow Corning again provides a successful example with Xiameter. As the Internet started to become a viable alternative channel to market, the senior-most members of the Dow Corning team considered the opportunities it might present in meeting the needs of increasingly price sensitive customers. To be profitable at lower prices, the new business unit, Xiameter, had to create a correspondingly lower cost model. Xiameter automated order entry and as many additional functions as possible. Using Dow Corning's existing SAP backbone made extensive automation easy while the early involvement of dedicated I/T professionals was essential in the development of the business concept. In the extraordinarily short timeframe of six months, Xiameter went from ideation to test markets; three months later it launched in full; three months after, that Dow Corning's entire investment had been recovered.

Not surprisingly, the Internet has also facilitated business model innovations in the payments area of financial services. In 1998, with the launch of PayPal, the Internet enabled a new payment processing network with a profit model different from that of the traditional credit card. PayPal is a peer-to-peer money transfer service where customers and merchants sign up for online accounts funded by consumers through transfers from bank accounts or credit cards and accessed by merchants through electronic funds transfers. Both customers and merchants are responsible for creating their own accounts, eliminating direct marketing and merchant acquisition costs. As the size of PayPal's network grows, the value to new customers and merchants of joining the network increases as well. By 2002, over half of eBay customers, the largest P2P marketplace, had opened PayPal accounts.[14]

Through low overhead from online operation and its direct relationship with customers and merchants, PayPal has entered the market with a profit model that can sustain profitability at a lower markup than its competitors. PayPal works directly with merchants and customers allowing direct

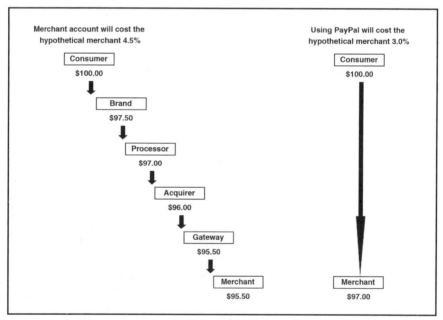

*Figure 5: Cost Comparison of PayPal vs. Hypothetical Merchant Account*

transfers between accounts without resorting to acquisition and processing intermediaries. With fewer players to support, the PayPal network can operate profitably at a lower cost than traditional payment networks.

In another example of technology-enablement, Charles Schwab moved from selling the human investment expertise of its staff to executing trades on command, thereby creating a discount brokerage firm. San Francisco-based start-up Schwab went to the market with a different profit model. Instead of wooing high net worth customers, Schwab reached out to a broader group of customers with low markup offerings, supported by a low overhead structure and high resource productivity (brokers in a back office). Using the new AT&T toll free number service, Schwab began offering discounted trades over the phone. The company worked to gain the scale it needed to offset overhead, but kept the operation lean. Schwab brokers were confined to executing trades and prohibited from giving specific investment advice in part to keep up resource productivity and also to allow Schwab to hire less expensive workers who would accept a fixed salary rather than the typical commission structure that full service brokerages paid. In 1975, a Schwab trader earned roughly $10,000 a year, a figure that a Wall Street broker could make executing only a few full-commission trades a day.[15]

There is little doubt that the introduction of new technologies has created growth opportunities through business model innovation. New processes, new application of resources, and the ability to leverage new profit models are all enabled by I/T. Given the accelerated speed of change in business today and in the future, I/T creates the tipping point for companies to achieve the competitive advantage needed to overtake their competitors and stay ahead of the industry curve.

# CONCLUSION

Business model innovation is an important and highly valuable lever of change that both large and small companies should consider as they seek growth opportunities. Perhaps less comfortable and natural to product and process-oriented firms, developing a corporate competency in fostering and nurturing new business models could pay dividends for years to come, enabling the firm to re-invent itself to match the ever-changing market for its products.

*We'd like to acknowledge the contribution of Joshua Suskewicz and Alex Leichtman in writing this chapter.*

**Editors' Note:** The content of this chapter is the result of a collaborative Business Model Innovation research effort by SAP AG and Innosight, LLC. Stacy Comes and Lilac Bernicker co-directed the project.

# ENDNOTES

1   Innosight analysis (11/06).
2   "The Quest for Innovation: A Global Study of Innovation Management 2006-2016," American Management Association (2006).
3   Economist Intelligence Unit. "Business 2010: Embracing the Challenge of Change." 2005.
4   "Expanding the Innovation Horizon: The Global CEO Study 2006", IBM Business Consulting Services. (2006).
5   Innosight analysis (11/06).
6   "History and Architecture." *Marshall Fields. n.d.* 02 January 2006. http://www. fields.com/common/history_architecture.jsp.
7   Christensen, Clayton and Richard Tedlow. "Patterns of Disruption in Retailing" in "The Future of Commerce." Ed. Nicholas Carr. *Harvard Business Review.* February 2000: 39.
8   Walton, Sam. *Made in America.* Bantam: New York, 1993.
9   10 Retailers commonly use a metric called Gross Margin Return on Inventory Investment (GMROII) to optimize their operations. GMROII is generally calculated as Gross Margin * (Sales/Average Inventory) which is equivalent to Markup * Inventory Turns. This demonstrates the relationship between these three elements quite clearly.
10  Bhatnagar, Parija. "The K-Mart – Sears Deal." *CNN Money.* 17 November 2004. 22 January 2006. http://money.cnn.com/2004/11/17/news/fortune500/sears_kmart/.
11  Lovelock, Christopher. "Southwest Airlines (A)," HBS Case No. 9-575-060. Boston: Harvard Business School Publishing, 19 February 1985.
12  Lovelock, Christopher. "Southwest Airlines (A)," HBS Case No. 9-575-060. Boston: Harvard Business School Publishing, 19 February 1985.
13  Lovelock, Christopher. "Southwest Airlines (D)," HBS Case No. 9-575-135. Boston: Harvard Business School Publishing, 21 June 1984.
14  Keung, Paul and Apurva Shah. "Addressing the PayPal Opportunity: Disruptive Technology or eBay Add-On?" CIBC World Markets. 10 July 2005. After attempting to develop a competing payment processing function called BillPoint, eBay bought PayPal in 2002 for $1.5 billion, its largest acquisition to that point. In 2005, PayPal had penetrated over 75% of eBay accounts.
15  Schwab itself has fallen prey to changing market dynamics in recent years as well.

# 2.3

# PROCESS INNOVATION THROUGH OPEN BPM (Business Process Management)

**Mathias Kirchmer,** *Chief Innovation and Marketing Officer, IDS Scheer Global; Affiliated Faculty, Center for Organizational Dynamics, University of Pennsylvania*

Innovation has become a core focus area for all successful organizations. To ensure long-term survival, an enterprise must make innovation part of day-to-day business, thus enabling desired revenue stability and growth. Two major forms of innovation exist: Business Model Innovation and Technology Innovation. Both require the change of existing business processes or the development of new business processes. Business Process Innovation is a key success factor for the next generation enterprise. Companies need to create an environment that encourages and enables process innovation.

Open BPM delivers a business process infrastructure that provides optimal flexibility at the lowest cost level through the use of business and technology standards. This enables efficient and effective business process innovation. The main components of Open BPM are holistic Enterprise Architectures (EA) and the supporting software, Service-Oriented Architectures (SOA), an effective business process change management plan focused on the individuals involved, and a comprehensive process monitoring and controlling approach, including Business Activity Monitoring (BAM).

This chapter discusses characteristics of innovation and explains the importance of process innovation for most forms of innovation. You will learn how Open BPM serves as an enabler for business process innovation. Short case studies support the significance of process innovation through Open BPM and demonstrate the theory in practice.

## INNOVATION AND BUSINESS PROCESSES – A CLOSE RELATIONSHIP

Today, more and more companies are built on the principles of process innovation. Dell, for example, did not invent the PC. However, Dell did invent new business processes to bring PCs to market, eliminating unnecessary steps in the supply chain while offering more flexibility and control to the customer. These processes have become Dell's main differentiator in the competitive marketplace. Amazon.com did not invent the book, but it introduced the now-popular process of buying books online from the comfort of your living room. eBay did not invent the auction, but its online, easy-to-use processes increased the popularity of the auction. Traditional companies are also focusing on process innovation. For example, enterprises in the machinery industries offer more convenient and reliable service processes. Airlines have simplified the ticketing process to reduce cost and increase, or at least stabilize, service levels through online-ticketing.

Business process innovation is clearly of the highest importance for every company. But what is it all about? How do "innovation" and "business processes" really fit together? Innovation is defined as the act of introducing something new. Within innovation in general, there are two major directions:

- Business Model Innovation
- Technology Innovation

Business model innovation includes new or modified value propositions, new business processes (especially in the supply chain), or new target customers and markets.[1]  In their PC offerings, Dell's value proposition was the convenient custom configuration and ordering of products — the supply chain processes eliminated dealer networks and enabled individual configuration by the client, while the target customers remained more or less the same as those of competitors. Sometimes the profit formula is mentioned as an additional component of the business model[2]; however, it may also be seen as part of other elements (e.g., vendor-related aspect of the general value proposition).

Technology innovation has the following levers: offerings, including products and services; process technologies; and enabling technologies.[2] New product technologies (e.g., the introduction of digital cameras) are some of the most obvious forms of innovation. Process technologies support efficient and effective business processes. Enterprise Resource Planning (ERP) systems, for example, were able to make specific processes more efficient and effective. Supporting technologies improve either product or process technologies. For example, the development of efficient relational databases supported the development of integrated application software, especially the aforementioned ERP systems.

Innovation in the fields of processes and process technologies show the direct link between "process" and "innovation", but the other forms of innovation also lead to new processes. New value propositions and the expansion into new markets require appropriate processes. A product innovation generally leads to new production or distribution processes, resulting in an indirect link between "business processes" and "innovation". Almost any form of innovation requires business process innovation: processes with new structures, more accurate data, new organizational responsibilities, new activities, or better deliverables of the process.

The levers of innovation are shown in Figure 1: Levers of Innovation

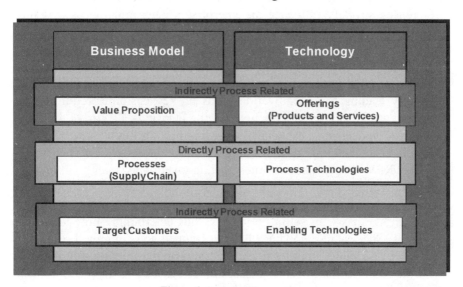

*Figure 1:* *Levers of Innovation*

The close relationship between innovation and business processes is reflected in various innovation theories that are applied in practice, such as Christensen's "Value Chain Evolution" (VCE) theory and his "Resources,

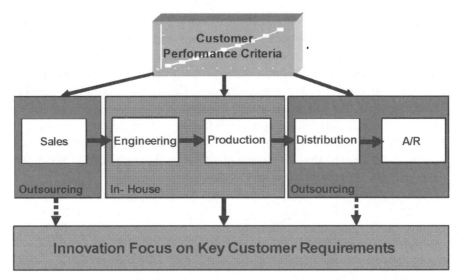

*Figure 2: Value Chain Evolution (VCE) Theory*

Processes Values" (RPV) theory.[3] The VCE theory is defined around a company's value chain, which is the process beginning with marketing and sales and ending with distribution and accounts receivables. Customer preferences strongly influence an enterprise's determination as to which parts of the value chain process are outsourced and which are executed in-house. The more important the process steps are to the customer, the more likely the enterprise will execute the related process parts in-house. Innovation initiatives are focused on the sub-processes executed in-house, indirectly leading to an innovation focus on key customer requirements. Consequently, business process outsourcing decisions also drive the focus of innovation decisions, especially regarding process innovation. The VCE theory is visualized in Figure 2: Value Chain Evolution (VCE) Theory.

The RPV theory demonstrates that innovation is mainly influenced through a company's resources, processes, and values. Resources are transformed through processes from an input into an output. Company values are the basis for setting priorities, thus determining how to use the resources. Successful companies have developed and combined resources, processes, and values in order to clearly focus on the existing offerings that make the organization currently successful. The result is sustained innovation that constantly improves existing offerings. However, if other enterprises introduce disruptive innovations, focusing on new market segments with completely new solutions, the existing companies are faced with challenges. Their focus on sustaining innovation makes it difficult to handle disruptive innovation. Their business processes are generally not flexible enough to

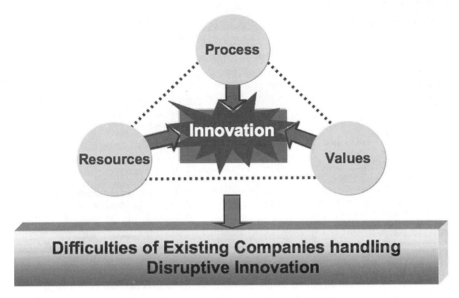

*Figure 3: Resources, Processes, Values (RPV) Theory*

deal with disruptive innovation or to produce innovations that are really addressing new markets. Effective business process innovation can now become a real question of long term survival. The RPV theory is shown in Figure 3: Resources, Processes, Values (RPV) Theory.

The management of innovation within an organization is a business process in itself. This process must be defined, implemented, executed, and controlled just as any other process. It goes through the same process lifecycle. An example of such an innovation process is shown in Figure 4: Example of an Innovation Process. The process develops from the preparation of an innovation initiative, to the idea finding, and finally to the execution of the innovation idea. Due to the importance of process innovation, the "innovation process" must support that form of innovation effectively to ensure the success of the organization. The biggest challenge is to combine creativity in the generation of ideas with the structure necessary to ensure systematic innovation activity. In most cases, this involves external organizations that may form an innovation network to be integrated in the processes. In section 3 of this chapter, we will discuss how a company can build an infrastructure that supports the goal of an effective innovation process.

"Collaboration innovation" is an extension of business process innovation. In this case inter-enterprise processes are implemented to support unlikely "innovative" collaborations between organizations.[4] For example, ING is a bank that collaborates with coffee shops. When customers

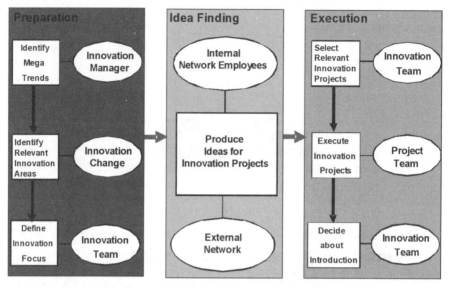

**Figure 4:** *Example of an Innovation Process*

visit an ING location, they feel like they are in a coffeehouse — with some terminals in the back for your banking transactions. Therefore, the BPM infrastructure has to support this collaboration between organizations. Processes of different organizations must be integrated to deliver value to the final client. Thus, process innovation is again the underlying principle of collaboration innovation.

An important and very specific form of process innovation is the innovation of service processes. A service, as rendered by a consulting company or financial services company for example, is also a process. Therefore, the innovation of the offering (the service), which is consumed directly by the customer, must be a process innovation. Product Innovation in a service company is essentially always process innovation.

It is clear now that business process innovation is a topic that every organization should address. How can we provide an environment within the enterprise to support this innovation? This question leads us to the notion of Open BPM.

## OPEN BPM ENABLES BUSINESS PROCESS INNOVATION

Open BPM provides a business infrastructure with the flexibility necessary to facilitate innovation, especially business process innovation. In general, it is helpful if an organization is able to react to change efficiently and effectively. Process innovation is a special driver of such change.

## The Principles of Open BPM

Open BPM means the consequent use of business and technology standards around the process lifecycle, resulting in an infrastructure that provides optimal process flexibility at the lowest cost level. The use of standards to support process management allows changes (e.g., regarding the design of a process) with minimal effort because the information about the change can be seamlessly transferred to all aspects of the process lifecycle (e.g., to ensure the necessary IT support and execution of the new process). The resulting flexibility is the key enabler for business process innovation.

In order to achieve the greatest possible number of benefits, the philosophy of Open BPM must be applied in each phase of the process lifecycle. The phases of the business process lifecycle are shown in Figure 5: ARIS House of Business Process Excellence.[4,5,6,7] BPM begins on the strategy level of an organization, where the business processes of an organization are identified. Next, planned innovations and their process impacts are defined, delivering the basis for the definition of the business process structure and the related business goals. The underlying application system architecture is planned accordingly. All aspects combined set the guideline and strategic direction for a process-centered organization.

This guideline is passed from the strategy layer to the process specification layer, where the business processes are specified in detail. The blueprint for the process-centric organization must be defined using techniques like simulation or ABC costing, in combination with process modeling methods. Processes reflecting next business practices are designed from scratch. The specification of best practice-based processes can be supported by using templates, or so called "business process reference models". On the specification layer, all necessary business processes must have detailed descriptions, which can be used to drive the process execution. The result is a blueprint consisting of business process models.

Based on these process models, all physical and information processing activities are implemented within an enterprise and across organizational boundaries. Here, processes are either executed using standard application packages like ERP, Supply Chain Management (SCM), or Customer Relationship Management (CRM) systems that primarily support best practice processes. Alternatively, processes can be executed based on more flexible application solutions that reflect necessary next practice approaches or next generation business process automation solutions — based on an SOA.

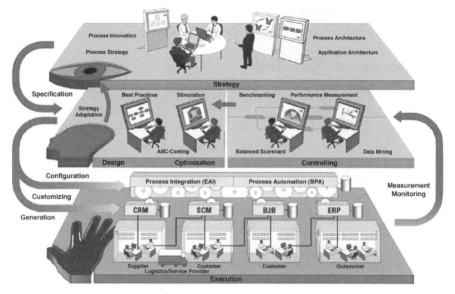

*Figure 5*: *ARIS House of Business Process Excellence*

The actual executed processes are measured and controlled on the controlling level. If there are differences observed between the actual values and the planned key performance indicators (KPIs) that were defined based on the goals identified on the strategy level, action must be taken. Either a continuous improvement process is initiated through the process specification layer or the situation is resolved on a strategic level if the business environment has changed significantly.

On one hand, all phases of the process lifecycle must be organized from a business point of view, thus the "process of process management" has to be defined. On the other hand, the required methods and software support must be provided. The use of open standards for all business and technology aspects of this business process lifecycle management leads to an Open BPM environment. Key components of an Open BPM approach are:

- EA (Enterprise Architecture)
- SOA (Service Oriented Architecture)
- Business Process Change Management
- Process Controlling

These components are positioned in the process lifecycle in Figure 6: ARIS House of Business Process Excellence with Key Components of Open BPM. Again, each of those areas has a business and a technology

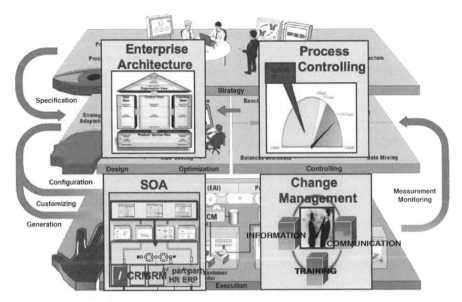

*Figure 6: ARIS House of Business Process Excellence with Key Components of Open BPM*

dimension. The discussion of BPM is often focused solely on technology aspects. However, creating a technology environment and infrastructure without the appropriate business input will not lead to any significant effects since the technology is not used in a business and strategy-driven manner. Innovation cannot be planned and actively driven; it is only the result of a coincidence. Therefore, the combination of business and technology components is crucial for the successful application of Open BPM.

The EA, especially the business process architecture, serves as the framework to describe all business process-related information in a structured way so the descriptions can be easily reused to drive the process execution. The use of EA is supported by the appropriate EA tools.[28] Business standards that can be applied here include the SCOR framework developed by the Supply Chain Council, the ARIS Architecture developed by Scheer, or the Zachman Framework.[8,9] Processes can be described using modeling standards, like the event-driven process chains (EPC).[10]

The execution of processes in an Open BPM environment is best supported by SOA[11,12,13], a highly flexible next generation process automation. The process design information, describing the business situation, can be transferred into technically oriented standards like the Business Process Execution Language (BPEL).[14] The BPEL (or similar standard-based) process models are loaded into the technical middleware of SOA, which is then configured based on the process information. The application software components, or the "services," are utilized according to process needs. This leads to truly process-oriented application software.

The main activities of change management are information, communication, and training. These activities can be supported by the same process models stored in the EA, provided that a consistent process modeling standard is used, such as the aforementioned EPC. Such formal process modeling methods can be transferred into process descriptions that are easy to understand and easy to use[7] even by less skilled employees. Change management encompasses the people side of process execution. Maximum flexibility in the technical execution of processes requires equal flexibility from the people working directly or indirectly with those technologies. Open BPM addresses both aspects.

Process controlling systems can be linked to the SOA (or traditional process automation environments) through standardized adapters in order to monitor and measure the business processes.[15] Information, such as cycle times or execution frequency, is monitored. Thus, it becomes more and more important to utilize Open BPM technology standards to provide real-time information about potential process issues, so that appropriate actions can be taken. This is the key goal of business activity monitoring (BAM). The result is the management of business events. In order to measure the appropriate processes or sub-processes, such controlling systems are configured based on the aforementioned process models.

The most important aspect of a functional Open BPM environment is the integration between process design and execution, facilitated by EA with structured process models and the process execution based on SOA. The use of standards in this field enables the integration of process execution solutions (mainly SOA platforms) from various vendors (e.g., those necessary to support mergers and acquisitions). This can be done without the high costs of development and maintenance for software interfaces.

While process design can be optimized for the simple formulation of successful business solutions, the SOA environment can be constructed for the efficient and effective technical execution of the resulting processes. The information from the process models is transferred to the SOA middleware, which is configured based on those models. Therefore, in the support of every process step, the right application component or "service" is applied. Services can be stored within an enterprise or at a third-party I/T environment. In the latter case, they are procured through the Web, thus called Web services. In the future, Web services may be selected from specific Web pages that offer such service components. The services are often described in a "business language," in the form of process reference models, which can be used as building blocks for the process design.

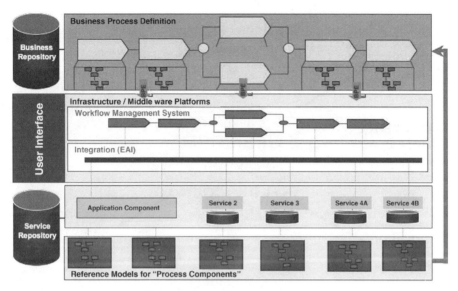

*Figure 7: Open BPM Empowers SOA*

The consequent use of standards within Open BPM also supports the management of processes across organizations, resulting in the collaboration of enterprises.[16] Therefore, collaboration innovation (e.g., in form of new, more efficient supply chains) is well supported through this approach. Interactive Web based applications as they are offered by the "Web 2.0"[17] movement can be integrated into business processes through EA and SOA and can effectively support a collaboration environment within and across the organization.

Open BPM empowers SOA to deliver real business value through the integration of business and technology aspects. The entire design and execution environment based on SOA is explained in Figure 7: Open BPM empowers SOA.

SOA can be built based on products like SAP NetWeaver[18], Oracle Fusion[19], or Microsoft BizTalk.[20] The process descriptions and EA frameworks are delivered through business-oriented BPM environments, such as IDS Scheer's ARIS Platform[21,22,23,24,25,26,27,28], which is integrated based on open standards with SOA solutions.

## The Relationship Between Open BPM and Business Process Innovation

The flexibility delivered by Open BPM enables innovation, especially business process innovation. Directed by the guidelines defined in a business

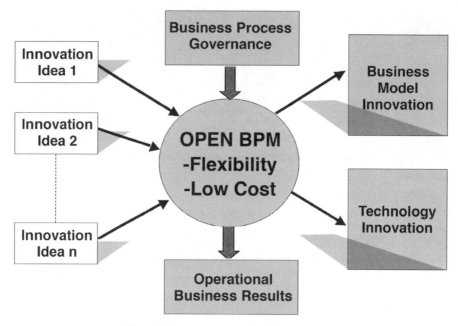

*Figure 8: Open BPM – Enabler of Innovation*

process governance approach[22], Open BPM facilitates the delivery of desired business results, especially process innovation, defined in process models. In addition, Open BPV provides the flexibility to evaluate innovation ideas by testing new processes in a simulation or prototype mode and measuring the results. Then, an enterprise can decide if an innovation idea should be implemented and rolled out to create business model or technology innovation, mainly delivered through the necessary business process innovation. This effect can be seen in Figure 8: Open BPM – Enabler of Innovation.

Technologies that support open standards can be interpreted as innovations themselves (e.g., SOA can be considered an innovative process technology). Sophisticated EA approaches, when combined with governance rules, may be seen as process innovation regarding the BPM processes.

Business-oriented BPM software environments, like the aforementioned ARIS Platform[21] and ARIS-based solutions, can be used to support and facilitate the innovation process in an Open BPM environment. These solutions enable process innovation definition in the form of process models and enable evaluation of the initial effects of the innovation before making larger investments. The integration of design and execution environments, based on previously discussed standards like BPEL, allow for a rapid prototyping of the innovation and an efficient rollout afterwards. The

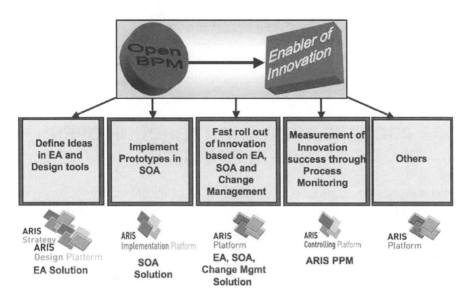

*Figure 9:* BPM Software Supporting the Innovation Process (Example)

process monitoring of Open BPM provides the measurement and control of the effects of the process innovation, resulting in a conclusion regarding the innovation's success. Additional aspects of process innovation (e.g., the compatibility with legal requirements) can also be evaluated via Open BPM components.

The support of the innovation process through Open BPM components is displayed in Figure 9: BPM Software Supporting the Innovation Process (Example). The design and implementation of an innovation process ensures that innovation becomes part of an organization's day-to-day business.

Open BPM and the resulting process innovations may become especially significant in the management of knowledge-intensive processes that are difficult to define and continuously changing. Those processes are often emergent processes, since the process is already executed but further process steps must still be modified or defined.[29] Emergent processes are typically found in R&D environments or large, unique projects (e.g., in the engineering industry) while those processes focused on knowledge workers have become increasingly important for most industries.[30] Open BPM delivers the necessary infrastructure and flexibility to enable the systematic input of innovation within those processes, including the set up of a collaboration environment for knowledge workers.

While Open BPM provides the necessary flexibility at a low cost level, there are still entrepreneurial tasks left to define the innovation content that is evaluated and implemented. Market, technology, and process developments must be monitored to define which innovation areas should be addressed.[23] For example, a structured formalized market and product description can be very helpful.[24,25] General strategies, such as the real time enterprise or the agile organization[26], or trends like globalization, mobility, etc., may be used to support the definition of an innovation focus.

# PROCESS INNOVATION THROUGH OPEN BPM IN PRACTICE

We have seen that process innovation has become increasingly important for the business success of companies. As discussed, process innovation is the enabler for more and more innovation initiatives, sometimes serving as the basis for the entire company. The support of process innovation through Open BPM has just begun to increase the effectiveness and efficiency of the innovation process. Some important components of Open BPM have only been available in an acceptable maturity level for a relatively short period of time. This is especially true for process execution technologies around SOA and their integration with the process design and EA environment. Therefore, many companies are currently still in the phase of preparation for a full Open BPM approach. However, many organizations have already established some Open BPM components to achieve early benefits, gather experience, and gain time that can lead to competitive advantages (e.g., through a superior innovation process).

A good starting point in process innovation with Open BPM is the structured design of business processes. Many organizations, including Nova Chemicals[27], combine this design with the introduction of an EA framework as a corporate standard. Nova is a producer of commodity chemicals, such as plastic foils. The company defined process innovation as a key corporate initiative and implemented it based on EA and the underlying BPM software. Process innovation ideas are therefore evaluated efficiently and the implementation of the approved innovation is also facilitated. The process models within the EA can also support a potential move towards SOA in the future. The focus of Nova is explained in Figure 10: Nova – Focus on Business Process Innovation[27].

Siemens and Intel, both high-tech enterprises, similarly facilitated the innovation of their mutual supply chain management (SCM) process. The inter-company collaboration processes were defined based on the SCOR standard delivered by the Supply Chain Council[8]. Innovations included in the supply chain structure enabled an efficient rollout of changes and standards across the organizations. Their approach is visualized in Figure 11: Intel-Siemens: SCM Innovation Based on EA.

**Focus on Business Process Innovation (BPI)**

**Develop a culture around process innovation**

- Establish an organization that promotes process ownership
- Establish an environment around continuous process improvement
- Establish an environment encouraging the generation of new ideas

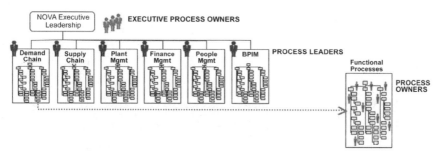

*Figure 10: Nova – Focus on Business Process Innovation with EA[27]*

Mitsui, a leading Japanese trading company, went a step further. The company also defined its processes based on an EA approach in order to identify innovations in various locations and implement them across the organization. The process models drive the implementation and management of an SAP ERP system. The process design is already structured to support a move toward SOA, (e.g., based on SAP NetWeaver).[18] Therefore, the process design can be considered a first step toward next generation process automation. Contrary to the prior cases presented, Mitsui also measures the performance of its implemented processes, using ARIS Process Performance Manager (PPM) of the ARIS Platform[15] as a component of their Open BPM approach. Change management is also conducted based on the process descriptions, which means that three of the four main components of Open BPM are already used to drive process management and innovation initiatives. Mitsui can use its existing environment to transfer innovation ideas from one location to another or to measure the effects of such initiatives.

Many organizations have chosen the strategy of process innovation and Open BPM reflected in the Mitsui case: they begin with process modeling initiatives in an EA environment and prepare systematically for the implementation and rollout of SOA while simultaneously implementing a traditional ERP solution. One such example is the US Navy.[27] Processes are designed within the Department of Defense Architecture Framework (DoDAF) using the ARIS Platform. From that point, the models, including SOA solutions, can be downloaded into the selected execution environment. In addition, those process descriptions are stored in SAP Solution Manager

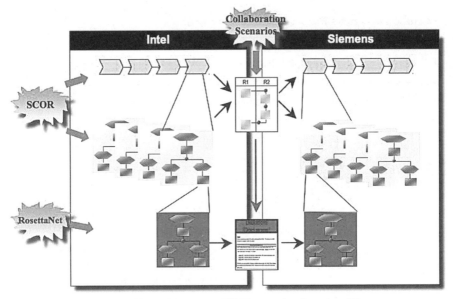

*Figure 11: Intel-Siemens: SCM Innovation Based on EA*

to drive the ERP implementation. Open BPM enables the seamless exchange of data between the ARIS Platform and SAP Solution Manager, resulting in short-term benefits, as well as the preparation for a more comprehensive Open BPM environment supporting the organization's continuous process innovation needs.

Early adaptors, such as Merrill Lynch[27], are already a step ahead. The company has built an integrated EA-SOA environment based on Open BPM solutions from various vendors, including the ARIS Platform as the basis for the EA solutions and MS BizTalk as the SOA environment for the integration of self-developed systems and application software packages (e.g., from Oracle). While the initial goal of such environments is often cost reduction and increased efficiency of software development, the real value only is delivered when process improvement and process innovation initiatives are supported through the new, flexible infrastructure. It is important to begin with a business focus from in order to build the EA and use the modeling methods in a manner supporting the definition of new innovative business processes. The example of Merrill Lynch is demonstrated in Figure 12: Merrill Lynch: EA and SOA of Open BPM for Process Innovation.

Business Process Innovation has also found its way into the educational and academic practice. Universities like Widener University in Philadelphia, PA offer certifications or master programs with a focus on business process

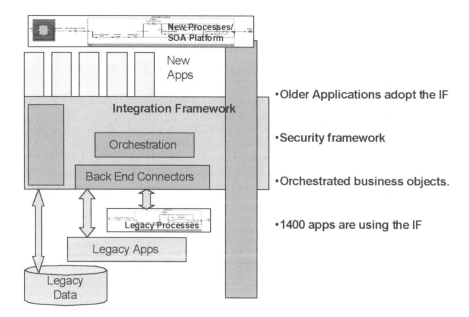

*Figure 12: Merrill Lynch: EA and SOA of Open BPM for Process Innovation*

innovation.[31] This allows enterprises to recruit people who are familiar with the management of innovation in a process environment and can help to put process innovation through Open BPM in practice.

The bottom line of business process innovation through Open BPM is reflected in the following four statements:

- The main types of Innovation are Business Model and Technology Innovation. Business processes play an essential role in both types; thus, business process innovation plays a pivotal role in all innovation initiatives. In order to ensure long-term business success, innovation must be part of daily business and an innovation process has to be defined, implemented, and managed.
- Through the use of business and technology standards, Open BPM ensures maximum flexibility at a minimum cost. The key components of Open BPM are EA and the supporting software (e.g., the ARIS Platform), SOA, Change Management, and Process Control.
- Open BPM can be an innovation by itself or an enabler of innovations, especially process innovation. Open BPM provides the necessary infrastructure for innovation initiatives and the innovation process.
- Innovation through Open BPM is in practice today.

# ENDNOTES

1　Davila, T., Epstein, M. J., Shelton, R.: Making Innovation Work. Upper Saddle River 2006.

2　Christensen, C., Johnson, M: Business Model Innovation. Report to the US Council of Innovation, The Conference Board, 01/2007.

3　Christensen, C.M: Raymour, M: The Innovator's Solution: Using good theory to solve the Dilemmas of Growth. Boston 2003.

4　Scheer, A.-W., Abolhassan, F., Jost, W., Kirchmer, M. (ed.): Business Process Excellence – ARIS in Practice. Berlin, New York, and others 2002.

5　Jost, W., Scheer, A.-W.: Business Process Management: A Core Task for any Company Organization. In: Scheer, A.-W., Abolhassan, F., Jost, W., Kirchmer, M.: Business Process Excellence – ARIS in Practice. Berlin, New York, and others 2002, p. 33-43.

6　Scheer, A.-W., Abolhassan, F., Jost, W., Kirchmer, M. (ed.): Business Process Change Management – ARIS in Practice. Berlin, New York, and others 2003.

7　Kirchmer, M., Scheer, A.-W.: Change Management – Key for Business Process Excellence. In: Scheer, A.-W., Abolhassan, F., Jost, W., Kirchmer, M. (ed.): Business Process Change Management – ARIS in Practice. Berlin, New York, and others 2003, p. 1-14.

8　Kirchmer, M., Brown, G., Heinzel, H.: Using SCOR and Other Reference Models for E-Business Process Networks. In: Scheer, A.-W., Abolhassan, F., Jost, W., Kirchmer, M. (ed.): Business Process Excellence – ARIS in Practice. Berlin, New York, and others 2002, p. 45-64.

9　IDS Scheer AG (ed.).: ARIS Design Platform – ARIS Enterprise Architecture Solution. White Paper. Saarbruecken 3/2006.

10　Scheer, A.-W.: ARIS – Business Process Modeling. 2nd edition, Berlin, New York and others 1998.

11　Woods, Dan: Enterprise Service Architectures. Beijing, Cambridge, Koeln, and others 2003.

12　Scheer, A.-W., Abolhassan, F., Jost, W., Kirchmer, M. (ed.): Business Process Automation – ARIS in Practice. Berlin, New York, and others 2004.

13　Kirchmer, M., Scheer, A.-W.: Business Process Automation – Combining Best and Next Practices. In: Scheer, A.-W., Abolhassan, F., Jost, W., Kirchmer, M. (ed.): Business Process Automation – ARIS in Practice. Berlin, New York, and others 2004, p. 1-15.

14　Wikipedia (Ed): Business Process Execution Language. In: wikipedia.org, 05/2007.

15　Hess, H., Blickle, T.: From Process Efficiency to Organizational Performance. ARIS Platform Expert Paper. Saarbruecken 3/07.

16　Kirchmer, M.: E-business process networks – successful value chains through standards. In: Journal of Enterprise Management, Vol. 17 No. 1, 2004.

17　Wikipedia (Ed): Web 2.0. In: wikipedia.org, 05/2007.

18　SAP AG (ed.): SAP NetWeaver helps put you ahead of the curve. In: sap.com 2007.

19　Oracle, Inc. (ed.): Oracle Fusion – Next Generation Applications. In: oracle.com 2007.

20　Microsoft, Inc. (ed.): Your Business – Connected. BizTalk. In: Microsoft.com 2007.

21   IDS Scheer AG (ed.): ARIS Platform. Product Brochure. Saarbruecken 2007.

22   Kirchmer, M., Spanyi, A.: Business Process Governance. White Paper, 2nd Edition. Berwyn 2007.

23   Christensen, C., Scott, A., Roth, E.: Seeing What's Next. Boston, MA 2004.

24   Kirchmer, M.: Market- and Product-Oriented Definition of Business Processes. In: Elzina, D.J., Gulledge, T.R., Lee, C.-Y. (Ed.): Business Engineering. Norwell 1999, p. 131-144.

25   Elzina, D.J., Gulledge, T.R., Lee, C.-Y. (Ed.): Business Engineering. Norwell 1999.

26   Pal, N., Pantaleo, D. (eds): The Agile Enterprise. New York 2005.

27   IDS Scheer AG (ed.): Documentation of the Presentations at ProcessWorld 2006. Berwyn, PA 2006.

28   Henry Peyret: The Forrester Wave: Enterprise Architecture Tools, Q2 2007. Boston 2007.

29   Majchrzak, A., Logan, D., McCurdy, R., Kirchmer, M.: Four Keys to Managing Emergence. In: MIT Sloan Management Review, Winter 2006, Vol. 47, No. 2.

30   Davenport, T.: Thinking for a Living. Boston 2005.

31   Widener University, School for Business Administration: Business Process Innovation. At: www.widener.edu, 5/2007.

## 2.4

---

# PRODUCT AND SERVICE INNOVATION

*Dan Trotzer,* VP Business Development, Bhootan Inc., LLC

As the pace of change continues to accelerate for firms across all industries, geographic locations, and markets, many companies are beginning to challenge the traditional view of what constitutes product and service innovation. In a sense, we are seeing the innovation of innovation. At a very basic level, product and service innovation is the enhancement, reconfiguration, or replacement of anything that generates revenue for a company. A product and service innovation strategy provides the guidelines for individuals throughout a company to understand the way forward for their company and shape their activities to contribute toward a defined goal. In response to the current environment of accelerated change, we have witnessed somewhat of a paradigm shift away from linear innovation strategy models to non-linear, more complex and creative models. In a traditional, linear model of product and service innovation, companies remain competitive by making incremental improvements and adding new features to comparable products serving similar markets. In this general category of product and service innovation strategy, the primary question driving the strategy is "how do our products and services perform relative to other companies doing the same thing?"

- How many cup holders does our mini-van have vs. others in its class?
- How much memory does our chip have vs. other chips on the market?
- How many pixels does our digital camera have vs. others on the market? Etc.

In an environment where technology, customer demand, market dynamics and economic drivers can change overnight, staying ahead of the curve and sustaining competitive advantage in a "product feature war" has become an increasingly daunting task. Product life cycles are shortening dramatically leaving firms with much less time to derive adequate returns on their R&D investments. New products can be easily copied, produced, and distributed cheaply and efficiently forcing firms to remain ever vigilant in pushing the product innovation process forward while continuing to deliver the next new big thing. Large multi-national firms invest vast sums of capital to create innovation engines that never stop, operating around the clock and around the globe by leveraging advanced communications and data management systems to connect geographically dispersed development centers. Despite the fact that technology and infrastructure enhancements such as the internet, satellite, and wireless communications have made it possible to create innovation empires upon which the sun never sets, many businesses do not have the necessary resources to do so. Borrowing from the old adage that necessity is the mother of all invention, in this day and age, necessity has become the mother of all innovation. In order to establish or maintain a competitive advantage, many firms have begun to look at product and service innovation in entirely different ways. New questions are emerging as the primary drivers of innovation strategy development and execution such as:

- What does my customer want to accomplish with my product or service?
- How well is my product or service accomplishing the end result desired by my customers?
- Is there a better, faster, or cheaper way to accomplish that end result than the way it is being done now?
- Can we deliver that end result better, faster, or cheaper than the customer can on their own?

Looking to the customer as the primary measuring stick as opposed to the competition can have a profound effect on the development and successful execution of a firm's innovation strategy. As firms have begun to use these and other consumer oriented questions as the primary decision drivers, firms are exploring new and creative ways of fulfilling customer demand through product and service innovation, opening the door to new opportunities for competitive advantage and unveiling new revenue models that deliver high returns.

Take for example the evolution of the automobile from simply a vehicle for transportation into a vehicle for delivering travel and entertainment services. For the majority of the auto industry's history, competition has been based on price and features. Luxury and high performance models have traditionally pushed the envelope with new technology features and performance enhancements delivering everything from seat warmers to windshield wipers that automatically sense the amount of rainfall and adjust their speed accordingly. Many of these features may go far beyond the general consumer's vision of what is necessary and desirable in an automobile; however, the feature and performance war between the auto manufacturers rages on. At the same time, production technology and techniques have focused on extracting as much cost out of the process as possible driving the other end of the spectrum... the price war. Regardless of whether we're looking at a luxury vehicle with all the bells and whistles or an economy model that has rolled off the assembly line as quickly and cheaply as possible, the end result has traditionally been a finished product to be purchased in a single transaction (all financing models aside).

Recently, however, a new concept has begun to evolve that changes the nature of the automobile as a finished product and introduces a new recurring revenue model. Services such as, On-Star, satellite radio and GPS navigation systems are being bundled with the finished product and customers are paying monthly fees to maintain those services. The automobile has become a delivery vehicle and a distribution channel for subscription services. In most cases, a customer does not buy a car simply because they want to have the experience of owning a vehicle. Rather, at the core of their purchase decision is a desire to do the things that a car enables them to do. When we begin to break down the key drivers of a customer's decision to purchase a car, you can see how these new opportunities emerged. At the very basic level, consumers buy cars in order to travel from point A to point B, but they also want to be safe, they want to be entertained and they don't want to be late. As such, customers may buy the car to get from point A to point B, but they are also willing to continue to pay for services such as On-Star, satellite radio, and GPS navigation systems because these services help them accomplish the additional desired outcomes of having a safe, enjoyable, and fast trip.

The tactic of transitioning from selling products to providing services, or, integrating services with products (which is often most likely the case), is one of a number of emerging models of product and service innovation that move beyond the linear, incremental improvement model. This paradigm shift can provide new ways of establishing and maintaining competitive advantage for firms of all sizes. Of course every situation is unique and will require the development of individually relevant tactics to accomplish the desired end result; however, as an overarching framework, the process of categorizing your firm's product and service innovation strategy can help guide your decision making. This chapter will focus on a few key categories of product and service innovation including:

- Building a better mousetrap – Addressing an existing need better, faster, or cheaper
- Changing the rules – Addressing an existing need in a different way
- Changing the game – Addressing a previously unrealized need

You may find it odd to define the process of innovation because it is, by nature, a process that tends to defy categorization. However, using a framework and categorizing the type of innovation strategy that your company is pursuing can help focus all the creative minds with big new innovative ideas and get them pointed in the same direction and get working towards the same end.

## "Finding the Job to be Done"

With a seemingly infinite combination of categories and tactics available to create a product and service innovation strategy the challenge becomes where to start. The common denominator and starting point for any strategic planning process should be to develop a clear understanding of where and how your customer derives the most value as a result of their transaction with your company. Clay Christensen, in his work on disruptive innovation, describes this process as "finding the job to be done".[1] It seems an intuitive concept but is something that can easily be overlooked, particularly when trying to come up with a new creative idea.

To illustrate this process I will use the example of a chemical company selling specialty cleaning agents to labs, restaurant kitchens, operating rooms, and other sterile environments. These facilities are regulated by strict health code standards which mandate minimum levels of sterility; failure to meet these standards can result in hefty fines or closure. In this example, the concoction of chemicals and cleaning agents needed to clean each facility is customized for each type of facility and will vary from location to location. The chemical products are themselves commodities and widely available from any cleaning supply company. Each month the chemical company puts together the individual chemicals and cleaning agents for each location, packs up the boxes, and sends them off on a truck for delivery. It is then the responsibility of the customer to combine and use the cleaning agents correctly when cleaning their sterile environment. As things stand, this chemical company is operating a commodity business competing purely on price because these same chemicals can be ordered in the same fashion from any number of suppliers.

In the situation described above ask yourself, "What is the job to be done?" The customer is buying cleaning agents and chemicals, but what they NEED is assurance that their kitchen or lab is cleaned and sterilized to a level that will meet the requirements dictated by health code standards. The true value derived by the consumer from the transaction with the chemical company is that they have been given a method of meeting those standards. So the question then becomes, "Is there another way that the chemical company could accomplish the job to be done in a better, cheaper, and more efficient or more reliable way?" Perhaps the chemical company has skilled staff with extensive training in the handling and use of the cleaning agents and chemicals. Perhaps the customers have had a few occurrences where human error in handling the chemicals has resulted in fines from regulatory agencies and health risks to their patrons or patients. Perhaps rather than buying commodity products and relying on their own staff, the customers would rather buy a cleaning service that guaranteed code compliance and completely eliminated the risk of being fined for non-compliance with the health codes. In return for that peace of mind and the elimination of risk exposure, perhaps the customer would be willing to pay a premium because they would derive far greater value from this service transaction than they would from simply buying cleaning products.

Alternatively, perhaps the chemical company has only a limited number of trained staff in the handling of the chemical products and would be better served by pre-mixing chemicals in their own specialized mixing facility to create the customized cleaning agents for each customer. They may also be able to offer employee training and certification services for the cleaning staff so that customers can reduce the chance of human error and potential fines or health risks to patients and patrons.

Ultimately, the specific innovation strategy implemented to change a product or service should depend on a careful analysis of a company's strengths, weaknesses, and assets. Regardless of the specific tactics employed however, we see in this example how a commodity business can be transformed to a premium business by getting to the core value derived by the customer from their transaction with a vendor: this is the process of finding the job to be done. Once you identify what is at the core of value that your customers derive from you, you can unleash the innovators to tackle the challenge of developing new and creative ways to fulfill that need and deliver greater value.

In the following sections we will focus on the evolution of the media and entertainment industry to illustrate three of the key innovation categories and provide an overview of the many different, interconnected influences and circumstances that can drive product and service innovation. The intent of this section is to illustrate how each category of product and service innovation plays a role in one specific industry eco-system so that you can begin to identify the characteristics and drivers for the different types of innovation strategy.

## "BUILDING A BETTER MOUSETRAP" – ADDRESSING AN EXISTING NEED BETTER, FASTER OR CHEAPER

When we hear the term "product innovation", we may think of a mad scientist or crack team of engineers emerging from the depths of a research lab with a new invention that will revolutionize the world as we know it. Or perhaps these words conger up the image of Steve Jobs standing at a podium announcing the "iEverything", a new device that allows people to store every song ever recorded, watch any movie ever made in high definition, take pictures of outer-space, and shoot full length feature films, all with a device that fits in the palm of your hand.

The notion of product innovation as a process for inventing a new widget or building a better mousetrap is the most traditional and most widely practiced strategy in many different industries. In this category of product/service innovation, firms are focused on altering their existing products or services to address a known and existing need in a better, more efficient, or cheaper way. Because this form of product/service innovation is the most common among businesses across all industries it is also fiercely competitive. Given the current environment of rapidly declining product life cycles, ease of product imitation, and round-the-clock/round-the-globe development up time, the level of competitive intensity continues to rise. Companies that rely on their ability to constantly improve their products or invent new ones in order to maintain differentiation from their competition are facing ever increasing challenges to maintain leadership positions and derive premium pricing for their products and services.

The dramatic impact of our current environment of accelerated change on traditional product innovation strategy is illustrated very well by the

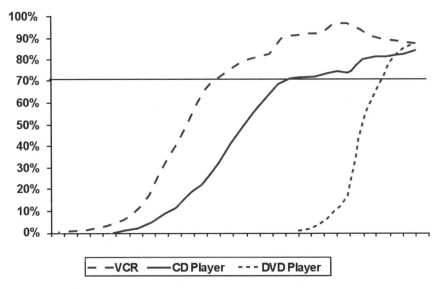

*Figure 1:* Penetration of Consumer Electronics US TV Household 1979-2006.
Source: Consumer Electronics Association eBrain Market Research statistics and MPA
Worldwide Market Research and Statistics

evolution of consumer electronics used for media and entertainment. A strong representation of how dramatically things have changed in terms of product life cycle time frames can be seen in the consumer adoption rates of new technologies that are in the same general category of home media and entertainment. In the late 1970's, VCR technology became widely available to the general public and household adoption of this new home entertainment device grew steadily over the following 12 years reaching 70% of U.S. households in 1990. Similarly, CD players were introduced to the mass market in the early 80's and reached 70% penetration of U.S. households 14 years later. Both of these home media entertainment devices followed a relatively steady adoption rate and elongated adoption curve. However, when you compare those curves with the adoption rate of DVD players, you see a very different story; when DVD technology was introduced to the mass market in 1998, it took only 7 years for the device to make its way into 70% of all US households.[2]

Although there were many different factors that influenced the rapid rate of adoption for DVD players – which we analyze in more detail – this does not appear to be an isolated incident. The pattern of rapid consumer adoption for new technology is continuing with the introduction of flat screen TVs, DVRs, digital music players, and other consumer electronic devices indicating that, although a new product innovation can very quickly displace a predecessor, they can just as quickly be displaced by the next big thing.

When we compare the market adoption rates of VHS and CD players with that of DVD players, DVR's, and flat screen TVs, we get a very clear snap-shot of how dramatically the world of consumer electronics has changed in the past 15 years. More importantly, when we begin to dissect the broad spectrum of disparate but interconnected factors that are driving the greatly increased rate of new technology adoption we can begin to understand the challenges and opportunities associated with a product and innovation strategy that is based on linear incremental improvements to products that serve the same basic demand or need.

## Consumer Demand

One of the key influences for rapid DVD, DVR, and flat screen TV adoption is simply a general consumer familiarity with what the new technology provides. By the time DVD's came around, VHS technology had already established and solidified the market demand for home movie viewing. Consumers were already familiar and comfortable with home movie entertainment as a regular part of their daily lives. As such, DVD technology was not the introduction of something new; it was a substitution of something better. DVD, DVR, and flat screens all provide quality and feature improvements in terms of the picture and sound clarity, navigation capabilities, smaller device size, etc., all of which are incremental upgrades to the VHS players and bulky big screen TVs of the past. In this scenario, when the new technologies were introduced, consumers were again already convinced of the core value proposition of the end product; the stage was set for rapid uptake of newer and better solutions from a demand point of view.

## Product Supply

On the supply side of things, there were a number of important factors that came together to make newer home entertainment technologies accessible to a much broader segment of the population much more quickly than their predecessors. The cost of technology development and production has declined dramatically as high tech production capabilities have increased in developing economies such as China and India. The combination of low labor and manufacturing costs with an abundance of highly skilled engineers has made it dramatically cheaper for companies to make and manufacture high tech products; we can see this in the dramatic increase in high-tech imports coming from China in the past six years.[3]

$ in Billions

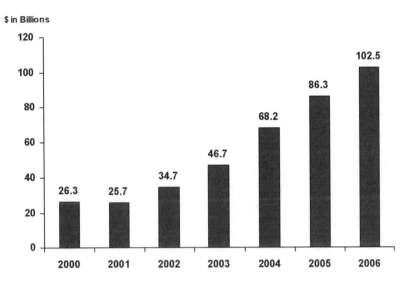

**Figure 2:** *Hi-Tech Imports from China to U.S. 2000-2006*
*Source: US Census Bureau*

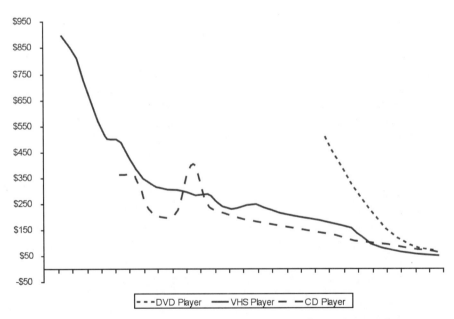

**Figure 3:** *Average Sale Price of Consumer Electronics Hardware 1980-2006*
*Source: Data compiled from multiple industry reports and media publications.*

Additionally, improvements in communications and transportation technology have made it easier to manage supply chains around the globe and efficiently operate global production processes. The ability for fast followers to enter the competitive arena and provide similar or "good enough" technology products has also created a situation where companies have to compete on price very quickly. This in turn has reduced the amount of time that new technologies can sustain premium pricing and increased the need for companies selling higher end products to continue releasing new products with more and better bells and whistles.

When you look at the average sale price of the same group of consumer electronics over time you can clearly see how the rate of price decline mirrors the rate of adoption with a gradual decline in price for products released in the 80's following the gradual rate of consumer adoption and a rapid decline in price corresponding to rapid adoption rates.

## Product Distribution

When we look at the situation from a distribution perspective, the emergence of the big box retailers as the dominant players in the consumer products space also contributed to the rapid uptake of newer consumer electronics. Premium consumer electronics that were once only available in specialty retail stores are now available at high volume, lower margin, large footprint retailers like Wal-Mart and Target. As destination retail locations, the big box format stores can deliver more products to more people in less time and do so at dramatically reduced prices, more than compensating for the reduced profit margins with increased volume and unprecedented efficiency.

These are just some of the many factors that influenced the rapid adoption of DVD technology and illustrate the rapidly evolving business environment in which we operate where:

- demand for new products and advanced features remains high due to general consumer familiarity with advanced technology,
- the global capacity to develop and manufacture high-tech products at dramatically reduced prices has increased at an incredible rate, and
- the retail distribution infrastructure can get products from anywhere to anyone in the world more efficiently and inexpensively than ever before.

The pace of change and rapid adoption of new technologies continues to spiral upward. From VHS to DVDs to DVRs; from big screen, to flat screen, to hi-def flat panel TVs; new products in the consumer electronics media and entertainment world continue to show how quickly a new product can enter the market, skyrocket to the top, and, just as quickly, be displaced by something new. The underling message here is that product innovation strategies based on the delivery of new features and incremental improvements will face the challenge of reduced product life cycles and intense price point competition right out of the gate. On the bright side, however, if you do happen to have the resources and capacity to drive a relentless product innovation engine with:

- round-the-clock, round-the-globe research and development up time,
- highly skilled low cost development and distribution facilities around the world,
- access to global markets through integrated and highly efficient supply chain operations and retail channels,
- ubiquitous brand awareness and marketing power, etc…,

then all the pieces are in place for your company to make the most of an innovation strategy focused on constantly developing and releasing new and cutting edge products.

But what if you don't have all of those things? Luckily, for the rest of us, the rapid pace of change and highly evolving global economy has opened the door to new and creative ways of looking at product and service innovation to drive growth. You don't always have to build the best mousetrap; it may be more profitable to forget about the trap, develop a method for luring mice out of people's homes, put them in cages with runner wheels and open up a shop for small pets. In the next section we'll look at a different category of product and service innovation strategy that focuses on serving an existing need in a different way. We will continue to look at the consumer electronics and entertainment industry and discuss how this new category of innovation strategy has spawned some of the most notable and compelling business success stories in recent years.

## CHANGING THE RULES – ADDRESSING AN EXISTING NEED IN A DIFFERENT WAY

With the introduction of new and innovative products to the mass market comes the opportunity for the second category of product and service innovation to develop. Companies that can recognize the core demand of their customer and leverage new advances in technology to serve that demand in new and innovative ways can disrupt established market dynamics and experience rapid growth. We have often seen this domino effect occur in the consumer electronics and entertainment sector when a new innovative technology or consumer product is introduced. When a new gadget starts to proliferate in the mass market, it often spawns a host of new businesses that are set up to capitalize on the fact that millions of people have the device in their homes or in their pockets. For example, as soon as home video players were introduced to the mass market, the video rental industry was born. Most communities saw local video shops popping up where they could go every weekend, grab the latest new releases and enjoy a night at the movies minus the trip to the mall, parking hassles, ticket lines, sticky theatre floors, and, of course, the feeling of anxiety and disappointment when one realizes that the only seats left are in the front row. The introduction of the video rental industry was an example of a technology enabled service innovation that changed the rules and fulfilled an existing demand in a different way. As you can see from the chart below, throughout the 80's consumer behavior began to change rapidly as consumers began to spend fewer and fewer dollars at the movie theatre as a percentage of the total amount they spent on recreation and entertainment activities.

Compare that trend line with the forecast amount of spending per person per year at the box office and on home video: you can clearly see that consumers chose to replace trips to the theater with trips to the video store.

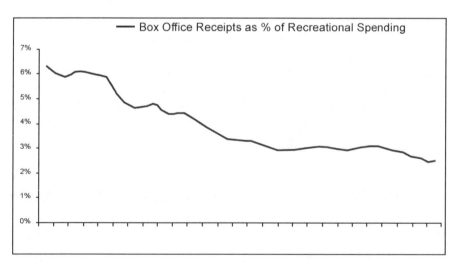

**Figure 4:** *Box Office Sales as a % of U.S. Consumer Recreational Spending 1980-2006*
*Source: Boxofficemojo.com. US Dept. of Commerce: Bureau of Economic Analysis*

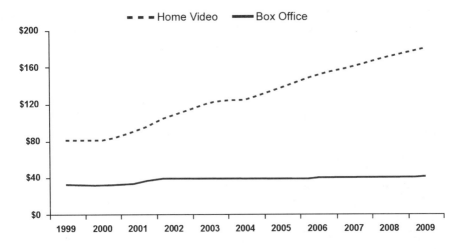

*Figure 5: Annual US Consumer Spending Forecast through 2009.*
*Amount Spent Per Person Per Year*
*Source: US Census Bureau*

In this example, the core demand of consumers to watch movies didn't change, but the rules defining how, where and when they could fulfill that demand changed dramatically.[4]

As VHS technology became ubiquitous to television homes over the course of the 80's and 90's, the video rental industry experienced incremental innovation as national chains such as Blockbuster and Hollywood Video capitalized on operational efficiencies of scale. Although the consolidation of the video rental industry drove growth and pushed cost out of the value chain through efficiency gains, the basic business model remained the same. The physical shape and somewhat bulky size of the VHS tape required relatively large physical locations in order to display the wide and ever growing selection of movies and facilitate a positive customer experience. The video store remained essentially a single purpose destination that required a minimum of two trips by the customer per rental experience. As such, there was an inherent ceiling to the number of retail locations that could be supported and a floor to how much cost could be eliminated..... enter DVD technology.

With the meteoric rise of DVD player adoption, an entirely new world of opportunity emerged for innovative companies to once again change the rules and fill an existing demand in a different way. As the national video rental chains were forced to transition their inventory from VHS to DVD, new innovative companies such as NetFlix and Redbox recognized the opportunity to deliver the movie viewing experience in a completely different way. The smaller physical size of the DVD, ubiquitous internet connectivity, and advances in data management software all came together to create an environment conducive to product and service innovation that altered the movie rental industry dramatically.

In the case of NetFlix, the online subscription DVD rental service, the video rental experience was brought into peoples' homes utilizing the ubiquitous connectivity of the internet and the distribution channel of the postal service. Customers could browse the rental "store" on a PC at home or – more often than some managers would like – at the office, and have access to a vast library of movies far greater than could possibly be maintained in any one physical location. Additionally, due to the small size of a DVD, the cost of sending an item through the mail was reduced to $0.31 compared to the $1.75 it cost to send a VHS tape. Improvements in parcel delivery services with advanced data processing, transportation, and logistics technologies made the receipt and return of movies through the postal system efficient and economically feasible. Although each of these factors was necessary for the successful execution of the NetFlix model, the foundation of the true service innovation that ultimately led to this success came from insight into consumer behavior as opposed to insight into technology. As Mitch Lowe, Co-Founder of NetFlix describes:

> *When NetFlix was getting started, we had all of the pieces in place for customers to rent or buy movies online and receive them through the mail but customers were not responding in any substantial and scalable way. We struggled to overcome the hurdle of requiring a full day or more between customers making a movie selection and the delivery of the movie watching experience. We were continually re-inventing ourselves every 90 days trying to find a solution to the problem. It wasn't until we initiated the subscription service and established and patented the concept of the "queue" that we were able to truly address the needs of the consumer and create a successful model. The real value of the subscription model was to move our inventory out of our warehouses and into our subscriber's homes where they were ready to watch on impulse.*

The NetFlix service innovation strategy was originally driven by the widespread adoption of DVD technology, the smaller physical size of the DVD, advances in infrastructure and I/T technology, ubiquitous internet connectivity, and improvements in communications and data processing capabilities. Like many companies that were founded during the dot-com boom, the primary driver of the NetFlix business innovation was initially technological capability. However, unlike many of the dot-com era companies that fell by the wayside, the executives at NetFlix were able to re-focus their innovation strategy to address the needs and behavior of their customers; this customer foucs led NetFlix to become the successful company they are today. The subscription model combined with the movie selection queuing system solved the problem of lag time between selection and movie viewing experience and dramatically changed how consumers approach the movie rental process. Because consumers have a consistent supply of movies that they have chosen to watch coming to their door, it no longer matters to them that they see a new release the week it comes out. Once a movie is in the queue customers don't have to think about it anymore; they know it will be at their doorstep eventually. NetFlix has created a different type of immediate gratification because, although you may have to wait a few days for a specific movie, you always have a selection of movies waiting for you in your living room. Furthermore, NetFlix is able to provide the widest selection of movies to a fragmented and diverse community of movie fans, offering virtually any movie they want to see from any genre right down to the independent foreign film that was all the rage ten years ago at Cannes. While NetFlix still delivers on the core consumer demand of wanting to have a movie watching experience, their service innovation changed the rules by which that experience is delivered.

Redbox, a leading DVD rental kiosk company, also took advantage of the small size of DVDs, internet connectivity, and advances in data processing systems to deliver a product and service innovation in the movie rental industry; but with a very different focus. The Redbox fully automated kiosk technology has brought the movie rental experience into multi-purpose consumer retail locations. Responding to the increasingly busy lifestyles of today's consumer, the Redbox DVD rental kiosks are located in grocery stores, restaurants, pharmacies, and other retail locations allowing consumers to accomplish multiple tasks in a trip to a single location. The small size of a DVD and the internal computing capability of the Redbox kiosks allow for a broad enough selection of the most popular and frequently rented movies to serve the needs of customers who value convenience and immediate gratification over limitless selection. Additionally, since a Redbox can serve the same core demand of the average movie renter from a box the size of a coke machine as opposed to a fully staffed, 7,000 square foot video store, they can offer that service for a much lower price. Although you probably won't find the 1995 Cannes Film Festival winner for best independent documentary at a Redbox, you will find any of the more popular new releases which you can grab on your way out of the grocery store for only $1.00.

Describing the inception and evolution of Redbox as an innovative company that is revolutionizing the DVD rental space, Matt Sheehan, Vice President of Sales and Business Development, said:

> To find products and services that are truly viable in the marketplace today, it is crucial for companies, whether start up or global, to continually listen, understand and respond to consumer needs. We (Redbox) are a very good example of this. Redbox was created, as an innovation group within a global organization, to find products and services that attract consumers more often to the retail locations. We were not originally sanctioned to improve DVD rental distribution. It was only after analyzing multiple consumer demands and industry trends, along with significant testing, that we recognized how changing the DVD rental offering would offer significant revenue streams to us and also increase a retailer's core business. The first step in this, however, was to truly understand the consumer influence in the marketplace. The mere volume of rentals we see on a daily basis is the clearest indication that we have answered the need well.

Both NetFlix and Redbox recognized an opportunity to take advantage of the characteristics of a new product on the market – the small size of a DVD – and deliver on an existing demand in a new way. Additionally, they were both able to capitalize on the introduction of new technology and infrastructure improvements that were happening in industries outside of their own to execute their innovation strategy effectively. Most importantly the basis and primary driver of each successful innovation strategy was not the technology, it was the ability of NetFlix and Redbox to address the needs and behavior of the customer. In defining or developing an innovation strategy that falls into this category, there can be a tendency to focus on changing technology capabilities or shifts in the general marketplace as the primary drivers of opportunity. As such, it is critical to constantly ask yourself of every decision, "What is the core customer demand we are addressing, and how does this deliver on that demand?" On the strategy execution side of the equation however, the technology capability and changes in the market do become critical areas of focus. There are of course many moving parts that will impact a company's ability to successfully execute an innovation strategy, many of which are not directly controlled by the primary business entity. To address this challenge, it is important that firms first take a 30,000 foot view of the landscape, identify the key drivers of success, and then take a deep dive to understand the changes occurring with each of those drivers and the implications of those changes. This can often require that firms develop understanding and a level of expertise on industries that are not directly related to their business. For this reason, the establishment of strategic relationships that give you access to expertise outside your realm of understanding can be a critical step in the execution of a new innovation strategy.

As complex as the above scenarios are, at least they have the benefit of addressing a defined and proven customer demand. However, what if that demand is not defined? What if a company is entering the marketplace with an entirely new product or service that is addressing a demand that customers don't even realize they have yet? The challenge of convincing customers that they need something that they have never thought of before and then executing the fulfillment of that need is a daunting challenge that, if successful, can be an incredible opportunity.

# "THE PERFECT STORM OF INNOVATION" – ADDRESSING AN ENTIRELY NEW, PREVIOUSLY UNRECOGNIZED NEED

As was the case with the rapid adoption of DVD players and the evolution of the DVD rental industry, there are always many different factors that come together to set the stage for a product or service innovation opportunity. The challenge is in connecting the dots between seemingly disparate factors and across multiple industries in order to identify new, previously un-tapped opportunities. When you look at isolated changes in a particular market – such as the introduction of a new technology or a shift in consumer behavior – the impact of that change can certainly represent a new growth opportunity and provide the foundation for successful product or service innovation. However, when a number of distinct shifts begin to impact each other and fuel the rate of change across the entire group, product and service innovation becomes even more complex. This scenario can best be described as a "perfect storm of innovation" where changes occurring across distinct but inter-connected aspects of a value chain happen at the same time and generate monstrous waves of opportunity and game changing product and service innovations. In this category of innovation, the demand itself is often entirely new because, prior to the changes occurring in the market, the new product or service was either impossible to deliver or completely unnecessary. As such, the challenge becomes first convincing your customers that they do actually need this never before seen product or service, and then delivering the product without completely derailing the existing flow of business.

For example, when Fred Smith first began Federal Express, the demand for overnight parcel delivery was virtually non-existent because no one had ever considered it necessary. Everyone just accepted the "fact" that it took a few days to send an item from one location to another by mail; it was beyond the scope of what the general public thought possible so there was no demand for it. Not until overnight service began to propagate into the general flow of business operations was its value recognized. It is important to note that game changing innovation strategies can easily fall into the "because we can" category rather than the "because it delvers value" category. If companies didn't see a real return for the higher cost of sending something overnight, there would be no FedEx Corporation today with a $34B market cap.

It is this kind of game changing product and service innovation that often represents the greatest opportunity for growth but also the greatest risk. However, as the pace of change accelerates throughout the global economy, the windows of opportunity to develop game changing innovations are increasing. In an environment where there are more opportunities for this category of innovation to occur, there is increased familiarity and levels of expertise in the marketplace to recognize and effectively execute successful, game changing product or service innovation strategies. The emergence of the CIO (Chief Innovation Officer) as an official role in many companies represents a recognition of both the challenges and the opportunities inherent in today's business environment. It may be advantageous to have individuals – or even entire teams – whose job it is to come up with ways of completely disrupting the way a firm does business and constantly challenging the way things are being done. This does not mean that companies need to change their business model every time a new idea hits the white board, it simply means that since the game is changing more frequently in this environment than ever before, companies who pay attention to the fringe may have a better chance to capitalize on those game changing innovations.

The emergence of a game changing innovation and the "perfect storm" that made it possible can be illustrated very well by analyzing the evolution of the out-of-home, digital entertainment and advertising industry. Recently, you may have begun to notice hi-definition flat screen TV's popping up all over the place. Flat panel digital displays have migrated out of living rooms and sports bars, and into seemingly odd places like your grocery store check out lane, your local bank, the corridors of shopping malls, or even outdoors in lift lines at ski resorts; each of these locations provides a new channel for

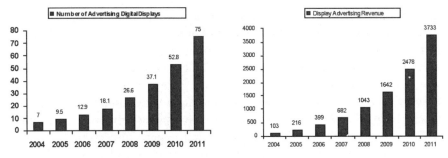

**Figure 6:** *US Digital Signage Market Forecast 2004-2009*
*Source: North American Digital Signage Markets: Frost & Sullivan, 3 May 2005*

**Figure 7:** *LCD TV Average Sale Price Jan '05 - Nov '05*
*Source: Current Analysis Industry Report. Plasma Vs. LCD: Retail Collision Course Digital TV Industry December 21, 2005*

advertisers to reach consumers. As you can see from the forecasts below, the out-of-home digital display advertising market is poised for explosive growth in the coming years.[5]

This dramatic jump from a relatively obscure market of a few hundred million in revenue per year to a projected $3.7 billion market in only a few years provides a sense of the incredible upside potential for companies that can successfully identify these types of opportunities before they emerge. In order to do that, it is important to understand the underlying forces that have come together to create this perfect storm of innovation. On the surface you may see the emergence of digital, out-of-home advertising as primarily driven by the screen technology itself. As a new consumer product, the flat screen TV has undergone the same pattern of rapid adoption and rapid price decline driven by intense competition among manufacturers as seen in the story of the DVD player. In the flat screen TV case however, the rapid decline in price of this consumer electronics product gave rise to an opportunity that has very little to do with consumer demand for a better home entertainment device. In the case of digital out-of-home advertising networks, the decline in flat screen prices has brought the capital expenditure requirement for wide-scale deployment of screens down to an economically feasible level.[6]

This is certainly a reasonable explanation for the rapid increase in screens deployed and it is a very important component of what is happening here. However, when we dig even deeper, it is clear that declining screen prices is only one of many factors driving this market towards its forecasted phenomenal growth. Using our "perfect storm" analogy, picture a meteorologist storm tracker map up on the screen and imagine a storm front approaching. That storm on the meteorologist map represents the declining cost of hardware including flat screen TV's, PCs, Wireless Routers, Media Players, and all of the other electronic devices needed to build a digital signage network. This storm front is large and is gaining strength, but by itself, it is not anything more than a normal weather pattern.

Once again, we see how declining product life cycles – driven by fierce competition, increasing production capabilities, decreasing production cost, and highly efficient global retail distribution systems – are driving the supply side of a product and service innovation equation. However, the flat screens and other hardware are not the only supply side changes that are feeding into this tempest on the horizon. Beyond the physical hardware cost of deploying a digital media network, the ongoing operating costs of connectivity, data storage, and data transfer, which also play a critical role in managing a digital media network, are declining and are forecast to continue on that trajectory.[7]

This decline in costs driven by rapid advances in computing speed and memory capacity, bandwidth and wireless connectivity, and other aspects of the digital infrastructure have made it possible for many innovative businesses and markets to emerge. In our case, it has made the prospect of deploying and managing a distributed network of media screens over the internet much more attractive. Going back to the storm-tracker visual, you can add a low pressure system of declining network and data management costs coming in just behind the hardware front, adding power and speed to the building storm.

At this point, we have set the stage for a very significant weather event and we have only considered the forces that have made out-of-home digital

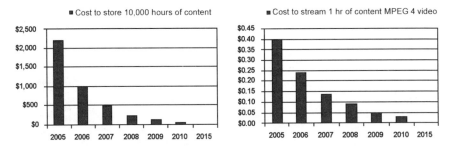

*Figure 8*: Operating Costs for Digital Media Storage and Streaming 2005-2015
Source: Sanford C. Bernstein Research, Media time running out: February 25, 2005

media networks economically feasible. As such, it is now time to turn to the demand side of the equation. Just because we *can* cost effectively install flat screens and send out vast amounts of data in the form of digital content over the internet doesn't necessarily mean that anyone will pay for it.

With the advent of home entertainment technology and services such as DVRs and TiVo, the rapid growth in popularity of video gaming, the ever increasing amount of time consumers spend on the internet, the introduction of satellite radio, etc.; the media landscape has become incredibly fragmented. Consumers now have a seemingly infinite number of options when it comes to receiving information or being entertained.[8]

When consumers were basically limited to network television, newspapers, magazines and local radio stations for their news and entertainment, advertisers were essentially dealing with a situation where everyone was in one room and they could deliver their message with a single megaphone. This, of course, is no longer the case as more and more people exit the mass media room in favor of smaller, more personalized media chambers; the megaphone has become a less than optimal method of delivering a message. These shifts in consumer behavior and media consumption have dramatically changed the landscape for advertisers and it has created a growing demand for new and innovative ways of delivering an advertising message.[9] Nathan Gill, co-founder of Bhootan, a company in the out-of-home digital media industry, describes how he saw the dramatically changing consumer landscape that is contributing to the growth of this industry:

> *The introduction of new technologies such as the Internet,*
> *Tivo, and Satellite radio are fundamentally changing the*
> *media habits of consumers. With billions of content channels*
> *to choose from, today's digital consumer is empowered to view*

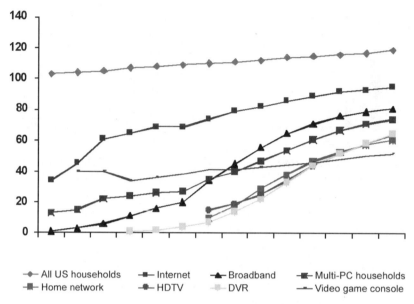

*Figure 9: Media and Entertainment Device Saturation of US Households Forecast 1998-2010*
Source: Forrester's North American Consumer Technology Adoption Study
2006 Benchmark Survey

content on their terms, resulting in highly fragmented media consumption habits. Consumers can save media for later viewing, skip commercials, and even share their favorite media with friends. Device proliferation has also helped fuel this fragmentation with consumers routinely utilizing multiple devices such as television, computer, mobile phone, and iPod to view media. This changing consumer landscape creates a new frontier for marketers and media companies alike struggling to reach consumers in this new digitally fragmented media marketplace of ad-skipping multi-taskers.

This media fragmentation brings additional pockets of disruption to our weather map causing hurricane force winds of change and further fueling the perfect storm of innovation.

Finally we need to consider the activity and spending patterns of the customer as an additional driving force behind any innovation storm. In the case of out-of-home digital networks the customers are advertisers, the massive corporate institutions that spend billions of dollars each year in order to reach their customers and establish a meaningful connection between their customers and their brand.[10] With the media landscape evolving at an ever

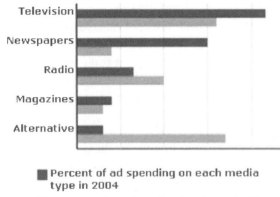

*Figure 10:* Consumption vs. Ad Spend
Source: Forrester's Consumer Technographics 2004 North American Benchmark Study, Mc-Cann Erickson, IAB

■ Percent of ad spending on each media type in 2004

■ Percent of total media time households spend with each media type

increasing rate, an imbalance between ad spending and media consumption has developed.[11]

Consumers have moved away from traditional media faster than most large advertisers could change their ad spending patterns, creating a situation in need of an adjustment. It is in that adjustment that we see another major driving force behind the out-of-home digital media industry growth. Advertisers are increasing their ad spending in alternative channels to adjust for evolving patterns of consumer media consumption providing the economic engine to drive explosive growth in this industry.[12]

On our storm-tracker map we can visualize this as an unstable air mass entering the picture; it is beginning to cause thunderstorms to drop a

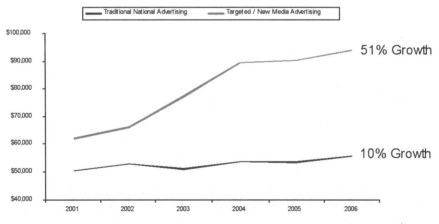

*Figure 11:* U.S. Advertising Spend 2001-2006 In Millions
Source: TNS Media Intelligence Media Reports 2001-2006

downpour of revenue into the system. This inflow of capital coming from a large source is not likely to dry up anytime soon and represents the final, and possibly most important, driver for our perfect storm of innovation. As was the case with the NetFlix and Redbox innovations, it is the needs of the customer that truly drives the development of any successful innovation and it is the external factors that enable the execution of any successful innovation strategy.

In the case of Bhootan, Inc., an interactive media company that introduces contemporary media to public environments via high definition digital television and mobile handsets, the company was spawned from the realization of a problem and the recognition that many changes in technology, the marketplace, and consumer behavior were coming together to provide a solution to that problem. As Matthew Stoudt, co-Founder of Bhootan describes:

> *The genesis behind all great concepts stems from the recognition of a problem and the application of a creative solution. Bhootan's foundation lies in that fact. McDonald's recognized that it's ability to reach consumers was declining precipitously due to media fragmentation and the advent of ad-skipping technology. If McDonald's, one of the top 10 brands in the world was having this issue, then we figured that most other advertisers must be facing similar difficulties in reaching their core customers. Once we clearly defined the problem, we began to analyze consumer behaviors to create the solution. In McDonald's case, the first half of the solution resided within its 4 walls. Averaging over 30 million American customers daily (or more than 10% of the US population), McDonald's was its own media outlet.*
>
> *Unfortunately, most retailers lack the market ubiquity of McDonald's. The question then became "how do you amass all of the retailers so that each one can become its own media outlet." The twin trends of declining flat screen prices and increasing ubiquity of broadband access delivered the solution. As the central aggregating force, Bhootan could acquire critical mass by deploying low cost LCD screens to retailers and networking the retailers with an IP based solution. As a digital network, Bhootan could empower individual retailers to come become "media giants" and could enable advertisers to harness the targeting efficacy of the internet. With $140 billion in adverting dollars in flux, Bhootan is poised to capitalize on the pending massive shift.*

With all of these different forces coming together at the same time it becomes a bit more clear and reasonable to believe that an industry can go from relative obscurity to a multi-billion dollar opportunity in just a few years.

It is important to recognize that this kind of brand new, high growth product or service innovation is still the exception rather than the rule. Perfect storms do not typically happen everyday, but given the current environment of rapidly accelerating change, the windows of opportunity for storms to develop do seem to be increasing in frequency. Just as a meteorologist tracks and maps the developing weather patterns that may affect a particular geographic region in order to tell you if you should bring an umbrella with you tomorrow, it is important to keep a watchful eye on the changes occurring both in and around your industry so you will know what your company will need to bring to the market in the future.

## CONCLUSION

As we have discussed, the concept of product and service innovation is evolving rapidly in response to the current environment of accelerated global change. This chapter has provided three different categories of product and service innovation that can be used to define how your firm sets your own innovation strategy. While this is in no way an exhaustive list, the examples illustrate a few different ways to think about how to most effectively enhance, reconfigure, or replace your current products and services to maintain competitive advantage and drive growth. For the purpose of illustrating these concepts we focused on the consumer electronics and media and entertainment industries because they provide highly publicized and widely recognized examples of major shifts in technology and consumer behavior. However, the practice of mapping the impact of new technologies and services across multiple industries is applicable to virtually any business sector. As we have seen across all categories of product and service innovation strategy, the key to the development of a successful strategy still lies in the needs and the behavior of your customer. Innovations that fall into the "because we can" category must be re-evaluated and re-focused to become "because it serves a need". Once the innovation is clearly tied to solving a customer problem or addressing a changing behavior, the effective execution of a product and service innovation strategy then relies on the accurate definition and deep understanding of new technologies and changes in the market that will serve as the key driver. Regardless of whether your business is B-to-C or B-to-B, retail or manufacturing, local or global, the changes occurring throughout your business ecosystem can be tracked, analyzed and leveraged to develop and execute the most effective innovation strategy for your company.

# ENDNOTES

1   Clayton Christensen, Scott Anthony, and Gerald Berstell, "Finding the Right Job for your Product," *MIT Sloan Management Review*, Spring 2007.

2   Judson Coplan, "Diagnosing the DVD Disappointment: A Life Cycle View," *The Leonard N. Stern School of Business*, April 3, 2006.

3   High tech in developing countries story. Data from the US Census Bureau Statistics, 2000 – 2006.

4   US Entertainment Industry 2006 Market Statistics, MPA Worldwide Market Research and Analysis.

5   North American Digital Signage Markets: Frost & Sullivan, 3 May 2005.

6   Steve Kovsky, "Current Analysis Industry Report. Plasma Vs. LCD: Retail Collision Course," *Digital TV Industry*, December 21, 2005.

7   Sanford C. Bernstein, "Media time running out," **[Was this part of a larger publication?]**February 25, 2005.

8   Forrester's North American Consumer Technology Adoption Study 2006 Benchmark Survey.

9   "The end of television as we know it: a future industry perspective," *IBM Business Consulting Services*, January 2006.

10  "Alternative Media Research Series II: Alternative Advertising & Marketing Outlook 2006 Executive Summary," *PQ Media*, June 2006.

11  Forrester's Consumer Technographics 2004 North American Benchmark Study.

12  TNS Media Intelligence Media Reports 2001 - 2006.

# 2.5

# AGILE STRATEGY EXECUTION – CREATING STRATEGIC ALIGNMENT

**Ryan Nichols,** Corporate Strategy Group, SAP
**Ranga Bodla,** Director, Solutions Management, Corporate Performance Management, SAP
**Chris Mark,** Corporate Strategy Group, SAP

In Sun Tzu's *Art of War*, the Chinese general laid out five simple requirements for victory in battle. Military metaphors do not always translate well in the business world, but one of the five will resonate powerfully with any CEO contemplating strategy and execution. As Sun Tzu put it: "He will win whose army is animated by the same spirit throughout all its ranks."[1]

Sun Tzu was talking about alignment, which is just as hard to achieve today as it was two thousand years ago, despite the number of tools, processes, and technologies that organizations now have at their disposal. Yet alignment has grown even more important to achieving success, especially given the accelerating rate of change facing most organizations. Time after time, companies have been overtaken by competitors or failed to deliver on expectations because different groups of people at different levels of the organization were not on the same page. Indeed, research shows that companies on average realize only about 60 percent of the potential financial performance their strategies promise – and more than one-third of executives place the figure at less than 50 percent.[2]

On the other hand, when alignment is there, you know it, and you see it in the results. It is what we call agile strategy execution, and in our experience this is an almost unbeatable advantage in today's competitive environment.

# CLOSING THE GAP

We came face-to-face with this need for strategic alignment recently at our own company, SAP AG, the leading provider of business process solutions. The resulting strategic transformation was documented in a Stanford Graduate School of Business case study that summarizes our story of striving for strategic alignment.[3]

In 2005, Henning Kagermann, SAP's CEO, tasked our strategy team with preparing an analysis of the opportunities and challenges we could expect to face between 2006 and 2010. The trends that we anticipated impacting SAP's business going forward will sound familiar to executives at many organizations: we were facing a rapidly consolidating industry characterized by fierce competition and high levels of M&A. The lines were blurring between our suppliers, our competitors, and our go-to-market partners. Our relationship with our customers was growing broader, with our role changing from a supplier of software to that of a co-creator of business process solutions. We were faced with both opportunities and threats from powerful, low cost talent pools in emerging nations. While these trends are common in many industries, the rapid – and accelerating – pace of change in the high tech industry meant that SAP would need to manage the impact of each of these trends more than most.

The most powerful trend we anticipated came from a powerful set of potentially disruptive technologies. We came to believe that emerging Internet-based technologies and standards known collectively as "web services" would transform the $79.8 billion enterprise software applications industry, in which SAP is the market leader. As a result, Kagermann committed SAP to deploy new web services-based technology on a massive scale. He also announced several growth initiatives that hinged on the implementation of the newly defined strategy, which was based on a new software framework called enterprise services-oriented architecture.

A sweeping internal transformation was required in order to achieve our goals. In addition to requiring a costly research and development effort, capitalizing on the new growth initiatives required far-reaching change that would test the very core of the company: our leadership, our culture, our values, and our processes. On the one hand, most people felt confident that SAP eventually would make the adjustments necessary – indeed, SAP had weathered several technology and market cycles over its 33-year history. On the other hand, powerful and deep-pocketed companies including Oracle, Microsoft, and IBM were investing billions of dollars into similar growth initiatives.

Given the context, Kagermann recognized that speed was critical:

> *Execution is a question. How long will it take, how efficient and fast can we be? Can we actually be the first in the market to deliver on the promises of the new architecture? We do not have room to make many mistakes. We must break down the barriers imposed by the old power structure.*

Having been at SAP since 1982, Kagermann had experienced firsthand our company's rapid headcount growth (which had increased more than thirty-fold since his arrival) as well as its steady transition from a single-product company into a multi-line, multinational software giant. Yet such growth had come at a price. Now that SAP had become a large and complex organization, coordinated execution on our strategy across groups and regions quickly proved to be a significant challenge.

## THE STRUGGLE TO CREATE ALIGNMENT

Why is it so difficult to create alignment around a strategy? One reason is an artificial gap that many organizations create between strategy and execution. Strategy can never account for the massive complexity and myriad of unexpected events that define what happens in the "real world." This is precisely what another great military strategist, Carl von Clausewitz, was referring to when he spoke about "the fog of war." As he explained:

> *In war, countless minor events – the sorts of things that can never be properly taken into account on paper – conspire to decrease efficiency, and one always falls short of the goal. These difficulties happen over and over again, and cause a sort of friction that only those who have experienced war can accurately understand.*[4]

Strategy, then, is not about delivering step-by-step instructions for achieving a goal. When people approach it that way, reality always gets in the way. Instead, strategy is more about preparing people to act appropriately in the face of the unexpected. This requires that a strategy be crystal clear to every one of us, in a way that is relevant to our day-to-day work. We need to understand where the organization intends to go, and what our own role within it should be. With that, we have alignment.

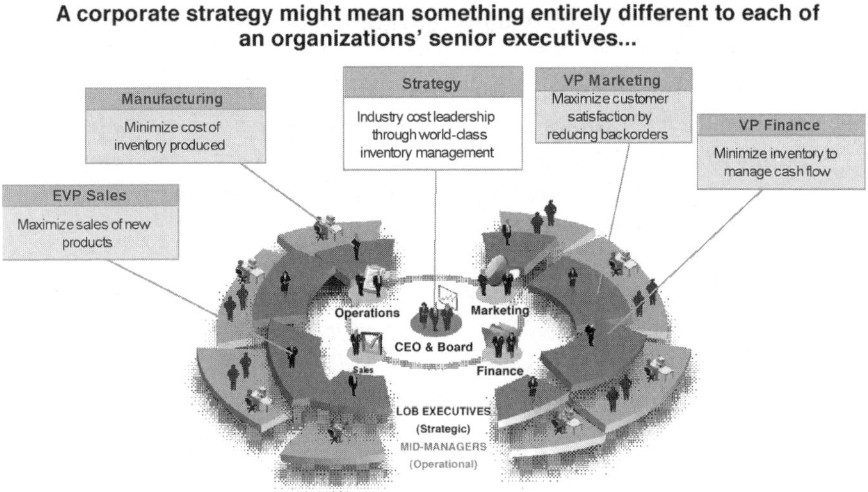

**A corporate strategy might mean something entirely different to each of an organizations' senior executives...**

*Figure 1: The Gap Between Strategy and Execution (Part 1)*

In most organizations, however, there is often a structural disconnect between the people formulating the strategy and the people charged with carrying it out. Indeed, the formal strategy development process as we have seen it usually goes something like this: first, a small team is put on the case. A set of smart, informed people are interviewed and the findings are used to inform decisions by top management on a set of goals and a plan to achieve them. However, as this plan is communicated into the organization, it runs head-on into they way people currently do their jobs. Most of the organization wasn't involved in generating the plan – and rightly so as many key decisions need to be made at the top of an organization. Yet for the most part the strategy is communicated top-down, using high-level slogans and targets. Too often the strategy doesn't mean anything specific to the people whose collective actions define the course of the company, and who operate in a complex and ever-changing environment. This artificial distinction between the process of creating a strategy and the process of carrying it out creates misalignment – when once-a-year top down guidance conflicts with real-time, bottom-up feedback and stale broadcast communications conflicts with rich collaboration across the network, misalignment is the natural result.

When we looked around, it quickly became clear that we were not alone in recognizing this problem. One study indicated that less than 5 percent of employees, and only 50 percent of managers, believe they have a clear understanding of their organization's strategy[5] – especially their role in making it happen. Most troubling is that this is not happening intentionally; most people are not purposely choosing to ignore strategy or make decisions

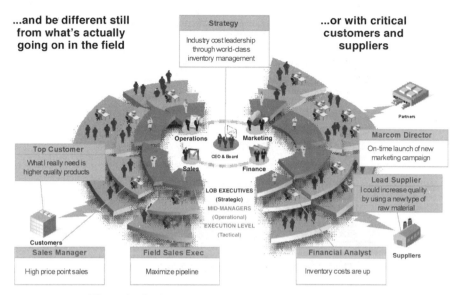

**...and be different still from what's actually going on in the field**

**...or with critical customers and suppliers**

*Figure 2: The Gap Between Strategy and Execution (Part 2)*

against the best interests of the organization. If they were, the problem would be easy to remedy. Rather people are using the information they have at their disposal to make what seems to be a locally optimal decision.

To address this disconnect, many organizations attempting to execute on a new strategy spend significant amounts of time, money, and leadership talent on projects and processes to create alignment. As an intuitive first step, they will start a communications campaign to get the word out through executive speeches, posters, and placards. More importantly, they will also try to ensure that every new project has an explicit tie to the new plan, and they will encapsulate this new plan in a set of scorecards to measure progress – ideally tied into with individual performance and compensation plans. All of these programs, projects, and best practices can be an important step toward achieving true alignment. This, too, was what we experienced at SAP as we began our own transformation.

## CASCADING STRATEGY AT SAP

In launching SAP's strategic transformation, Kagermann knew that aligned execution of the new growth strategy would be impossible without the "prepared minds" that result from improved communication, planning, management, and employee engagement. He kicked off a series of internal

*Figure 3: Essential Elements of Best-Run SAP*

process initiatives collectively known as "Best-Run SAP" to communicate the new growth strategy to all levels of the organization and to strengthen the "culture of execution" within SAP. As part of the launch, Kagermann identified focus areas for Best-Run SAP and allocated resources – including Executive Board members – to support each one.

One process element of Best-Run SAP was dubbed the "Cascade" effort, whereby we worked to propagate understanding of the corporate strategy throughout the organization. More specifically, the Cascade project aimed to tie strategy to execution within each business unit, align business units that needed to execute together, and generate feedback regarding the push for strategic change. As a part of this effort, each business unit developed its own strategic business plan (SBP) that identified and documented organizational goals, an execution plan, success measures, and critical dependencies. Each SBP also had to clarify linkages to and support of the Corporate SBP, tying back to a set of central goals that were important for every part of the organization: first, create value for customers, partners, and employees, and then capture value by leading our industry – owning our core markets and growing from that base into new markets in an efficient and effective way.

To enhance high-level communication around these goals and our plans to achieve them, Kagermann added an annual two to three hour session with each business unit leader (in addition to existing quarterly review sessions with the Executive Board) as a part of the strategic management process. Finally, the Best-Run SAP initiative defined new requirements stemming from our cultural values and placed increased emphasis on evaluating

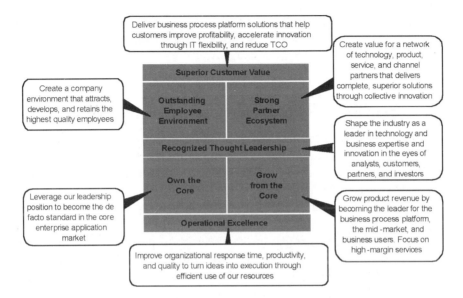

*Figure 4: Corporate Goals Used to Facilitate Alignment*

manager performance. To measure progress toward our goals, a survey-based mechanism called "Pulse Check" was created to solicit periodic feedback from employees.

Kagermann knew that thousands of lower level implementation issues lurked beneath the surface of our growth initiatives, and that he needed strong commitment from all employees in order for SAP to have any chance at achieving its goals. As Herbert Heitmann, Senior Vice President, Global Communications, remarked, "At the board level, it is often easy to achieve an agreement. The tough part starts when you are in the implementation process and nobody has told the rest of the organization that there is a need for change management. Why are we doing this and why are these changes necessary?"[6]

By the beginning of 2006, Kagermann was confident that senior executives at SAP shared a clear understanding of our strategy and what was required to execute it. The impact of the alignment at this level cannot be understated. Meetings and discussions with the top executives became more focused and, at the executive level, all were headed in the same direction.

At lower levels of the organization, however, achieving understanding and alignment required more work. In some functional areas, translating the vision into concrete tasks that people could do to help the company deliver on its goals was extremely difficult. Indeed, one chief platform engineer, observed that some individuals seemed more "fascinated" by the options the strategy offered than aligned to execute upon it. As another executive noted, "If you are as loosely organized as SAP is, and you try to do things top down, you will not get what you expect."[7]

## SUPPORTING STRATEGIC ALIGNMENT

The takeaway from our experience was that the projects, programs, initiatives, and processes used to jumpstart this type of effort are just the starting point to a true corporate transformation. There was clear communication about what the strategy was and what it was intended to accomplish, but in order to truly transform the organization there was much more to be done. For one, while people "understood" what the strategy was, making it relevant required a collaborative element that was missing. Person-to-person discussions of the changes required and the real impact on day-to-day operations were critical. So, while the top-down effort was effective, it needed to be complemented with an effective grass-roots adoption of its key principles.

Henning's first strategy whitepaper was a great mechanism for forcing difficult discussions between the most senior executives, but no mechanism existed to translate the strategies, goals, and objectives laid out in the paper into requirements for SAP's 40,000 employees. The same could be said for the first round of the "Cascade" process – while conversations between Henning and his senior managers were a powerful first step toward ensuring aligned execution at the highest levels, our transformation required having these conversations at every level of the organization. Each aspect of SAP's efforts to turn strategy to execution needed to be rolled out into the organization. We needed to scale these processes quickly to fully support the alignment of execution with strategy.

Organizations have spent the last 20 years leveraging information technology to solve exactly this problem for dozens of other business processes – SAP itself has made a living by developing solutions for automating the business processes at the core of large enterprises: Idea to Offering, Market to Order, Order to Cash, Forecast to Delivery, Issue to Resolution, and Hire to Retire. Why would "Strategy to Execution" be any different?

What we discovered was that a significant gap exists in the information technology tools required to support the process of executing on a strategy: the traditional enterprise applications most helpful for efficient execution can't handle the flexibility required of a strategic transformation, yet the office-productivity tools most helpful for initially articulating a strategy break when it comes to aligning with execution.

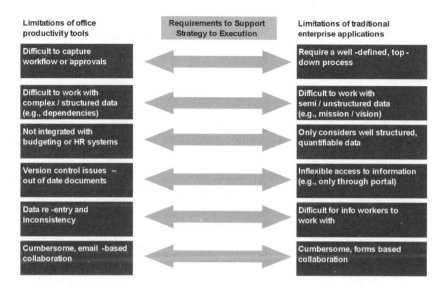

*Figure 5: Gaps in Traditional Tools to Support Strategy to Execution*

Why have traditional enterprise software tools failed at supporting the "Strategy to Execution" business process? In short, they aren't flexible enough to support strategic alignment. While a company's essential sales or manufacturing business processes can be enormously complex, they are rarely as dynamic as the processes required to actually develop and execute a strategy. Much of traditional enterprise software is built for top-down management based on quantitative data and structured processes. This simply doesn't reflect how strategy is actually developed at most companies. For example, at our company:

- **Traditional tools that required a well-defined, top-down process for setting objectives were simply not useful.** While Kagermann's vision 2010 was ultimately driven top-down into the organization, many key elements of that vision were driven from the bottom up. In some areas, Kagermann had a very concrete idea of what needed to be accomplished, and the chief objective of the Cascade process was to communicate this vision to his lieutenants. In other areas of the business, Kagermann needed to have his lieutenants propose the strategy to him, and the chief objective of the Cascade process was to ensure that these proposals were consistent with other elements of the vision.

- **Traditional tools with sophisticated rules to calculate status based on quantitative data tolerances were not effective.** While the discipline of regularly measuring progress against the agreed upon KPIs was an important of the Cascade process, the flexibility to reflect management's judgment in communicating the true progress in executing on the strategy was extremely important. The KPIs to measure progress against the new strategy were immature – and management was uncomfortable making hard commitments to specific targets unless they could also include their "color commentary" for why a target was missed but the status was green. In the end, the learning from going through this process was one of the chief benefits of the process.
- **Traditional tools that required hours to architect a KPI's information structure in a data warehouse before it could be used were simply not useful.** While some KPIs came directly out of an existing metric, others started as nothing more than vague concepts of what needed to be achieved (e.g., high partner satisfaction). The exact measure, data source, and target levels were defined over time. However, it was important to maintain a placeholder for these KPIs right next to KPIs that had been tracked and audited for years.
- **Traditional tools that only lived in the corporate intranet or required the assistance of trained users to operate were not useful.** Strategy at SAP was a collaborative, consensus driven process that often happened around a table in the coffee corner or at the airport – the process demanded the flexibility of a document that could be printed out, annotated, and edited, not hard-to-access pages in a traditional enterprise application.

Even if there were a traditional enterprise application that overcame the problems above to support strategic alignment, you would face the challenge that the knowledge workers responsible for defining the strategy nearly always start by using the tools they are most familiar with – Microsoft Office. And when users find the traditional tools that they are offered by the IT department inadequate, they'll again make-do with the tools they are most familiar with – stretching these tools well beyond their intended use. This was certainly true at SAP: the key strategy documents were simple Microsoft Word documents. The Cascade conversations were based on three-page PowerPoint presentations, with accompanying data in Excel. This was a perfectly appropriate approach for the corporate strategy group – there was an entire team of strategy professionals supporting this effort, managing the creation and revision of these documents. But this approach didn't scale –

even when extended to the most senior level of management, SAP outgrew the capability of office-based tools to support strategy management. For example:

- **Richer visualization capabilities were required.** Attempting to visualize and capture the relationships between the goals and objectives of different organizations became a time consuming task – before each round of strategy discussions, the strategy team would tape printouts of each strategic business plan to the walls of a conference room and use markers to draw different color lines between different organizations to identify conflicts and inter-dependencies.
- **Integration into the actual process of running the business was required.** It was difficult to turn the PowerPoint files into living documents – given the speed of change in the technology industry, the actual strategy being pursued by a business unit often differed significantly from the version last inputted into the business plan template and submitted to the central group.
- **Richer two-way collaboration capabilities were required.** It was difficult to collaborate around a single office-based template – different versions would be emailed around a department for input or commentary. Opportunity was lost for colleagues to build on each others thinking, and consolidating this feedback was a nightmare. This was true during the initial development of a strategy, but even more critical during its execution – managers and employees needed to have the opportunity to give feedback on the specific aspects of a strategy that they were being asked to act on, and share their experience in execution with others asked to perform analogous tasks.
- **Better tie-ins to existing data sources were required.** The office templates required lots of time re-entering data. Not only was this inefficient, but the resulting inconsistencies made it difficult to interpret and process the resulting business plans. Was one region really setting more ambitious targets for their customer satisfaction strategy, or were they simply using different metrics?
- **Tight links to financial and HR systems were required.** It is difficult to tie the strategy contained in an office document to an organization's budgeting or performance management process. A strategy can only become real when investment is allocated to the required activities and employees are measured on the outcomes that result from its execution. Unless this link can be made, the strategy is destined to become a whitepaper that sits on the shelf.

But where does this leave an organization like SAP, trying to transform their business by driving a new strategy to execution throughout a large, complex organization? Existing enterprise software offerings are tied to traditional ways of thinking about financial performance management: rigid command and control-oriented processes without enough flexibility to accommodate ad hoc processes, unstructured data, judgment-driven rules, and rich collaboration. Office documents are flexible enough to handle this richness, but are not robust enough to support organizational transformation. Strategy to execution is caught between individual productivity tools and enterprise applications, supported well by neither.

SAP did what every other company has done when confronted with this dilemma – we did the best that we could to cope using the existing tool set. But the costs to this approach were serious: the Cascade process wasn't carried as far into the organization as our team would have liked due to its inability to support the process. Dependencies between different parts of the organization were missed due to the amount of manual work required. Decisions were made using out-dated information, and valuable opportunities to enrich the strategic thinking across the company through collaboration between senior executives were missed. It became clear to SAP that there had to be a better way.

# THE NEXT STEP: STRATEGY 2.0

As SAP's management team struggled to create strategic alignment across the organization using traditional enterprise and productivity applications, many of SAP's employees were starting to use an entirely different set of tools and technologies to support the way they interacted with information in their day-to-day work and personal life. This wasn't just happening at SAP: last year, 22 million blogs were tracked on Technorati, one third of all internet traffic was generated by users of BitTorrent, five million pictures were tagged on Flickr, and more than one million articles were written by users of Wikipedia.

But what does all of this have to do with turning strategy to execution? After all, managing photos is a very different task than managing a complex organization. As a company, SAP started to wonder what it could learn from the way it saw its own employees engage in these emerging consumer internet applications. These employees weren't just consuming information – they were participating in the creation of surprisingly complex and high value content. What if the "architecture of participation" seen in these consumer applications could change how companies aligned to execute on a new strategy?

| Characteristic | Description | Example |
|---|---|---|
| Self-published | *Users, not editors, create the most relevant content.* | • Blogger<br>• Wikipedia |
| Self-structured | *information is best structured dynamically by the people using it* | • Flickr<br>• del.icio.us |
| Self-assessed | *Users are best at assessing the usefulness of information* | • Google's PageRank<br>• Amazon |
| Self-policed | *Users are best at policing themselves* | • Craigslist<br>• HotOrNot.com<br>• eBay |
| Self-sustained | *Users can financially sustain non-traditional interest areas directly* | • Google AdSense<br>• eBay<br>• Pod-Casting |
| Self-powered | *Users can technologically power non-traditional interest areas directly* | • Google's Hello<br>• BitTorrent<br>• Joost |

*Figure 6: Social Computing Represents a Dramatic Shift in How People Interact with Information*

After all, these applications are strong where traditional enterprise applications are weak. Social computing applications are so intuitive to use that they require almost no instruction; traditional enterprise applications are not. Social computing applications are flexible enough to be used in mash-ups never envisioned by their creator; traditional enterprise applications still require complex and costly integration. Most importantly, social computing applications are designed to increase in value as others use them, while most of the information in traditional enterprise applications is underutilized and the vast majority of enterprise users do not benefit from the activities of other users.

This last difference is driven by a simple philosophy: information is most effectively and efficiently generated/structured/displayed by the people who are using it. As a result, this new generation of social computing can be:

- Self-published: users, not editors, create the most relevant content. Blogger empowers individuals to publish their own journals; Wikipedia broadens this to collective publishing by groups; Ning. com applies this same thinking to user-published applications, allowing users to freely combine common social website building blocks into applications of their own design.
- Self-structured: information is best structured dynamically by the people using it, not through a centrally-defined taxonomy. Flickr

applies this approach to the collective tagging of photos; del.icio. us applies this approach to book-marking internet content more broadly.

- Self-assessed: users are best at assessing the usefulness of the information they consume. Google's Page Rank algorithm uses this concept to prioritize search results; Amazon uses this concept to make tailored product recommendations.
- Self-policed: users are best at policing themselves. Craigslist and HotOrNot.com have users screen for inappropriate content; eBay's reputation ratings formalizes this concept.
- Self-sustained: users can financially sustain non-traditional interest areas directly. Google AdSense has enabled a "long tail" of content that would never be of interest to traditional advertisers; eBay has done the same for markets of physical goods; Pod-Casting has the potential to do the same for music.
- Self-powered: users can provide their own hardware and bandwidth to support peer-to-peer applications. Google's Hello applies this idea to photos while BitTorrent applies this to video and music file sharing.

What if the tools to support strategy management shared these same characteristics? "Information is power" used to mean that he who had the information had the most power. As a result, people guarded information to increase their power. In certain areas of their life, however, people are discovering the power that results from getting the appropriate information into the hands of the appropriate broader audience. If an organization could take advantage of this increased willingness of ordinary people to move from simple consumers of information to providers of information, the resulting dynamic could allow an organization's strategy-to-execution content to be self-published, self-structured, self-assessed, and self-sustaining.

Think about what this might look like. Today, strategic priorities are often defined in an ivory tower without organizational involvement. What if instead, elements of strategy emerged from self-published feedback, debate, and interaction of employees at all levels? At SAP, this would mean that managers could directly collaborate on the "Sun Tzu" strategy whitepaper through a collaborative wiki.

Today, strategy often only affects behavior at top levels of organization. What if instead, it was possible to have a self-powered strategy process that could reach the "long tail" of the organization, blurring the distinction between strategy and tactics? At SAP, this would mean a clear link between

| Element | Traditional process | Process with architecture of participation |
|---|---|---|
| **Strategy definition** | • Strategy defined in an ivory tower, then sits on a shelf until next planning cycle | • Collaboration: Elements of strategy emerge from feedback / debate / interaction of employees at all levels<br>• Live content: Event -driven strategy re -definition |
| **Objectives, targets, and initiatives** | • Command and control objective setting without input from below | • Negotiated multi-party objective setting through strategy dialogues<br>• Wisdom of crowds: Distributed prediction of performance through information markets<br>• Collaborative resolution of misalignment |
| **Cascade into business** | • Strategy only affects behavior at top levels of organization | • Long tail: Possible to cascade strategy down to every individual in the organization, blurring the distinction between strategy and tactics |
| **Risks & depend- encies** | • Inadequate assessment of performance and risks; unknown dependencies between organizations and objectives | • Tagging: Interdependencies emerge from individuals identifying their own major risks factors<br>• Network map: many -to -many connections based on mutually expressed dependencies<br>• Wisdom of crowds: Distributed prediction of risk probability through information markets |
| **Analysis & assessment** | • Centralized assessment of performance | • Performance issues raised by those depending on results<br>• Live content: Alerts if new data impacts strategy and may require a change |

*Figure 7: Overview of Bringing Architecture of Participation to Strategy 2.0*

individual MBOs, and the team, board area, and corporate objectives that were part of the Cascade process.

Today, companies often don't know the dependencies that exist between different organizations and their objectives, or rigidly structure this information along the organizational relationships defined in the org chart. What if these interdependencies emerged from individuals mutually self-identifying and structuring their own major risks? At SAP, this would mean that managers could tag their peers' Strategic Business Plans (SBPs) as they read, to highlight dependencies on or with their own goals.

Today, most companies set the targets for their objectives in a command and control setting, without collaborative input from below. What if these objectives were self-policed, through collaborative negotiation to resolve misaligned targets? At SAP, this would mean that misaligned – or unrealistic – target levels could be flagged by managers to be resolved in the quarterly strategy dialogues.

Today, most companies use an annual strategy setting cycle. What if this process were self-powered, driven by external events or new incoming data that impact the existing strategy and may require a change in the current strategy? At SAP, this would mean that survey results could automatically trigger the need for the revision of the related strategic business plan and all dependent strategic business plans.

Today, most companies rely on an undifferentiated mass communication of their corporate strategy. What if this content could be self-assessed, and delivered to individuals in a highly contextualized fashion based on each individual's requirements for information? At SAP, this would mean that the relevant strategy documents would be delivered to individuals based on an assessment of the contents of their strategic business plan.

Today, most companies perform an inadequate assessment of their expected performance and risk factors. What if these risks could be self-assessed, leveraging the wisdom of crowds? At SAP, this would mean that the best prediction of performance and risk might emerge through broad participation in information markets, where employees could compete in an internal marketplace to assess likelihood of product delay or competitor action.

What impact would be achieved if strategy management were supported by an architecture of participation?

- Insight: individuals in every corner of an organization already have access to different bits of strategically critical information, yet few organizations effectively tap the "wisdom of crowds" inside and outside the organization.
- Real-time adaptability: a network is far more responsive to change than a hierarchy – a strategy based on an architecture of participation would result in an organization that is highly responsive to new pieces of information.
- High flexibility: strategy management supported by an architecture of participation could handle the real-life messiness of ad hoc strategic decisions where there is high variability in the process and in the roles played by different individuals

## THE ARCHITECTURE OF PARTICIPATION AT SAP

Will these tools fill the gap in capabilities between strategy management based on office templates and strategy management supported by traditional enterprise applications? It is too early to tell, but there are encouraging signs, even in SAP's own experience in transforming its business:

- "Enterprise Services Community" is a first step towards using the architecture of participation to set key elements of SAP's product strategy. Rather than having product managers determine what services to provide and how to provide them, SAP's customers and partners can join a community to collectively determine the highest priority services for a given industry and the most useful way to define those services.

- "SAP Developer Network" leverages the wisdom of crowds to collect real time feedback on SAP's execution of its strategy. Over 900,000 developers have joined SDN for community-provided technical information and support. In addition, the SDN provides a forum for SAP's management team to first expose emerging elements of our technical strategy. These executive blogs, and the lively online discussions that follow, give SAP invaluable insights very quickly around key decisions.

- A tool called Harmony uses the power of social networks to build communities among SAP's 40,000 global employees. Employees share what they want to share about their personal and professional interests and abilities, and find unexpected connections with co-workers. These connections facilitate the information sharing across geographies and organizational boundaries. In the initial pilot, more than 1,500 employees filled out profiles.

- Even the team managing SAP's formal strategy cascading processes has found it useful to leverage the architecture of participation in its work. Up-to-date knowledge on the status and methodology behind the calculation of SAP's key performance indicators is distributed across the organization – decentralizing the maintenance of this information to these groups would be a real time saver, but traditional document management systems were too cumbersome. The better answer: a secure enterprise wiki that allowed for this information to be maintained in a far more flexible manner.

- SAP also acquired Pilot Software to bring a platform for collaborative strategy management to its customers. Pilot already had success in the marketplace as a provider of strategy management solutions, and by acquiring Pilot, SAP can advance its plans to make next generation strategy management tools a reality for our customers.

## WHAT COMES NEXT?

It is clear that these steps are just the first of many toward next-generation strategy management for SAP, and that even these steps won't be appropriate for every organization. No two organizations are alike, and the alignment challenges are often unique. Every organization will require a different mixture of traditional top-down strategy management and strategy management powered by an architecture of participation. Furthermore, certain tools can only be useful in scaling processes and will never be able to replace the power of inspirational leadership or a well-managed in-person strategic discussion between well-informed individuals.

However, the potential power of increased collaboration is driving even the most conservative businesses to start to move beyond the traditional processes for strategic thinking: strategy gurus, top-down command and control, mass communication, and need-to-know closed book management are being slowly replaced by decentralized information flows and bottom-up coordination. This is driven by the reality that strategy management, business planning, and performance measurement processes of complex enterprises demand collaborative thinking. When critical knowledge is distributed throughout the organization, strategic alignment requires far more than communicating a centrally defined strategy – strategic alignment requires the infrastructure to allow two-way collaboration on strategy throughout the organization. After all, encouraging active participation in the process of defining and executing a strategy is surely the best way for an organization to be, as Sun Tzu put it, "animated by the same spirit throughout all its ranks."

## ENDNOTES

1   Sun Tzu, *Art of War*, Shambhala, January 2005.
2   Michael C. Makins and Richard Steele, "Turning Great Strategy Into Great Performance," *Harvard Business Review*, July-August 2005.
3   Thomas R. Federico and Robert A. Burgelman, "SAP AG in 2006: Driving Corporate Transformation," Stanford Graduate School of Business, 2006.
4   Tiha von Ghyczy, Bolko von Oetinger, and Christopher Bassford, "Calusewitz on Strategy," John Wiley & Sons Inc., 2001.
5   Robert S. Kaplan and David P. Norton, *The strategy-focused organization*, Boston: Harvard Business School Press, 2001.
6   Thomas R. Federico and Robert A. Burgelman, "SAP AG in 2006: Driving Corporate Transformation," Stanford Graduate School of Business, 2006.
7   Thomas R. Federico and Robert A. Burgelman, "SAP AG in 2006: Driving Corporate Transformation," Stanford Graduate School of Business, 2006.

## 2.6

# FROM STRATEGY EXECUTION TO PERFORMANCE MANAGEMENT

**Sanjay Poonen,** *Senior VP and GM of Analytics, SAP*
**Nenshad Bardoliwalla,** *VP, Solution*
*Management, Corporate Performance Management*
*Products, SAP*
**Adam Thier,** *VP, Development, Corporate Performance*
*Management Products, SAP*

## INTRODUCTION

The fundamental business goal remains constant: make a profit and return value to shareholders. The objective is straightforward: sell a product or a service to customers for more than it costs to produce and deliver it (profit = revenue − cost). Executing a strategy to achieve this objective in today's unforgiving business environment is not nearly as straightforward. Global markets, intense competition, compliance constraints, disruptive technologies, and talent shortages are all pressuring companies to become more agile so that they can constantly adjust to a world of accelerated change. This condition of constant adjustment forces companies to embark on a non-stop cycle of strategy development, execution, measurement, and refinement. Companies that can effectively manage their performance within this steady cycle of change are well positioned for success; companies that can't are likely to suffer a less fortunate fate.

In this chapter, we will examine why corporate performance management (CPM) is a vital part of a company's ability to manage its success. We will also discuss the roles, methodologies, and tools that help companies execute, measure, and refine successful business strategies. Along the way, we will give examples of how real companies have succeeded and failed at this undertaking.

# FACING THE REALITY OF ACCELERATED CHANGE

The market conditions pressuring companies today are well documented in other chapters of this book. Globalization, regulatory constraints, and disruptive innovation are all contributors. There is no need to add to that analysis here; instead, we will focus on what a business needs to do to understand how it is performing in this quickly changing environment and what it needs to do to assure its future success.

Business, today, is undergoing faster and more profound change than ever before. Evidence of this change is most readily perceived along five fundamental dimensions that present both challenges and opportunities.

**1. Increased Risk**
- Businesses have come under increasing public scrutiny due to cross-border operations and the advent of stringent regulations in the wake of 9-11, Enron, Parmalat, trade disputes, environmental issues, and other catalyzing events. Regardless of size, enterprises participating in the global economy will face the same challenges as they grapple with new and often inconsistent regulations. Additionally, activist stakeholders are aggressively challenging management on social responsibility, ethical leadership, and privacy.
- Factoid: Only 65% of executives are confident that they are compliant with foreign regulations.[1]

**2. Customer Power**
- Entry of new customers in the global market and the increased market transparency enabled by enhanced access to information has triggered a tectonic shift of power to the customer. First, customers – both consumers and businesses – are increasingly influencing the design and delivery of products and services, as well as influencing business models. Second, developing nations are emerging as the main drivers of growth in global GDP. Savvy multi-nationals are localizing products and services to gain market share.

## 3. Pervasive Technology and Information Explosion

- The world continues to see an explosion in digital information that is bombarding modern day executives – both structured business data that requires their attention (reports, charts, etc.) and unstructured data (e-mails, Web pages, etc.) – all coming at them on a variety of devices (computers, mobile devices, etc.). Putting this growth in perspective, the world produced an estimated 12 exabytes of information in the first 300,000 years of civilization. By 1999, we were producing around 2 exabytes per year or 800 MB per each of the world's population of 6.3 billion people. This growth in data production has been driven by lower communications costs, the exponential growth of computing power, and the improved price performance ratio for storage. It is also being driven by new technologies – modeling, RFID, etc. Turning this raw data into actionable information requires computer systems can rapidly integrate silos of data and automatically correlate and predict trends without full-time analysts having to troll through the data. The result is that executives can make quicker decisions in order to improve their performance.
- Factoid: Today's research estimates that information doubles every 11 months in 2007, but will double every 11 hours in 2010.[2]

## 4. Global Competition

- The world has rapidly changed to a single global integrated market. This integration is ushered in by plentiful capital with emerging markets serving as both recipients and providers of capital, and record levels of M&A activity transforming industries by creating efficient global giants. These trends have produced an intense global competitive environment with companies simultaneously facing low-cost and high-end niche competitors.
- Factoid: M&A activity has accelerated with acquired assets growing by over 35% in 2005 and a predicted record of over $3.3 trillion for 2006.[3]

## 5. Global Workforce

- Tacit and transactional work has eclipsed transformation as the primary lever for value creation. This shift in economic activity towards information-oriented work will create a shortage of 10 million information workers in developed nations. As a result, global recruitment is targeting 33 million college educated professionals in 28 emerging nations that have invested in a qualified, accessible information worker talent pool.

- Factoid: Emerging nations have 4 times the amount of qualified young professionals as the top 8 developed nations. Emerging nation college graduates will grow at 5 times the developed nation rate.[4]

Business leaders who seize the opportunities and alter their practices to capture new competitive advantages, will sustain a winning trajectory in the global marketplace. Conversely, executives who treat the challenges as threats are destined to be market victims – followers who have ceded leadership to competitors.

# BALANCING THE PRESENT AND THE FUTURE

Sustained success requires a focus on winning the present while simultaneously focusing on adapting to the future. Focus on the future puts current financial performance at risk while focus on the present sacrifices future opportunities. The challenge is to set the proper balance between these two potentially conflicting efforts.

## Winning the Present

Winning the present involves:
- Flexible execution – flexibility is critical for minimizing the latency between business strategy and execution. Additionally, in the non-stop cycle of strategy development, strategies must be continuously refined.
- Predictable performance – financial markets will not tolerate unexpected surprises; therefore, companies must set realistic financial and operational targets and then monitor and manage the business to these expectations.
- Compliance – globally integrated capital markets, rising fiduciary responsibilities and accountability, workforce expectations, and more powerful external stakeholders exert more governance and compliance pressure on companies. Compliance with regulations and the broader governance of companies is now under scrutiny and must be unquestionable.

## Adapting to the Future

Adapting to the future involves:
- Strategic agility – the business environment has become unforgiving and the consequences of a single misstep or delay in pursuing a

strategy can be severe. Executives must be alert to emerging threats and opportunities. They must swiftly adapt strategies to new conditions.

- Business model innovation – sustained leadership requires innovation not only on products and services, but also on processes and business models.
- Flexible networks – being competitive no longer requires optimally managing a firm's processes and resources; it requires having access to complementary processes and resources. Our global world is becoming a modular one where joint ventures, alliances, outsourcing, and shared services are common tactics.

# FINANCING THE RIGHT STRATEGY

Good performance is the responsibility of everyone in an organization. A strategy cannot be executed successfully unless everyone understands their role in making it work. There is however one piece of the business that plays a more central role in managing performance: the Finance Department. Finance allocates the oxygen for all operations: the budget and resources. Without sufficient amounts of either of these, initiatives are starved and will ultimately fail.

## The Changing Role of Finance and the Strategic Role of the CFO

What makes finance different today, and why is the role of the CFO moving from historical number crunching to forward looking strategic planning? The simple answer: businesses have undergone fundamental change, yet the processes by which they are supported haven't caught up – in fact, they aren't even close. The symptoms are all right there in front of us – huge demands for better compliance, better decision support, and better profitability analysis – yet these are just that: symptoms. The problem is that businesses have evolved; and the processes to support this evolution have not.

At the turn of the industrial age, businesses tended to do one thing and do it well. Banks were banks; not banks, *and* insurance companies, *and* investment banks, *and* brokerages. Steel companies made steel. Aluminum companies made aluminum, car companies made cars….ad infinitum. These companies also operated on smaller scales than they do today; banks couldn't operate in all 50 states because – without computers – there was no way to keep track of all the different regulations.

The point is, businesses were much simpler, and they actually operated – and looked like – the way their finance systems (paper ledgers) depicted them in the chart of accounts. Likewise, the processes that were built around those finance systems – like the budget – actually reflected the operations of the business and, as a result, were actually useful. Compare that to today's operations, and it couldn't be more different.

Back in the 1950/60s, businesses, looking for ways to grow but having tapped out the "one thing" they did, needed to pursue new adventures. Some companies expanded up and down their value chains – such as car companies going global and starting their own finance arms and banks moving from regional to national or global (invariably through acquisitions) – while others simply invested in whatever markets were attractive, no matter how alien they were to current operations – such as General Electric, Minnesota Mining and Manufacturing (3M), Honeywell, and Asea Brown Boveri.

Given the lack of technology and processes, most of these new operations functioned autonomously – and many of the early conglomerates still operate this way. GE, with businesses ranging from broadcasting, to plastics, to appliances, to aircraft engines, is famous for its management model of driving targets to subsidiaries and allowing them to execute independently without complex interdependencies such as joint sales forces.

Today however, many companies have opted for a more vertically integrated business model – and as a result have become highly interdependent. The problem is that none of their systems, still based on the linear account structures of old, reflect these interdependencies well. Further, efficient shared services models, such as those for HR and transactional accounting (i.e. centralized payables) further blur the classic top down lines of management. The end result is that the "budget," the primary tried and true management tool, no longer actually works.

For example, once upon a time, if a car company sold three different car models, each operation – from design, to production, to marketing, to distribution – was hierarchically integrated, and the interdependencies were clear cut. Unfortunately, each group was making its own engines, designing different taillights, etcetera, and cross group efficiency wasn't even a thought. Compare that to today where assembly lines run multiple different cars down the same production line at the same time, and everything from chassis and engines, to switches and gauges are all shared. How would you budget for such a scenario with anything remotely resembling accuracy?

In actuality, the classic management techniques, still based on the classic budget, are actually corrosive to operations. For example, let us look at a classic – and simple – interdependent model tied together through shared services: a new product introduction. When a company introduces a new product, they have to look across a variety of operations to develop a plan. The sales organization has to come up with target revenue numbers; marketing then has to come up with appropriate marketing plans; human resources has to look at staffing new sales teams; training has to develop new programs to train those new salespeople; and so on. Yet, nowhere in the budget is there a valid representation of this actual business model; instead, it is all rolled up in generic buckets called "training" or "human resources"

Where this goes very wrong is when the organization tries to use its old management techniques. For example, everyone can relate to the two most common cost control mechanisms: "hiring freeze" and "no non-billable travel." If either (or both) of these get implemented during the new product's introduction, the repercussions across the interdepencies are painful. How does HR fill the potential new sales employee slots if there is a hiring freeze? How does training get people up to speed on the new products if no one can travel? Although the revenue target for that new product hasn't changed, the plan for achieving it has been hopelessly snarled.

Ultimately, these examples indicate that the classical management systems are potentially more damaging than useful and need to be quickly replaced with CPM systems that actually reflect how modern businesses operate. Without CPM systems, companies will never achieve an accurate view of operations and will never have the processes they need to effectively manage themselves.

Today's finance departments increasingly need to become business partners with the lines-of-business. Gone are the days where the lines-of-business are satisfied getting a green-bar financial report that is outdated as soon as it arrives on the desk of the general manager. With the automation of transaction processing, accounting has become a much more organized process, and ERP systems, a novelty in the early 80s, are now relatively commonplace in every growing company. The wave of compliance regulation in the late 1990s and early 2000s, of which Sarbanes-Oxley is probably the most widely discussed legislation, made the role of finance even more critical. Finance became the key department that needed to certify compliance standards, and the consequences of any failure or mistake became dire – fines, damage to shareholder value, and, of course, people could land in jail.

While transaction processing was the topic of every finance department the 1990s and control systems grabbed the headlines in the 2000s, performance management systems have always been a necessity. However, with the faster pace of business change and the increasing role of M&A, the need for flexible and adaptive performance management systems has taken higher priority. The successful finance organizations of 2010 are those that

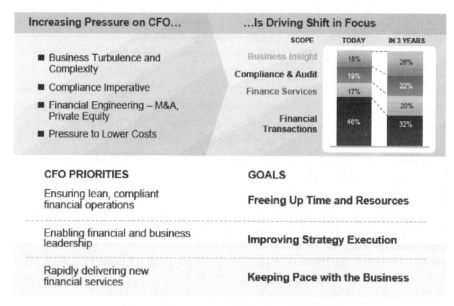

*Figure 1: Pressures and Priorities of the CFO*

will combine the effective use of transaction processing (ERP); governance, risk and compliance (GRC); and corporate performance management (CPM) into systems that give them competitive advantage and make them a better business partner to the lines-of-business that they serve.

A recent survey in CFO Magazine indicated that the current top prioritites of finance executives cause them to focus on: 46% on transaction processing (ERP), 19% on compliance and audit (GRC), and 18% on decision support (CPM). In the next 3 years, their focus is likely to morph to: 32% on ERP, 22% on GRC and 26% on CPM. Corporate Performance Management is the area with the largest increase in focus – clearly an indication of how important this is to the CFO today.

To put this all into a tangible example, imagine a CFO of a multi-billion dollar company that could a) integrate a sizeable new acquisition into the acquiring company's core transaction processing order systems within two quarters, b) run an adaptive and dynamic risk-adjusted financial plan every month if necessary, c) model customer and product profitability at arbitrary levels of granularity, and d) close the books within 2-3 days at the end of the quarter with full confidence of having met compliance standards. These are the finance organizations of some of the best run businesses today.

CFOs of such organizations are increasingly seeing more operational responsibility come their way, as they move from pure finance roles to broader

corporate leadership. Increasingly CFOs with this level of competence are
becoming COOs and CEOs, probably best exemplified by Indra Nooyi,
former CFO of Pepsi and now CEO of Pepsi. Whether it is the physical
CEO of the business or the GM of a Business Unit, finance executives who
have made themselves a strategic partner of the business are often finding
themselves not just as a partner, but eventually running the business itself.

# BUSINESS INSIGHT: KNOW YOUR BUSINESS

To make good business decisions, you must gain insight into how your
business is truly performing. To gain insight, you must get accurate
information about how the different components of your business are
operating. For 20 years transactional vendors have focused on making
organizations more *efficient* with innovations like ERP, SCM, SRM, CRM,
and PLM that automate the lives of numerous task workers. Increasingly,
however, the focus for the agile enterprise is making the information worker
more *effective*..

However, an information worker can't make sense of all this new data,
much less convert it to information and knowledge, without a robust analytic
infrastructure. This infrastructure is what we call a business intelligence (BI)
platform. Solutions built on BI platforms are called "analytic applications."
They cover a wide range of functional areas and vertical domains. For
example, HR analytics might help the HR director analyze compensation
patterns versus industry standards. "Spend Analytics" might help the VP of
procurement reduce "maverick spend" and facilitate supplier rationalization.
If BI is the platform and analytic applications are the solutions, "performance
management" is the benefit that these solutions provide. In essence, analytic
applications built on a BI platform help you gain business insight.

## Performance Management Embedded into
## the Business Process

Early on, performance management belonged to I/T and business analysts
and required training on query and analysis tools. Typically, these tools
were created as "bolt-ons" to a business process. However, the future of
performance management is one where analytic solutions are embedded in
business processes.

You don't have to leave the business process that you are running (HR,
CRM, SCM) to launch a BI tool to find the answers you need. You expect
the analytics to be there. For example, analytics are increasingly built into

GPS systems so automobile drivers can find the fastest route between points A and B, even with traffic or weather hazards. Another example: Amazon. com uses sophisticated analytics to suggest the books a buyer might be interested in reading by correlating similar purchases from other buyers; the buyer hardly notices the power of analytics made simple in the purchase experience.

By extension, people expect that when working with business information, analytics will seamlessly guide them through their jobs, making their decisions smarter without requiring a Ph.D. in mathematics or an understanding of an alphabet soup of acronyms (DSS, OLAP, EDW). Nirvana is when analytics are embedded in every decision making process, making every decision a "smart" one.

# LOOKING AHEAD: HOLISTIC PERFORMANCE MANAGEMENT

Traditional information systems that support the finance organization have suffered from obvious perils that force the finance organization into dysfunctional behavior. With businesses continuously changing, the need for information systems that can be adapted just as quickly has always lurked on the horizon but has never been more necessary. The challenge that businesses have is that traditionally, the ownership of these information systems has been driven by the I/T organization, whose management – with their linear development methodologies and natural technology skill-set – lacks the capacity and the nuanced understanding of business changes to be able to modify I/T systems in a timely fashion. By the time the I/T organization has implemented the changes that the finance organization has requested, the business requirements have already evolved dramatically, forcing the finance users to resort to their own means to solve their information deficiencies.

Of course, it is no secret what the weapon of choice for the finance professional is the disconnected, desktop spreadsheet. With unlimited modeling flexibility and, most importantly, complete ownership and control of the system, the disconnected spreadsheet represents *the* de facto information system of choice, not only for most finance professionals but also, in many cases, for the entire enterprise. And yet, there are such severe deficiencies with running an entire business on spreadsheets – whether from undocumented errors; GRC concerns; links that are maintained manually between networks of spreadsheets; or even the legitimate security concerns of valuable corporate data residing on the laptops of workers – that this practice can not continue indefinitely. Companies would ideally like to empower their finance organizations with the modeling flexibility and business system ownership that spreadsheets provide, but with the auditability, manageability, and security of an enterprise wise information system.

What capabilities would that information system contain? Every performance management system is supported by three legs with a unifying layer on top. This is best described as a unified set of strategy, plans, and actuals that drive profitability models throughout the enterprise. With a strategy system in place, the organization's goals, the initiatives that help the organization to achieve those goals, and the metrics that are used to track the success of achieving those goals, can be unified in a single environment that can be placed on the desktop of every user. These initiatives spawn plans, budgets, and forecasts which describe how the organization's precious resources will be allocated in service of the organization's strategy. And the tracking of the progress towards these goals – the actuals of the business – are sourced from the underlying transactional systems like ERP, CRM, and SCM system and are consolidated for management and statutory reporting purposes, leading to their expression in the corporate P&L, balance sheet, and cash flow statement that the business is judged upon. Ultimately, all this information serves to drive profitability models for the business to determine which customers, products, partners, channels, segments, etc. are those the business should continue to invest in and those which it should no longer do so, which ties back to the ultimate goal of delivering shareholder value.

Many businesses have these kinds of capabilities today – in one form or another – but lack the critical elements that allow these systems to respond to the business environment of 2010. The first critical element is unification. Having independent strategy management, planning, actuals, and profitability solutions that are patched together in a point to point fashion will never allow the finance organization to be responsive enough to change. In today's information systems, all of these capabilities must form elements of a holistic performance management system that can model the flow of information throughout the entire business to allow decisions to be made in rapid fashion. For example, the moment that it is clear from the management reports (the consolidated actuals) that the sales of products in the western region is double what was expected (the plan), the finance user should immediately be able to evaluate the impact of this change on the revenues and costs (the components of profitability) and decide whether the original goal (the strategy) of keeping expenses flat in the western region should be maintained. With a unified performance management system, this kind of responsiveness and scenario modeling is entirely possible.

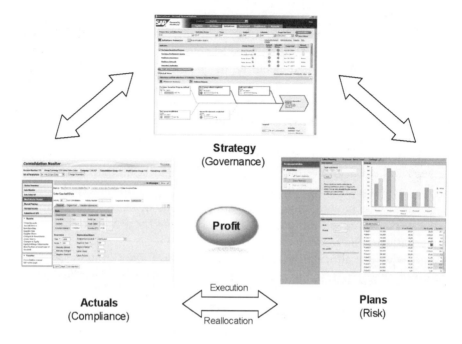

**Strategy**
(Governance)

**Profit**

Execution

Reallocation

**Actuals**
(Compliance)

**Plans**
(Risk)

*Figure 2: Decision Model Drivers*

The second critical element that allows these systems to respond to the business environment of 2010 is having GRC built into the performance management system. In each one of the axes of a performance management system, GRC needs to be interwoven to provide a balanced and unified view of the state of the business. If a strategy describes "what" a company must do to achieve its goals, governance describes "how" the organization will achieve its goals. Similarly, there has long been an implicit link between plans and risks. Traditional financial planning and scenario modeling have long incorporated the notion of an "optimistic", "expected", and "pessimistic" version of the plan. By tying in the key drivers of this optimism/pessimism continuum – that is, the risks of the business – it becomes possible to not only prepare for the downside implications of making strategic resource allocations via plans, but to actually *take* risks to achieve certain performance goals for upside gains. Thus, instead of the pessimistic scenario of an oil company buying a year's reserves in advance to protect against the risk of price inflation, the same company may in fact decide that the risk is worth the price and decide to allocate that money elsewhere for a greater return to shareholders. This notion of the "risk-intelligent enterprise" is currently being championed by Deloitte & Touche5 and is certainly germane to this discussion here. Finally, the most tangible example of where GRC must be integrated into the performance management systems of 2010 is certainly the compliance angle. The amount of money – in the billions of dollars – that companies have spent on professional auditing and compliance certification in the wake of Sarbanes-Oxley is well known. Additionally, the overhead costs of professional auditors, combined with the frequently changing regulations, make the case for software-based compliance solutions quite clear. By providing process and access controls around the delivery of the actuals of the business – manifested through the management and statutory reports that are submitted to governing bodies like the SEC via technologies like XBRL – it is possible to wrap the entire process of financial information dissemination in a lattice of control that was not possible even half a decade ago. With today's information systems, it is possible to trace the entire history of an individual item on the consolidated balance sheet back through the system with complete knowledge of who touched the system and when, what data elements were changed, and why the change was made. This gives performance management a degree of certainty in information quality that just is not possible using manual, paper-based systems and controls.

The third critical element that allows these systems to respond to the business environment of 2010 is having collaboration as a central technology component – which we will see as a recurring theme throughout this book. Capabilities such as search, threaded discussions, commentaries and annotation, tagging, wikis, etcetera, fundamentally change the paradigm by which performance is managed. Why is this the case? Because collaboration allows the individuals closest to the situation to assess it and respond accordingly in a manner that quantitative indicators, whether leading or lagging, can never do. As an example, imagine the CEO who looks at their performance scorecard and observes that the KPI of customer satisfaction is trending downward and is currently assessed as "red" based on an index of qualitative and quantitative indicators. A classic "drilldown" capability can give the CEO an indication that the primary dissatisfaction is in the western region, perhaps due to the unexpected increase in demand (see above example) that has caused a massive amount of backorders. But with collaboration capabilities, the CEO can go directly to the source of information, the team in the western region, and understand from their dialogue exactly what the root cause of the problem. The CEO may be able to look at the comments that the team in the western region has placed in the supply chain plan that clearly indicates "we're already at risk for capacity in this region because of the materials shortfall in our Malaysia plant and don't have much legroom if our demand estimates are off in this region". This also works in the other direction: with collaborative capabilities in a holistic

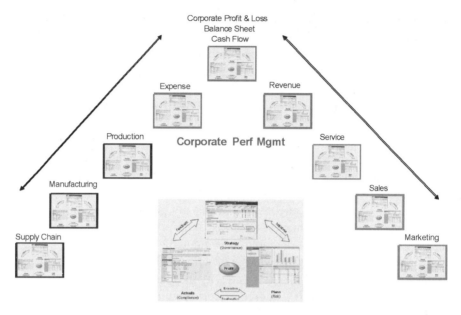

*Figure 3: Comprehensive Performance Management*

performance management system, individual line workers are suddenly empowered to make strategy relevant to them instead of *just* the C-level employees, as has traditionally been the case. The ability to layer personal context on shared business objectives allows employees to explicitly make the link between the outcomes they wish to drive for their own success and the outcomes that drive the success of the business as a whole.

Most critically, while the discussion here has primarily been focused on how information ultimately rolls up to the finance organization, the entire set of strategy, plans, actuals, and profitability models utilized by the finance organization must itself be integrated in a network of models across the entire organization's value chains – from the demand side of the business with sales and marketing performance management capabilities to the supply side of the house with production and supply chain performance management capabilities. Concepts like "Integrated Business Planning" identify the integrated nature of value drivers within one component of the performance management suite, but what is being described here takes this concept much further by ensuring all the elements of the performance management capabilities (strategies, plans, actuals, and profitability models) are being layered on top of the organization's value chain.

The intersection of Strategy Execution and Performance Management finds itself most clearly manifested in the concept of StratEx, or Strategic

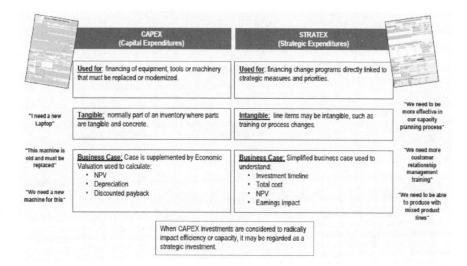

| | CAPEX (Capital Expenditures) | STRATEX (Strategic Expenditures) | |
|---|---|---|---|
| | **Used for:** financing of equipment, tools or machinery that must be replaced or modernized. | **Used for:** financing change programs directly linked to strategic measures and priorities. | |
| "I need a new Laptop" | **Tangible:** normally part of an inventory where parts are tangible and concrete. | **Intangible:** line items may be intangible, such as training or process changes. | "We need to be more effective in our capacity planning process" |
| "This machine is old and must be replaced"  "We need a new machine for this" | **Business Case:** Case is supplemented by Economic Valuation used to calculate:  • NPV  • Depreciation  • Discounted payback | **Business Case:** Simplified business case used to understand:  • Investment timeline  • Total cost  • NPV  • Earnings impact | "We need more customer relationship management training"  "We need to be able to produce with mixed product lines" |
| | When CAPEX investments are considered to radically impact efficiency or capacity, it may be regarded as a strategic investment. | | |

**Figure 4:** *Differences between CAPEX and STRATEX*
*Source: David Norton[6]*

Expenditures. David Norton talks about the ability of a company for the first time to be able to cost the business based on the tradeoffs between what it takes to keep the business moving along the current trajectory (measured by CapEx and OpEx) versus what it takes to move the business along a new strategic initiative (measured by StratEx)[6].The ability to generate a P&L, Balance Sheet, and Cash Flow statement based on a business's strategic goals allows the business to effectively estimate the cost of a strategy and the scenarios by which it should be operationalized. When tied with the governance frameworks and risk assessment methodologies described above, this becomes an entire new way to manage business that has been hitherto impossible with previous generations of technology.

# ENDNOTES

1    PricewaterhouseCoopers data.
2    IBM Research.
3    CNN Money.
4    McKinsey.
5    Deloitte & Touche USA LLP.
6    David Norton, "Strategy Execution – The Next Source of Competitive Advantage," *CFO CPM Conference*, February 12, 2007.

# 2.7

# GAINING COMPETITIVE ADVANTAGE FROM COMPLIANCE AND RISK MANAGEMENT

*Amit Chatterjee, SVP, Commercialization, SAP*
*David Milam, VP, Solutions Management, SAP*

## INTRODUCTION

Risk management has been around for decades in financial services, using highly evolved risk modeling and analysis to manage market and credit risk. As businesses across all industries contend with globalization, the increased use of outsourcing, and the operational and financial demands of regulators, it is more important than ever for corporations to take a strategic approach to effective risk mitigation and management.

Risk is generally defined as the potential for loss caused by an event – or series of events – that can adversely affect the achievement of company objectives. However, organizations are realizing that effective risk management can create opportunities as well as mitigate problems. In other words, a successful risk management philosophy focuses not only on risk avoidance and protecting existing assets, but also on enhancing future growth opportunities and creating competitive differentiation. Unfortunately, many organizations fail to fully achieve these risk management benefits. A combination of manual processes, siloed approaches, and reactive responses can limit visibility and the ability to adequately assess critical risk interdependencies.

The greatest threats to a company can arise when multiple risk factors combine to blindside management – often with disastrous results. Consider a life-threatening fire at a refinery that results from overdue machine maintenance and poor employee training, or a massive product recall caused by inadequate quality tests combined with faulty analysis of customer complaints.

How can you avoid such disasters? By automatically identifying and monitoring top enterprise risks, giving lines of business (LOB) the tools to effectively mitigate risks, and presenting risk in the context of corporate strategy and performance. With this approach, you provide executives with a clear understanding of the most important – and potentially damaging – risks your company faces.

This chapter will establish the need for a holistic approach to governance, risk, and compliance (GRC); discuss the challenges many companies face with respect to risk management; describe a comprehensive risk management process; and provide examples of common risk management scenarios you may be facing.

# GOVERNANCE, RISK, AND COMPLIANCE: WHY A HOLISTIC APPROACH WILL HELP

Many companies react tactically to the growing demands of regulatory agencies, stakeholders, and even customers. Unfortunately, this tactical response – which often includes extensive manual effort and one-off compliance solutions – is costly and becoming even more expensive. AMR Research reports that companies will spend $29.9 billion in 2007 alone for GRC-related activities – up 8.5 percent from the previous year. Approximately two-thirds of this cost is in people – because fragmented GRC efforts tend to result in "people-powered GRC," where inefficient processes are often duplicated across departments.

Companies that have relied on relatively informal, manual processes to identify and assess risks are now realizing that this approach is not only expensive but unsustainable. As external expectations increase, so does the cost of compliance as companies allocate more people to risk and compliance management – taking away resources from other revenue-producing areas of the business. AMR reports that "companies are turning the corner and adopting a systemic approach to risk management, using technology to support the process. Risk management is emerging as a structured, strategic approach to identifying, assessing, and potentially remedying issues before they become public problems."1

AMR's observation means that leading organizations aren't simply reacting to the newest compliance regulation with a project-based response. Instead, they are adopting a unified risk-based GRC strategy that guides employees, standardizes processes, and uses technology to embed risk management into business processes at every level of the organization. A comprehensive GRC solution should encompass not only risk mitigation but also risk taking as a means to value creation. By taking a holistic approach to GRC, you can increase shareholder value, minimize costs, master uncertainty, and optimize the opportunity to free resources for innovation and growth.

---

A best practice approach to managing GRC:

- Automatically identifies and monitors top enterprise risks
- Enables lines of business to effectively mitigate risks by embedding risk management into existing business processes
- Plans for cross-enterprise risk scenarios
- Adds risk analysis to strategy and decision-making processes

---

## CHALLENGES: MITIGATING RISK AND MANAGING COMPLIANCE

For many companies, moving to a strategic, risk-based approach to GRC is hampered by poor visibility, fragmented operations, and after-the-fact responses. Let's take a moment to look at how these conditions affect risk management.

The first problem for many organizations is poor visibility into the status of risks across the enterprise. Since the majority of enterprise risks are owned by LOB managers, it is difficult for employees outside of that particular line of business to get knowledge about the status of those risks. Driving this lack of visibility is the substantial manual effort required by many risk management processes. Most risk managers send out periodic surveys to LOB managers, in hopes of better assessing the risks their

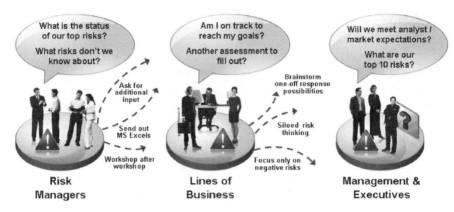

*Figure 1: Typical Fragmentation Impacting Risk Management*

organization faces. However, since the input is manually captured in forms or spreadsheets, it is difficult to track progress or follow up on errant responses. In addition, the potential impact of risks can change rapidly. This means that the information gathered by risk managers is quickly obsolete, making manual risk identification and tracking ineffective.

In addition, many large or diverse companies find that risks are managed within the walls of functional or departmental silos. Because of this siloed approach, there is little transparency across organizational boundaries and individual business managers can be caught off-guard by events happening in other groups. For example, a supply-chain risk leads to slowed production, which affects the ability to deliver product to customers, ultimately resulting in a risk to sales revenue. This fragmented approach to risk management makes it almost impossible to evaluate risk interdependencies and the potential impact of multiple risk events happening at once. Effective planning for risk scenarios that include the interaction of multiple risks can only happen with an integrated, cross-enterprise approach to risk management.

Finally, many organizations consider risks "after the fact" and separately from the overall strategy or goals of the organization. Most companies use a bottom-up perspective to tackle risk management, often identifying hundreds or thousands of potential risks in total. In that scenario, the challenge becomes seeing the big picture when overwhelmed with evaluating every individual risk exposure. The solution? Taking an approach that aligns risk management with well-understood corporate objectives, so risks are managed in the business context in which they occur. With this kind of proactive and "top-down" approach, risk management becomes infused into the corporate culture, and you can quickly identify gaps, track interdependent risks together, and allocate resources to mitigate risk for the greatest overall impact.

# THE COSTS OF A FRAGMENTED APPROACH

Without a holistic approach to GRC, companies can find themselves facing significant loss events. Consider a well-known high-tech manufacturer forced to take an inventory write-off equivalent to two quarters of earnings and resulting in a 6 percent loss in market capitalization. The write-off was triggered by multiple risk events happening simultaneously: an unanticipated and sharp reduction in orders, outsourced manufacturing operations locked into production plans stemming from long-term forecasts, and extremely long lead times for key components. The end result? A buildup of equipment the company couldn't sell. The sales organization didn't have visibility into the state of inventories in the supply network, and vice versa, leaving the company unable to anticipate its exposure to market fluctuations.

In another example, a military equipment manufacturer was fined $100 million because business unit managers weren't aware of export license requirements on certain equipment. The company was dealing with a supplier in Singapore, which in turn outsourced to China. The company didn't identify the link with the Chinese supplier, resulting in the violation and corresponding fine.

As illustrated by these two examples, if your risk management practices are disjointed, risks can slip through the cracks to become loss events. According to a Deloitte Research study[2], these problems have dramatic effects: in the past decade, nearly half of Fortune 1000 companies experienced a loss of over 20 percent of their stock value within a one-month period due to risk events, as shown on the left-hand side of the illustration.

It is equally staggering that it took half of the companies more than a year to regain their lost value – 22 percent of companies never fully recovered their stock prices, as seen in the right-hand side of the illustration.

What are the causes of this plummeting stock value? The study found that 80 percent of the losses occurred when several cross-silo risks became a reality at the same time. For example, a new competitor enters the market *at the same time* that your supplier can't deliver on time; or a sharp rise in product returns and customer complaints happens *at the same time* as a competitor launches a product upgrade; or air, water, or waste permit limits are exceeded, temporarily stalling production, *at the same time* that inventory levels drop to all-time lows.

In addition, the speed at which information travels has magnified certain loss events. As Lee Dittmar, Global Leader, GRC Consulting for Deloitte, explains, "Over the past few years, the real-time global spread of information has impacted enterprise risk significantly. Now an event can destroy value – or create opportunity – within an organization with incredible speed."

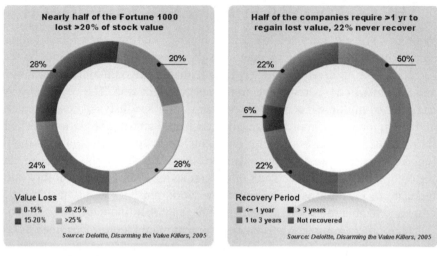

*Figure 2: Value Erosion as a Result of Disjointed Risk Management*

To prevent your company from experiencing drastic value loss, it is crucial to first understand the interdependencies among risks throughout your organization, and second, to set thresholds that will immediately trigger alerts whenever one or more risks are elevated at the same time. "More than ever, management must build in risk management so that they can proactively mitigate the impact of risk factors or take advantage of events in order to drive opportunity. If they do this well, they can actually turn uncertainty into a competitive advantage," concludes Dittmar.

# STRATEGICALLY APPROACHING GRC: THE BENEFITS

A holistic, strategic approach to GRC can form the basis for successful risk management and compliance. By providing a new level of transparency and confidence across the enterprise – and beyond – GRC delivers value to the board, LOB management, and key external stakeholders. When companies adopt a strategic approach to risk management, they can expect to generate significant benefits, including increased shareholder value and lower GRC spending.

As noted in the Deloitte Research study, 80 percent of the companies that suffered the greatest losses in value were exposed to more than one type of risk and failed to recognize and manage the relationships among different types of risks. It follows that if you rely on an integrated risk management solution to identify and manage interdependencies among all the risks facing your company, you will make better financial and operational decisions, reducing the likelihood of suffering major losses in value. In addition, institutional investors and rating agencies – which can significantly affect your cost of capital or market capitalization – increasingly reward an organization for its capability to understand and manage GRC.

"Whatever the organization's proxy for enterprise value, the most important contribution that risk management can make is to help managers make better operational decisions as their businesses face an increasingly uncertain future," points out David M. Johnson, managing director at Protiviti and head of the company's Technology Risk practice. "Therefore, risk responses should support the organization's value creation objectives by monitoring and managing risk and performance variability inherent in its future operations while protecting accumulated shareholder wealth from unacceptable losses."

A second major benefit of taking a strategic approach to GRC is the ability to lower the overall cost of your compliance and risk management initiatives. An integrated GRC approach can replace many separate projects, isolated tools, and – most important – the manual work of integrating the individual risks into a cohesive risk analysis. With a unified GRC approach, you can avoid duplication of effort, significantly reducing the number of people and the amount of time you need to be in compliance with regulations and manage your risks. As you progress along the maturity curve of a strategic, platform approach, you will merge more and more individual GRC projects into the holistic GRC framework, reducing the cost of GRC as you go.

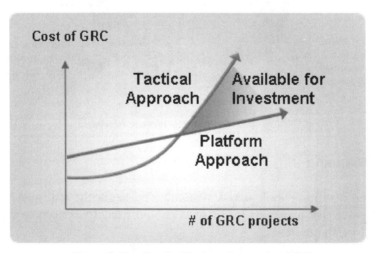

*Figure 3: Benefits of a Platform Approach to GRC*

# HOW TO IMPLEMENT A HOLISTIC APPROACH TO GRC

A unified, holistic approach to GRC starts with a strategic four-step approach to risk management. First is risk planning, setting the stage for risk management processes. Next is identifying and analyzing risks, by collecting information from business experts around the organization. Third is developing responses or mitigation plans for identified risks. Finally, continually monitoring ongoing risks using dashboard reporting and automated alerts to notify management at all levels of the company when a risk situation changes.

1. *Plan:* Enterprise risk planning
2. *Identify and Analyze:* Risk identification and collaborative assessment
3. *Respond:* Risk response and mitigation strategies
4. *Monitor:* Continuous risk monitoring

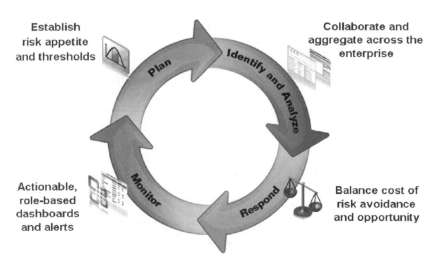

*Figure 4: The Risk Management Process*

## Risk Planning

Let's take a closer look at risk planning. To begin the risk management cycle, your risk managers, LOB owners, and executives need to consider the following questions:

- What types of risks can cause the greatest loss of value for your company?
- Which risks will keep you from reaching company goals?
- What key risk indicators (KRIs) do you need to track for each identified risk?

In the planning phase, you should evaluate and document the risk profile, or "risk-bearing appetite," for each business unit, as well as for your entire enterprise. For example, based on current capitalization, how much loss can your LOB absorb? There are some parts of your business where you may want to take more risks – for a new business area, for example – while you may want to manage other product lines more conservatively.

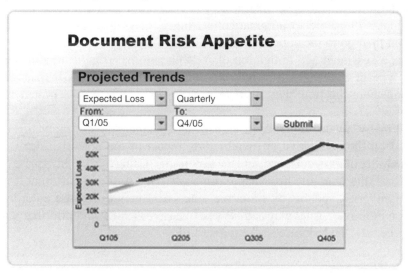

*Figure 5: Example of Documenting Changes in Risk Appetite Over Time*

## Risk Identification and Analysis

The next step within the risk management cycle is risk identification and analysis. In this step, your organization identifies and prioritizes all key risks – both internal and external to your organization. Effective risk identification and analysis is:

- Embedded into all key business processes
- Automated for early risk identification
- Evaluated in a structured and consistent manner

| Risk Overview | | | | | |
|---------------|------|-------|--------|-------|--------|
| Probability | Insign. | Minor | Moder. | Major | Catas. |
| Occasionally | 9 | 1 | 0 | 1 | 1 |
| Sometimes | 2 | 5 | 4 | 0 | 0 |
| Hardly | 5 | 2 | 5 | 5 | 0 |
| Very rarely | 2 | 3 | 5 | 0 | 3 |
| Almost never | 1 | 1 | 1 | 1 | 2 |

*Figure 6: Example of a Global Risk Heat Map Showing the Severity of Risks*

First, you should embed automatic risk identification and assessment into key business processes so that risk management is built in, instead of a reactive afterthought. For example, you may want all sales deals above a particular threshold to automatically trigger a risk analysis. A workflow would then go to the appropriate sales executive, requiring her to complete a risk assessment and mitigation plan. With automated indicators in place, this type of event would trigger alerts to the appropriate LOB managers, giving them the time they need to proactively decide on the proper next steps.

Finally, evaluating risk in a structured manner means analyzing risk based on the qualitative or quantitative impact of the potential event, the probability of its occurrence, and the timeframe. Using a cross-enterprise risk vulnerability map, or "heat map," can show risks sorted by different levels of granularity, such as by initiative, line of business, or entire enterprise. These intuitive, visual maps allow you to easily identify and prioritize risks and see how the risks are shifting over time.

## Risk Response

Step three in the risk management process is risk response. Once you have identified critical risks, the next step is developing an effective response strategy. The strategy could fall anywhere along a continuum, from "watch" or "research" to "actively mitigate" or "control." Your company's response strategy will be unique – and each risk may have several possible responses.

Addressing single risks may not always resolve the highest-priority problems. Instead, crucial issues are often the result of not being able to correctly identify what happens when multiple risks occur simultaneously and interact, combining to become a severe risk.

For example, a large consumer product manufacturer shared the following experience: The marketing group had worked overtime to

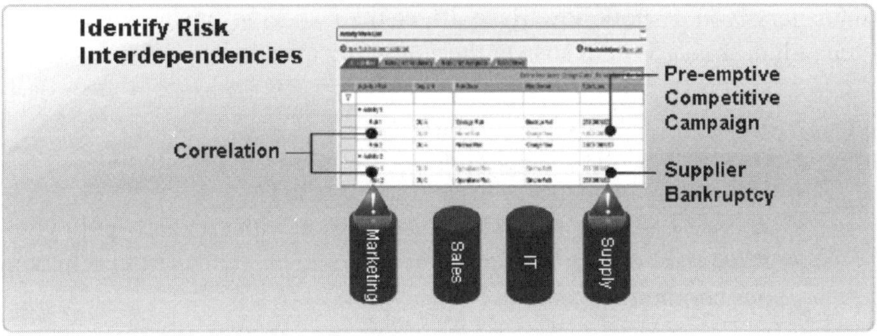

*Figure 7: Illustration of Identifying Risk Interdependencies*

develop a new advertising campaign to offset a competitive product launch. However, marketing wasn't aware that a key backup supplier had gone out of business and that purchasing was working to find a replacement. The purchasing department, not concerned that its search might take several weeks since the primary supplier could handle the historical demand, was oblivious to the new marketing campaign. The result? The new marketing campaign was a huge success and demand for the product soared, right at the time that the competitive product launched. Unfortunately, the main supplier could not meet the additional demand and store shelves quickly emptied, driving customers to purchase the competitor's product instead. The strategy backfired and was a costly lesson.

Clearly, these risks are related and should be evaluated together, not separately. However, in a siloed approach, the cross-company visibility needed to make the connection and develop mitigation strategies is missing. A single GRC system helps bring together risks from across your organization, making risk interdependencies easier to identify, as shown in the illustration.

## Risk Monitoring

The final phase in the risk management cycle is the proactive monitoring of ongoing risk. To be most effective, risk monitoring should be targeted and offer a risk-based approach to compliance with risk policies. This can help optimize opportunities while mitigating risks based on individual risk profiles.

Role-based dashboards can be an effective way to monitor risk and make more informed business decisions. For example, dashboards for risk management professionals may provide an enterprise-wide view of the status of the risk management process, while dashboards for business unit managers would show how risks affect their specific business targets. In general, dashboards help answer the following questions:

- What and where are our top risks?
- Have risk levels changed for key activities or opportunities?
- How many incidents or losses have we had?
- Are we assessing our risks in accordance with company policy?
- What risks or combinations of risks could prevent us from achieving our corporate objectives?

Another aspect of effectively monitoring risk is to incorporate a risk-based approach to financial and business controls. With Sarbanes-Oxley (SOX) and other regulations gobbling up management mindshare, the "checklist" approach that many companies take can result in uneven controls, such as over controlling low-level risks. Over controlling risks not only frustrates employees, it can lead to missed opportunities because it takes longer than necessary to react to a given situation. On the other hand, under controlling a situation leaves the company unnecessarily exposed to risk. Leading companies avoid both under and over controlling by adopting a risk-based approach to compliance and control management.

Finally, risk monitoring needs to accurately capture all incidents and losses. Many incidents are already captured in operational systems. For example, safety systems track the number of injuries that have occurred, sourcing software records the number of supply outages, and manufacturing software tracks the number of unplanned downtime occurrences. A complete loss and event database should integrate the information already in the I/T systems, while still allowing manual entry of events that may not be automatically captured, such as security breaches or natural disasters.

By implementing better evaluation, mitigation, and monitoring of risks, you are setting up your organization for compliance and risk management success. You will be able to automatically identify and monitor risks to the enterprise, enable lines of businesses to effectively mitigate risks by more easily alerting them to opportunities and risks, and present risks in the context of corporate strategy and performance.

## PRACTICAL EXAMPLES: STRATEGIC APPROACHES TO RISK AND COMPLIANCE

To see how this holistic approach to GRC affects a company in practice, let us consider a few examples of risks that commonly plague companies. We will show how an architected set of GRC applications and a unifying platform can help organizations identify and track key risk indicators that can be used to head off trouble before it gains momentum.

## Environment, Health, & Safety Risks

The environment, health, and safety (EH&S) umbrella contains many risks that pose potential threats to your employees and your company. If you don't comply with EH&S regulations, not only do you expose your employees to unnecessary harm, but you potentially face significant fines and penalties, disruption to production, and damage to your company reputation. However, if you handle EH&S issues effectively, you can generate benefits by lowering your operating costs and ensuring the safety of your employees.

Safety managers usually have an EH&S application to track, document, and monitor a variety of business practices, such as occupational safety requirements, employee incidents, and production waste disposal restrictions. To keep the company in compliance, the organization also needs to use enterprise-wide KRIs to ensure that EH&S processes are on track overall. Key EH&S risk indicators to track may include:

- OSHA recordable incidents
- Overdue safety inspections
- Employee training scheduled and completed

However, while the plant safety team may have access to pertinent EH&S information on their facility, the enterprise risk management team many times does not have visibility into this information. By monitoring key risk indicators, risk managers can be alerted when conditions change and can work with the safety personnel to ensure they are getting the corporate support and resources needed to address the situation. In addition, risk managers gain cross-department visibility by monitoring KRIs that can provide additional insight to correlated risks that could trigger a disastrous event. For example, safety and manufacturing risks often affect each other. If a particular manufacturing facility is experiencing an increase in the number of safety near-misses *and* an increase in the number of overdue equipment maintenance work orders, a proactive intervention should immediately occur to prevent a catastrophe.

## The Risk of Non-Compliance with Financial Regulations

The passing of the Sarbanes-Oxley Act (SOX) means that institutional investors, rating agencies, and regulators have started assessing GRC management as part of their evaluation of companies. Furthermore, the stakes for non-compliance with financial regulations such as SOX become more than just fines and penalties. Suddenly, your stock price and credit ratings are affected by your ability to comply with mandated regulations.

Heads of internal audit face a difficult challenge. They must ensure that controls operate as designed and work effectively while finding ways to reduce the high cost of compliance. Many audit managers rely on process control applications that automate the monitoring, testing, assessment, remediation, and certification of enterprise-wide business processes. With such an application, the auditors get complete visibility into the effectiveness of financial controls, and can ensure that the data reported to regulatory bodies and stakeholders is accurate. Common KRIs associated with process controls include:

- Number of internal control violations
- Increasing trend of failed controls

By approaching GRC strategically with KRIs in place, your executive team gains complete visibility into the company's overall compliance with internal controls, such as tracking accounts payable (AP) thresholds. For example, a company that has exceeded established AP limits for several months in a row may want to investigate related measures such as percentage of purchases off-contract, effectiveness of purchasing approval processes, duplicate invoice postings, or whether there were manual price changes to key direct materials in order to fully evaluate the risk facing the company.

## The Risk of Non-Compliance with Emissions Regulations

Another common operational risk for many companies is emissions control. The potential for political, financial, and public image fallout for non-compliance with regulations such as the Kyoto Protocol, the U.S. Clean Air Act, or the EU IPPC Directive is enormous. Non-compliance with greenhouse gas emissions poses an even greater risk to brand image and corporate goodwill for companies that operate complex, multifaceted manufacturing facilities.

Most environmental managers use an emissions application to manage, measure, and document emissions output – including plant emissions, compliance status, and performance benchmarks. However, in order to ensure that your emissions management controls are working as intended, you need an integrated, enterprise-wide approach to tracking KRIs such as:

- Permit limits exceeded for air, water, and waste

- Hazardous emissions levels that have crossed early-warning thresholds

By taking a holistic approach to GRC, you will create improved visibility of environmental risks at the enterprise level. This enables risk management personnel to track environmental and other key social performance measures and evaluate the impact KRIs might have on other parts of the business. For example, social and environmental responsibility can help protect brand value and form the basis for competitive differentiation.

## Global Trade Risks

Security concerns of the post-9/11 era have helped to create a host of new trade and transport regulations. To ensure that you are not trading with any entities on government-issued "watch lists" or "sanctioned party lists," you need to identify your business partners – and their outsourcing suppliers – throughout your global supply chain. Non-compliance with these trade regulations can be expensive; in extreme cases companies have even had their trade licenses or privileges revoked.

Under such strictly regulated conditions, having a complete global trade solution in place is crucial to facilitating business practices such as sanctioned party list screening, import and export license management, country embargo checking, duty and tax payment calculations, customs clearance, and electronic communications as mandated by local governments. In addition, to ensure proper risk management at the enterprise level, you may want to track specific KRIs such as:

- Non-compliance with trade regulations
- Goods-delay risk due to customs
- Outstanding duties or taxes owed
- Import and export license renewal management
- Accuracy of global trade documentation
- Accuracy of product classifications

By integrating risk management within your global trade strategy you can reduce the risks, time, and costs related to compliance with global trading regulations. Not only that, but you will get greater visibility into your global trade activities by identifying risk dependencies throughout your operations. With this information, you can take proactive action to eliminate import and export issues before they negatively affect your supply chain and ultimately customer satisfaction.

# CONCLUSION

Between the popularity of outsourcing, the speed of information, and extended global supply chains, the pace of business change has accelerated. New opportunities in new markets come into being every day, and with each new opportunity comes a new risk. At the same time, increasing regulations are impacting existing risks and creating new areas for compliance.

In the complexities of organizational, system, and geographic fragmentation found in most multinational companies today, it is no wonder that corporate strategies are not always reflected in ongoing risk management activities. In addition, risk management practices often suffer from poor visibility, manual efforts, siloed approaches, and after-the-fact analyses and responses.

The majority of risk identification and assessments are locked into disconnected silos, so that risk managers have a hard time prioritizing single risks, and – even more important, it turns out – identifying the cross-company interdependencies of risks and opportunities that can turn into a "perfect storm."

It is time to take risk management activities from reactive to strategic. To execute on this vision, you will need to:

- *Automate risk identification and monitoring*
  A risk management solution needs to help companies track risks, highlight significant changes in risk profiles, and ensure a balance of risk and opportunity that is suitable for your company and division. It should also include automatic notification of risk events based on predefined triggers and escalation procedures so that risks don't go unnoticed until it is too late.

- *Enable lines of business to mitigate risks*
  A holistic, enterprise-wide view of GRC is enabled by risk processes that are fully integrated into functional business processes and applications – such as financial, HR, or operations. A central risk repository can capture all risk-related data; helping to consolidate efforts among stakeholders, align risks with policies, and support the sharing of best-practice risk responses.

- *Deliver risk management in the context of strategy and performance*
  Finally, your GRC application should provide cross-enterprise, aggregated, and actionable risk analytics, regardless of the source system. It should allow you to link risks to corporate performance

management strategies and performance indicators, so that you can create new strategies with the associated risks in mind, and quickly see whether you are meeting existing performance targets.

With a strategic and comprehensive approach to risk management, you can align your corporate strategy with effective risk oversight, institutionalized policy setting, and business process controls. Consolidating enterprise risk efforts and providing visibility into opportunities as well as risks, your GRC platform should ensure that no emerging threat falls through the cracks. With the right practices and system, you will be able to proactively turn challenges into competitive advantages while you evolve your organization into a mature, risk-intelligent enterprise.

## ENDNOTES

1    John Hagerty, Eric Klein. "Compliance Is Still a Priority: Total GRC Spending Approaches $30 B in 2007 and Growing," *AMR Research, Alert Article*. February 22, 2007.
2    *"Disarming the Value Killers,"* Deloitte Research. 2005.

# SECTION 3:

## CULTURAL ASPECTS OF PERVASIVE RAPID CHANGE

# 3.1

# THE TALENT SUPPLY CHAIN: LEVERAGING THE GLOBAL TALENT MARKET

**Paul Orleman,** Director, Top Talent Management
Americas, Office of the CEO, SAP AG
**Harald Borner,** SVP, Global Top Talent Management, Office
of the CEO, SAP AG

## ROOTS

The consulting firm McKinsey & Company is a trend-setter in the business world. Their examination of "excellent" US companies in the early 1980's became a "search for excellence" that produced one of the best-selling business books of all time – *In Search of Excellence: Lessons from America's Best-Run Companies* – and turned a former McKinsey consultant – Tom Peters – into a business pop-guru.

In 1997, McKinsey & Co. released a report summarizing a one-year study which they titled "The War for Talent." The report stated that the ultimate corporate resource for the next few decades would be "talent," and that "battling for talent" would be more critical for an organization than managing capital, R&D initiatives, and corporate strategy.[1] Three years later, McKinsey issued an extension of their research called "War for Talent 2000," and in 2001, McKinsey consultants Ed Michaels, Helen Handfield-Jones, and Beth Axelrod produced a book entitled *The War for Talent* which stated that:

*...talent is now a critical driver of corporate performance and that a company's ability to attract, develop, and retain talent will be a major competitive advantage far into the future. "The only thing that differentiates Enron from our competitors is our people, our talent," said Enron Chairman Kenneth Lay recently. The whole battle going forward will be for talent. In fact, it has been that way for the last decade. Some people just didn't notice it.*[2]

Following the publication of the book, Kenneth Lay would prove to be an unfortunate choice as the talent war spokesman and illustrate that there are additional key factors in the business battlefield, such as integrity. However, his statement here appears to have been accurate. In the decade since the initial McKinsey report, "the war for talent" has been discussed and dissected in countless articles, books, conferences, boardrooms, and HR departments. In June 2007, a Google search for "war for talent" produces 268,000 hits while a search for "talent management," the concept outlined in the McKinsey publications, produces a staggering 1,050,000 hits. The synonym "Human Capital Management" (HCM) generates 1,030,000 hits.

In recent joint research by The Boston Consulting Group and the European Association for Personnel Management, published in June 2007, 1350 executives identified the key HR challenges through 2015, prioritized by future importance and current capability gaps. Out of 17 topics, talent management was a very strong first: "If both HR and other executives could have selected just one HR topic to excel at, managing talent would have been their choice."[3]

The war for talent... talent management... human capital management... what is this all about? This chapter will attempt to define these concepts – which is a challenge, as there are significant disagreements about the definitions of even the basic terms – and examine how different companies are taking different approaches to deal with "managing talent."

## WHO IS "TALENT"?

The first challenge of "talent management" is agreeing on who is being referenced in the term "talent." For some organizations, "talent" refers to an exclusive and elite batch of employees – or potential employees: the "best and the brightest," "high potentials," "top performers," or "A Players." For other companies, "talent" refers to all employees of the company. In this more democratic vision, every employee has talent, and all employees have the right – and responsibility – to develop their abilities. A 2004 Research Report from The Conference Board, "Integrated and Integrative Talent Management," defined "talent" as "Individuals who have the capacity to make a significant difference to the current and future performance of a company."[4]

Some organizations recognize that every employee needs to learn and develop, but that different types of employees require different types of development. For high potentials, development should focus on accelerating their readiness to make the move to test that potential. For top performers who excel and are in the "right" job, their development should focus on keeping them motivated and excelling, and perhaps include the responsibility to coach or mentor others to transfer the knowledge and practices that make them so successful. For people who are underperforming, development must focus on helping them reach an acceptable performance level, or if that is not possible, to find another role that fits their talents and abilities. For the bulk of the employee population, those individuals who successfully meet role expectations, professional development should focus on helping them continue to be successful and to become even stronger.

In recent years, many organizations have focused a higher percentage of their professional development budget and initiatives on their high potential population, believing that it is essential to nurture a "talent pool" of future leaders. Some organizations, such as General Electric, have actively worked to hire and retain "A Players" (top performers & high potentials) and eliminate "C Players" (low performers), with the goal of having teams with a very high percentage of "A Players." This approach of "building a talent advantage over your competitors" was described by authors Geoff and Bradford Smart in an article published in 1997, in which they dubbed the practice "topgrading." They stated that "Topgrading simply means proactively seeking out and employing the most talented people available, while redeploying (internally or externally) those of lesser ability or performance." They defined "A players" as "the top 10% of the talent available."[5] Bradford Smart expanded this concept in the 1999 book *Topgrading: How Leading Companies Win by Hiring, Coaching, and Keeping the Best People.*

# WHY A WAR?

In their initial studies, McKinsey & Company painted a challenging portrait of the future recruiting arena. In a 1998 interview, McKinsey consultant Ed Michaels stated:

*In 15 years, there will be 15% fewer Americans in the 35- to 45-year-old range than there are now. At the same time, the US economy is likely to grow at a rate of 3% to 4% per year. So over that period, the demand for bright, talented 35- to 45-year-olds will increase by, say, 25%, and the supply will be going down by 15%. That sets the stage for a talent war.*[6]

A number of dramatic changes have happened in the business world since Michaels made these observations. The dot-com bubble, which was in mid-stream in 1998, burst in 2001 and reduced the flow of top talent from bigger companies to start-ups – and left a fair number of talented ex-bubble people searching for new roles. Another key factor is that the quest for – and use of – talent has gone global, with lower-cost high-quality talent increasingly available in the "BRIC" regions (Brazil, Russia, India, and China), and other countries across the globe. And the fifty-something to sixty-year-old baby boomers, who often hold key positions in organizations, soon will be retiring in large numbers, opening up key roles.

The transformation from agriculture and manufacturing to an "information worker" and service economy continues to have a major impact on an organization's hunt for talent. Services as a percentage of GDP moved from 50 percent in the 1970s to 66 percent by 1995, and this continued shift is predicted to create a shortage of 10 million information workers in developed nations.[7] Business models depend much less on capital assets and place heavier emphasis on intangible and people assets. Most of the successfully growing corporations and start-ups today rely mainly on the excellence of these latter assets. Hence the importance of a high quality, creative, and motivated workforce has a greater and more measurable relevance to the success of a company than ever before.

## WHAT IS "TALENT MANAGEMENT"?

There are varied definitions of "talent management," but all refer in some sense, and in varying levels of detail, to a company's human resource supply chain. For example, Wikipedia defines talent management as:

*...the process of developing and fostering new workers through onboarding, developing and keeping current workers and attracting highly skilled workers at other companies to come work for your company....*

Companies that are engaged in talent management (human capital management) are strategic and deliberate in how they source, attract, select, train, develop, promote, and move employees through the organization. This term also incorporates how companies drive performance at the individual level (performance management).[8]

The processes required to recruit, onboard, engage, train, develop, and retain employees are many and complex. Add in processes for managing performance, rewarding success, dealing with non-performance, identifying potential, planning for succession, and future workforce planning, and things are even more complex. Try to design and implement these processes to align with and support the corporate strategy, and build a company culture that facilitates all the above, and the challenge becomes monumental.

There are few examples of companies that have achieved a truly integrated approach to talent management. A 2003 survey of companies in the UK found that:

> *Three-quarters of companies have invested in dedicated resources to manage their talent, according to the survey of 20 leading UK companies by recruitment and HR consultancy Astralis Group and Lancaster University Management School, but these resources have yet to make a major impact in most companies.*

The problem, the report says, is that talent management activity is typically delivered as a set of fragmented individual HR interventions rather than an integrated on-going process.[9]

The term "Talent Management" is now firmly planted in the business lexicon. There is even a magazine called *Talent Management* – a new name for an old magazine previously known as *Workforce Performance Solutions*. Their website is dividend in seven sections, which maps out their take on the components of talent management:

- Recruitment & Retention
- Assessment & Evaluation
- Compensation & Benefits
- Performance Management
- Learning & Development
- Succession Planning.[10]

The Conference Board's 2004 report, "Integrated and Integrative Talent Management," took a similar but slightly broader perspective, defining the components of talent management as:

- Recruitment (college recruitment, experienced hires, on-boarding)
- Retention (specific efforts, total rewards)
- Professional Development (professional development systems, assessment centers, learning and training)
- Leadership/High Potential Development (stretch and short-term/special assignments, high potential development, executive coaching, cross-functional and international opportunities)
- Performance Management (competency profiles, performance management systems, reward and recognition programs)
- Feedback/Measurement (exit interviews, regular employee surveys, Balanced Scorecard™)
- Workforce Planning (forecasting of talent needs and demand, talent skills development)
- Culture (corporate values, flexible workspace, diversity programs, internal communications)

However broadly or narrowly one defines "talent management," it always incorporates basic Human Resources processes. The broadest definitions of talent management incorporate all aspects of human resource management; in essence, "talent management" or "human capital management" may simply be the latest terms in the personnel/human resources evolution.

## RECRUITMENT: IN SEARCH OF EXCELLENT EMPLOYEES

The front end of the talent management supply chain is the recruiting process. Finding the "right" people always has been a challenge for any organization. And if an organization is aiming to hire top talent or A Players only, the challenge increases, particularly when an organization is looking to lure experienced talent – as opposed to new graduates. The issue, as expressed by Pat Fitzgerald, Senior Director of Executive Recruiting at SAP: "The ones we want are not looking for a job. You have to get their attention."

An organization needs top talent recruiters in order to recruit top talent. The recruiter needs an intimate knowledge of the hiring organization's strategy, culture, values, style, products and services, as well as intimate knowledge of the key job responsibilities, short and long-term goals, the hiring manager, and team. He or she also needs to deeply understand the market, and the hiring organization's chief competitors, which are often the source of the top talent the recruiting organization is trying to attract.

An organization must be skilled in both the science and the art of recruiting. The "science" covers recruiting processes, metrics, competency profiles, and job descriptions, whereas the "art" involves gaining a deep understanding of candidates' talents, aspirations, and motives. The recruiter must understand, before a candidate does, why moving to a new company makes sense for the candidate, gain the candidate's attention, and paint a clear picture of why changing companies makes sense. Effective recruiters also need to analyze what an initial "no" response means from a candidate, and decide whether, and how, to continue the pursuit. One recruiter stated "Sometimes I need to stalk someone, in a nice way."

New approaches to job hunting, such as Internet recruiting sites (monster. com) and job-related social networking sites (linkedin.com) can be a source for entry level and lower-level positions, but again, the top talent typically is not job hunting.

A valuable source of new top talent can come through an employee referral program. At SAP, 42 percent of all US new hires are individuals who have been referred by a current SAP employee. Employees who refer a candidate who is hired receive a referral bonus of $5000.

Another technique used by savvy recruiters: ask each newly-hired employee "Who are the five best people you ever worked with? What was their role? Would you be willing to give me their names?"

## WELCOME ABOARD

Once an organization brings a talented employee onboard, the next challenge is motivating them, and making them want to stay. First impressions are lasting impressions, so many organizations design thorough on-boarding process to welcome new hires and get them up-to-speed fast. On-boarding processes deal with the fundamental requirements of providing materials, equipment, clear job expectations, basic job training, benefit registration, etc. On-boarding also can provide a broader understanding of the overall organization's strategy, culture, and values. Many companies assign a coach or mentor for each new hire, to help them integrate rapidly.

## EMPLOYEE ENGAGEMENT

In 1999, Marcus Buckingham and Curt Coffman, consultants with the Gallup Organization, published a book summarizing intensive Gallup studies on "What do the most talented employees need from their workplace?" and

"How do the world's greatest managers find, focus, and keep talented employees?" The research, which involved more than 80,000 managers and over a million employees in over 400 companies, led to a definition of "engagement factors," and a tool to assess employee engagement, the Q12 (named for the 12 Questions in the assessment tool). Gallup defined "engagement" as employees' enthusiasm for and involvement in their work; an engaged employee is one who is enthusiastic, emotionally connected, and productive. Gallup's research confirmed the correlation between engagement level and key business outcomes: productivity, profitability, customer satisfaction, safety, and retention. In other words, an engaged employee is more productive, produces greater profitability and higher levels of customer satisfaction, has fewer accidents, and is more likely to stay with the company than a less engaged employee.

The twelve "employee expectations" in the Gallup engagement measure are:

1. I know what is expected of me at work.
2. I have the materials and equipment I need to do my work right.
3. At work, I have the opportunity to do what I do best every day.
4. In the last seven days, I have received recognition or praise for doing good work.
5. My supervisor, or someone at work, seems to care about me as a person.
6. There is someone at work who encourages my development.
7. At work, my opinions seem to count.
8. The mission or purpose of my company makes me feel my job is important.
9. My associates or fellow employees are committed to doing quality work.
10. I have a best friend at work.
11. In the last six months, someone at work has talked to me about my progress.
12. This last year, I have had opportunities at work to learn and grow.

In Gallup's view, the more strongly an individual can agree with these 12 statements, the more likely it will be that he or she is strongly engaged. The 12 statements "measure the core elements needed to attract, focus, and keep the most talented employees."[11] Another interesting observation was that an employee's responses to these twelve items were influenced more by the employee's direct manager than policies, procedures, and practices of the overall company. This research found widely varied engagement levels within a single company as well as within a single functional area of a company.

In the eight years since the initial research report, Gallup has continued their engagement studies, and now has engagement data on over 4.5 million employees. Their latest research shows strong correlation between engagement level and company share price.[12]

Managers who want to build an engaged workforce can use the Gallup Q12 statements as a guideline. By setting clear expectations, providing required material and equipment, putting people into roles where they can do what they do best every day, providing recognition and praise for good work, discussing progress, and providing opportunities for learning, development and growth, managers can increase the level of engagement of their direct reports.

## ALL THE STAGES OF THE GAME

Companies that take "talent management" seriously now focus on a broader, more systematic, and business-driven approach to the employee "lifecycle." Talent management encompasses brand awareness creation; attracting, recruiting and on-boarding the best; developing, motivating, engaging, and retaining them; discovering their potential and helping them realize it; and finally building an engaged and loyal community of retirees and alumni.

## ONE COMPANY'S JOURNEY

SAP is a software company founded in 1972 by five former employees of IBM Germany: Dietmar Hopp, Hans-Werner Hector, Hasso Plattner, Klaus Tschira, and Claus Wellenreuther. Their vision was to create software that would allow real-time business data processing. Over the past thirty-five years, SAP has grown from a small, regional player into a world-class global corporation that is the global market leader in collaborative, inter-enterprise business solutions. SAP is the world's largest business software company and the world's third-largest independent software provider, serving more than 38,000 customers worldwide. 2006 revenue was $12.2 billion (€9.402 billion).

SAP's phenomenal growth has required strong recruiting efforts around the globe, and the company continues to seek top talent worldwide. In 1991, SAP had approximately 2,500 employees. In 1997, that number rose to 13,000, and today, ten years later, SAP employs more than 40,000 individuals from 107 different countries. The increasingly-global nature of the company has required the development of new strategies, organizations, and processes to deal with talent management.

SAP has faced substantial changes and challenges over its 35 year life: retaining top talent, dramatic shifts in customer expectations, technology breakthroughs, new markets, changes in the customer base, fierce competition, a rapidly-growing and increasingly-global workforce, and new demands for strong management and leadership. The changes and challenges never stop though the pace of change seems to increase each year.

# GOING GLOBAL

In 1999, a small team of SAP employees from Denmark, Germany, the Netherlands, Singapore, Switzerland, and the United States worked together and proposed something that had never happened at SAP: a global leadership development program. Previously, all management and leadership development efforts had happened at the local or regional levels. This team, however, felt that there was now a need to launch a global leadership development program for SAP executives. The reasons they cited included:

- Changing business strategy – new products, markets, methods
- Changing customer expectations
- Competition from new "best of breed" software vendors
- Turnover: the loss of key players to dot-com start-ups and competitors
- Management development: due to the rapid growth of business and limited focus on management development in the past the level of management skill needed improvement

The team felt that a global approach to leadership development would:

- Lead to increased global understanding, teamwork, communication, networking, learning, and synergies among top management
- Strengthen the global talent pool for internal promotions and replacements
- Increase employee satisfaction with SAP management style and work environment
- Promote retention of valuable talent in the management team and improve manager satisfaction with SAP development opportunities and career paths

- Increase managers' effectiveness in leading strategic changes and producing results

The team presented their recommendations to the SAP Executive Board, and asked for approval to move forward with designing and launching a Global Leadership Development Program. The goals of the program were:

- To support the metamorphosis and business transformation of SAP
- To develop global leadership skills, particularly in the area of change management
- To strengthen managerial competencies and knowledge, primarily for understanding global competition and strategic management
- To develop a common "SAP Strategic Leadership" language
- To support increased global understanding, teamwork, communication, networking, and learning among senior management
- To provide a global forum for SAP's leaders to shape SAP's strategy
- To strengthen leadership skills to drive business results

The Board supported this proposal, and agreed to play a key role in the design and delivery of the program. Their first task was to nominate participants for the program, thirty-two senior executives who were direct reports of the Board – or the next level below – and were "top performers with global leadership potential."

After getting proposals from a dozen business schools and meeting with six of the schools, SAP choose to work with INSEAD in Fontainebleau, France. The SAP design team worked intensively with two INSEAD professors to custom-design a program that would address SAP's specific business and leadership development needs. An intensive program was designed, with a six-day opening module on the INSEAD campus, an interval of several months, a second module of seven days in the US (which included two days of benchmarking visits to other companies), and a third module of two days at SAP's corporate headquarters in Germany.

The SAP design team also charged the SAP Executive Board to identify four strategic topics that would be assigned to groups of participants. The program would have a strong "action learning" component – participants would be assigned to one of four project teams that would tackle one of the strategic topics assigned by the Board. Each team would have a Board member as sponsor/coach, who would guide the team as it addressed its topic. Teams would work on their topics for several months between the first two modules, and continue to work on the topic for several more months before the third module, which would include a day with the full Executive Board. The teams would present their ideas and recommendations relative to their strategic topic.

The first Global Leadership Development Program was delivered in 2000 although all 32 seats were not filled. Even though the Board had agreed to fund and sponsor the program, it was hard to get Board members to "give up" top talent for 17 days of "classroom" time and countless additional hours of project team work between modules. However, the first program was a major success, and after the first year, it was not a problem to fill the seats; one Board member alone wanted to send 25 participants in the 2001 cycle!

The program has now run once every year since 2000; to date, about 250 of SAP's top executives have participated. For the Board members, the Global Leadership Development Program (GLDP) has helped them get to know top talent outside their own functional area while the recommendations from the teams have made strong contributions to strategic challenges and opportunities for SAP. As desired, the leadership concepts have helped build a common leadership language at the top of the company. Two years ago, the program went through a substantial redesign, to better align it with the evolved strategy of SAP. The GLDP is now delivered jointly by INSEAD and Stanford, but continues as the "flagship" of SAP's global leadership development efforts.

## PERFORMANCE EXPECTATIONS, FEEDBACK, AND PROFESSIONAL DEVELOPMENT

As was the case with leadership development, performance management also operated in a decentralized fashion around the SAP world. When a project team began to consider a global performance management process, they discovered that there were more than 40 different performance planning and appraisal forms in use. The forms ranged from relatively short and simple forms in some countries to forms that were comprehensive and complex in other countries. When a global form was first proposed, several countries refused to consider it, stating that is was far too complicated and that it would be rejected outright in their organizations.

The design team faced a challenging change initiative. Finding the "right" process for use in all countries is difficult in any case, and when there has been a decentralized, "laissez-faire" approach for many years, it is even more difficult to impose a single global approach. Furthermore, in the absence of a global process, some countries had worked very hard to design and launch their own processes resulting in a strong sense of "pride of ownership" and additional resistance to any new global process.

However, as managers increasingly had global teams with direct reports based in several countries, managers began to express frustration that they had to fill out substantially different performance planning and appraisal forms. Their voices added to the push for a single, standardized process. An international team was formed to design a single performance planning and appraisal form, incorporating a form for professional development planning. In 2002, a global process was launched, to be used by every manager and employee worldwide. The process was piloted with a paper version of the planning and appraisal form, which since has been changed to an on-line process. Now all employees meet with their manager at the beginning of the year and discuss performance objectives and professional development activities. The employee then drafts a set of objectives and a development plan, which is electronically forwarded to the manager. The manager reviews the plan, makes any required edits, and approves the plan. At year-end, each employee completes an on-line self assessment, which is forwarded to the manager, and then the manager adds his or her comments and schedules a performance discussion, which focuses both on assessment of objectives achieved as well as development actions taken. The process then begins again for the following year's objectives and development planning.

## MANAGING MANAGERS

As the Global Leadership Development project team had observed, there was room for improvement in SAP when it came to management competence. Previously, technical specialists were promoted into managerial positions with little or no training in management skills and without clear, management-based performance expectations. Performance of managers typically was assessed based on what had been achieved but not on how it was achieved.

A global project team was formed to analyze the current situation and make recommendations for strengthening managerial effectiveness within the organization. The team proposed an initiative they called "Management Excellence @ SAP" which was designed to:

- Build a culture of Management Excellence alongside SAP's successful culture of Technical Excellence
- Provide a common framework of management philosophy, expectations, language, beliefs, and values

- Offer learning and development opportunities for SAP managers at all levels
- Strengthen the effectiveness of SAP by strengthening SAP management

The team believed that stronger managers would:

- Be better equipped to support SAP's strategic initiatives and align all employees around those initiatives
- Provide rapid integration of new employees as the company grows
- Build highly engaged, productive teams
- Help drive the strategic changes the company was implementing
- Increase customer satisfaction, productivity, profitability, and employee retention

The team worked with SAP Executives to define the role of the manager:

SAP managers are responsible for achieving results by **Creating the Future, Managing Performance, Building a Team**, and **Developing People**. Each manager is charged with understanding and shaping SAP's vision, mission, strategy, and values to create a productive, engaging environment where team members can use their talents, achieve their potential, and contribute to the success of our business.

For each of the four responsibilities, a set of "behaviors" helped clarify what managers need to achieve in order to meet that responsibility. For example, a manger who was successfully "Developing People" was one who:

- Provides orientation for new employees
- Delegates challenging tasks
- Provides opportunities to learn and grow
- Focuses on strengthening his or her effectiveness as a manager
- Supports learning from mistakes
- Ensures that people build and execute their own development plans
- Identifies and develops successors/creates future leaders
- Creates networking opportunities for others

As part of the launch of the Management Excellence @ SAP initiative, every manager worldwide received a letter from the Board and a copy of

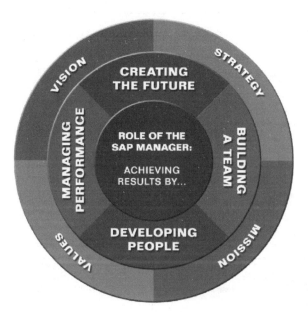

*Figure 1: The Role of the SAP Manager*

*The Manager's Guide to the SAP Galaxy*, a workbook that defined the managerial role, explained in detail the four responsibilities, provided tools to help each manager assess his or her strengths and weaknesses relative to management behaviors, and suggested development actions to become stronger in each area.

To reinforce the importance of the managerial role, the SAP Executive Board decided to assign two objectives to every manager around the SAP world:

1.  **Professional Development Planning**
    For each direct report, create a Professional Development Action Plan that specifies the skills, knowledge, and/or competencies to be developed. Identify development actions, including on-the-job activities, coaching, mentoring, and/or training. Ensure that development actions are carried out during the year and that individuals apply their learning.

2.  **Succession Management**
    Identify an individual who could be a potential successor for your current position. If the individual is a member of your team, ensure that this individual's Professional Development Action Plan focuses on accelerating development in areas that prepare the individual for this step. If there is no likely candidate on the team, establish a contingency

| Professional Development | MMT | MMM | MMO |
|---|---|---|---|
| Create an environment of continuous learning and individual growth | ● | ● | ● |
| Plan short - and long-term development with your direct reports and facilitate the implementation of their development plans | ● | ● | ● |
| Act as a coach for your direct reports | ● | ● | ● |
| Be a "net exporter of talent" by identifying individual potential and promoting your team members throughout the organization | ● | ● | ● |
| Provide opportunities to learn and grow for ALL High Potentials in your entire organization | ● | ● | ● |

| Succession Management | MMT | MMM | MMO |
|---|---|---|---|
| Identify succession candidate(s) for your own position, get your manager's approval, and develop candidate(s) accordingly | ● | ● | ● |
| Ensure that all your direct reports who are managers have approved succession plans in place and develop candidates accordingly | | ● | ● |

**Each manager's total incentive will be factored against the achievement of these objectives.**

*Figure 2: SAP Development Objectives for Managers*

plan (another SAP employee, an external hire, etc.). Ensure follow-up with any team member identified as "High Potential" in the Talent Management review.

This was the first time that managers had been assigned a universal performance objective on any topic and sent a clear signal that the Executive Board was taking the issue of talent management quite seriously. To reinforce the importance of these objectives, they would now constitute 10 percent of the potential bonus for all managers.

Letter from CEO Henning Kagermann to all managers:
To: All Managers
Subject: Management Excellence @ SAP Strategic Objectives 2004

Dear Colleagues,

As an SAP manager, you drive our company's efforts to reshape our business, capture market share, encourage innovation, and increase customer satisfaction. You are responsible for **achieving results by Creating the Future, Building a Team, Managing Performance, and Developing People**. In 2004, each manager's success in these four managerial responsibilities will be appraised in the new Performance Management process.

The talent of the people in our organization is the key to SAP's competitive advantage. Because every SAP employee must focus on building new skills, knowledge, and abilities aligned with the changes in our business, we will continue to place extra emphasis on your responsibility for **Developing People**—specifically, professional development and succession management.

For managers who receive variable compensation, the SAP Executive Board has stipulated that each manager's total 2004 bonus (paid in 2005) will be factored against the achievement of professional development and succession management objectives. Detailed information is available in a Virtual Classroom session.

To make SAP a stronger company now and in the future, we need to develop our future leaders from within and boost the learning of every employee. As a company, we believe in the value of investing strongly in people's growth. As a manager, you play an essential role in focusing professional development efforts. Purposeful development directs energy where we need it, helps people realize their potential, and powers systematic improvement in the competencies that are key for our organization.

Your Human Resources team will provide coaching and tools to help you accomplish these key managerial objectives. We look forward to the commitment and action of all managers as we build a culture of Management Excellence @ SAP.

With best wishes for the holidays and a healthy, happy, successful 2004,

Henning

---

# ALIGNMENT

Around the SAP world, training and development specialists began to redesign management development programs to align with the newly-clarified managerial role. The global performance management process was redesigned to incorporate the new management responsibilities, ensuring that these responsibilities would be a part of every manager's performance planning and appraisal.

# A GLOBAL HUNT FOR HIGH POTENTIAL TALENT

In order to have a clear picture of the talent around the SAP world, the Human Resources organization designed and launched a global annual Talent Management process that identifies high potentials globally. Unlike some organizations that identify high potentials only at the upper levels of the organization, SAP uses a "roll-up process" that begins with first-line managers – identifying high potential employees at the non-managerial/individual contributor level – and then moves up subsequent levels with directors identifying high potential managers, VP's identifying high potential directors, etc., ending with a final review at the Board level. This process occurs annually, and produces a comprehensive list of "High Potentials."

At SAP, a High Potential is someone who:

- Demonstrates an ability to learn and develop rapidly
- Meets the global Potential Indicators and Final Differentiators criteria (see below)
- Demonstrates professional maturity and personal caliber
- Lives the SAP values and new requirements
- Has the potential to take on greater responsibility or a more complex role within the next 12 months

During the Talent Review Meetings, management teams come together to discuss the potential of their employees and to commit to best-in-class development opportunities for SAP's most talented employees. A set of "Potential Indicators" and "Final Differentiators" is used to identify High Potentials:

## POTENTIAL INDICATORS

| Business Ownership | • Acts with the best interests of and demonstrates core values of the company; looks beyond the border of his/her business<br>• Demonstrates business acumen; acts and thinks economically<br>• Understands the value that SAP's solutions add to customers' business<br>• Brings the business forward; understands and can manage OR execute SAP's strategic direction |
|---|---|
| Drive for Results | • Is able to deliver results under difficult circumstances<br>• Makes things happen through personal drive and adaptability<br>• Sets clear priorities that simplify complexity and ensure focus on execution<br>• Delegates responsibility with clear expectations for the desired outcomes<br>• Sets ambitious targets and pursues them with speed and determination<br>• Monitors progress of others and redirects efforts as necessary to ensure execution |
| Intellectual Horsepower | • Seen as mentally "quick"; can get the "essence" of an issue better than most<br>• Is a solution finder; able to quickly analyze and resolve complex problems<br>• Shows a simple and smart approach in thinking and acting<br>• Constructively challenges the status quo |

| Change Agility | • Constructively engages in continuous product and process improvement<br>• Dares and drives to leave comfort zone and shows compelling results outside own area of expertise<br>• Initiates and implements new ways and methods; reviews the benefit for SAP's business<br>• Pragmatically deals with and works through resistance and/or obstacles<br>• Learns from past mistakes and experiences<br>• Proactively seeks feedback and acts on it |
| --- | --- |
| Interpersonal Relationships | • Seen as helpful and constructive even in disagreements<br>• Explores and considers the influence of different cultural backgrounds on interaction, communication styles, and work habits<br>• Adept at developing trusting relationships<br>• Operates with people from different cultures and backgrounds with fairness and respect<br>• Strong team player who inspires cooperation and team work from all<br>• Aware of how his or her behavior and actions impact others around them<br>• Shares knowledge and expertise with others.<br>• Strong team player who inspires cooperation and team work from all |

## FINAL DIFFERENTIATORS

- Is able to significantly stretch beyond current role in next 12 months
- Ambitious in own development
  o Actively involved in own career development and shows dedication to rapid advancement
- Flexible/mobile for future growth in personal career
  o Willing to move into a new role and accepts changes in his/her working environment (possibly in another county/region for a minimum of a few months)

- o Able to quickly develop additional competencies and skills and apply them in a multitude of situations
- Capable of working cross-functionally within a diverse team
  - o Capable of gaining the experience of working for cross-functional projects and topics in current Line of Business (LoB) or takes the opportunity of working in another LoB/ Board area (for at least a few months); e.g. Job Rotation via the Top Talent Fellowship
  - o Gets familiarized in new/different processes and topics out of other fields without any problems
- Demonstrates a pattern of success and accountability in new/ challenging situations
  - o Shows an effective and efficient approach to new/challenging situations
  - o Manages (nearly) all challenges that occur successfully
  - o Takes over responsibility for new/challenging tasks and works out a strategic plan to manage them
- History of exceeding performance expectations (can be monitored through global performance management)
  - o Consistently received performance ratings of "exceeds expectations" (except New Hires – comparable to quick on-boarding phase for New Hires within 6 months)

There are three basic phases of the Talent Review process that are followed by all managers worldwide:

- **Phase 1: Preparation**
  Managers complete a Talent Management Fact Sheet on each employee they would like to discuss during the Talent Review Meeting. Among other things, the Fact Sheet identifies an employee's Level of Potential. The Fact Sheet is used to ensure that each employee is discussed in a fair and consistent manner.

- **Phase 2: Talent Review Meeting**
  During these meetings, each management team discusses and evaluates all potential candidates against the Talent Review Potential Indicators and Final Differentiators. The Talent Review Meetings are facilitated by HR and involve active participation from all managers. Individuals can be proposed as "High Potentials" who are ready for bigger responsibility within the coming year, or "Top Talents" who will be ready for bigger responsibility within one or two years. Each year, approximately 2

percent of the global employee base is identified as "High Potential," and another 8 percent is identified as "Top Talent."

- **Phase 3: Feedback and Development**
  After the Talent Review Meetings, managers notify those employees who were identified as either Top Talent or High Potential. The manager then works with the employee to identify appropriate development activities. It becomes a joint responsibility of the manager and high potential employee to ensure that the appropriate development actions are taken to maximize the employee's potential. High Potentials are often asked to work on special projects, provide input into strategic topics, and participate in special meetings.

# MORE MANAGEMENT EXCELLENCE @ SAP

A new project team was formed to continue the Management Excellence @ SAP initiative. This team was charged with creating a set of measures to concretely assess managerial performance, and to identify training and development options to help managers be successful in achieving managerial responsibilities. There were several key products delivered by this team: the Management Excellence Evaluation (ME2), a regional management development program for middle managers, and Managerial coaching tools and training for managers at all levels.

## Measuring Managers: ME2

The Management Excellence Evaluation is a 360 degree assessment tool designed to assess a manager's management practices. The team first worked to identify the managerial competencies required to drive SAP towards the successful accomplishment of its long-term strategy – Vision 2010. The team interviewed Board members and managers at all levels who, through existing measures, had been identified as Top Performers or High Potential. More than 120 in-depth interviews were conducted, first to identify the competencies, and then to seek examples of successful application of these competencies in the SAP context. SAP partnered with Personnel Decisions International to build behaviorally-anchored rating scales to assess each competency. The end result, the Management Excellence Evaluation, is a brief (24 questions) feedback instrument that is a part of every manager's performance appraisal. The brief survey is completed by the participant, the participant's direct reports and direct manager, and, if the participant desires, additional managers and peers. A report is generated which indicates strengths, weaknesses, and development ideas. A copy of this report is electronically sent to the participant as well as the participant's manager, and the results are discussed during the performance appraisal. Thus a manager's management practices are assessed, along with results achieved, to determine merit increase and bonus percentage.

## The Regional Management Development Program (RMDP)

To continue the efforts that had been started with the Global Leadership Development Program, the Management Excellence @ SAP project team proposed launching a management development initiative for middle managers. Similar to the Global Leadership Development Program, the RMDP would help participants build a network across borders (country and functional area), offer common managerial tools, and help managers better understand the SAP strategy and their role in making it happen. INSEAD was again chosen as the partner. INSEAD's campuses in Singapore and France covered the Europe-Middle East-Africa (EMEA) and Asia Pacific-Japan (APJ) regions, and, for the Americas, INSEAD partnered with the Center for Creative Leadership. The regional programs offered design flexibility appropriate for the region (the Americas program was one week long, and the EMEA and APJ programs were two modules of one week each). The RMDP programs also incorporated action learning components, with teams making recommendations to panels of senior executives. The program focused on they key role of middle managers in communicating the corporate SAP strategy and translating it into actionable plans for their business units.

## The Manager as Coach

Now that the role of the manager had been clearly defined and mangers were being held accountable for talent management, it was important to offer managers tools and skills to help them be more successful in the role. There was a skills gap relative to providing open, honest performance feedback. There was also a need to help managers understand their role in coaching and developing any high potential employees they were managing. Again partnering with Personnel Decisions International, SAP began offering "Leader as Coach" and "Manager as Coach" workshops for managers at all levels. These workshops are based on the premise that managers need to coach direct reports based on each individual's performance and potential.

As discussed in the introduction to this chapter, the coaching and development for High Potentials should focus on "getting them ready faster" for taking on the envisioned broader responsibilities. The manager of a Top Performer needs to keep that individual engaged and challenged – and Top Performers are often ideal candidates for coaching less experienced individuals. A key to successful talent management is the ability to deal fairly, directly, and appropriately with poor performance, and the manager is the front-line defense in making this happen. The coaching workshops provided practical, effective tools for managers to achieve their responsibilities in performance management and people development.

SAP's focus on managerial coaching skills, along with the numerous other initiatives to strengthen leader and manager effectiveness, reflects the belief that strong managers are an essential ingredient in an effective approach to talent management.

## Talent and Strategy

SAP built an internal Corporate Strategy Group (CSG) to focus on projects that fundamentally impact SAP's strategy, services, and products. Organizationally, the CSG reports to the CEO of SAP, Henning Kagermann. Part of the CSG mission is to enhance and institutionalize SAP's capabilities to define, communicate, and consistently execute a strategy that enables SAP to outperform in a highly dynamic and competitive environment. CSG examined the core values that had made SAP a successful company in the past, identified which of these would help ensure future success, and also identified what values had to change, improve, or be emphasized even more strongly. "Talent development" was cited as one area requiring even greater emphasis.

Executive Board member Claus Heinrich describes SAP's approach to talent development as driven by an understanding of where we are going as a company – the strategic goals we are aiming to achieve – plus an understanding of each individual's strengths, talents, abilities, and weaknesses. SAP strongly emphasizes the need for every employee to learn and develop – not just High Potentials – but is also open about the fact that there are additional development options for High Potentials to accelerate their development. Claus Henrich expressed this in SAP's employee magazine: "…it's our entire workforce that makes SAP strong, not just our top talent. Of course we have special programs to promote our elite employees – they're the ones that are going to bring the company forward in the next five or ten years."

To boost its focus on Talent Development, SAP formed two new teams, Executive Development & Compensation (ED&C) and Global Top Talent Management (GTTM). The ED&C team focuses on the development of

SAP's global executives (150 managers in key global roles). ED&C's team of five HR professionals designs development initiatives for the global executive population and meets annually with each individual executive to discuss development needs and to help prepare professional development action plans. ED&C offers executive assessments, collective development opportunities (workshops and seminars delivered by INSEAD, London Business School, and IMD in Switzerland), as well as individual coaches (both internal and external).

## Global Top Talent Management

To provide additional development opportunities focused on High Potentials, SAP Created the Global Top Talent Management Team. This team of four individuals sits organizationally in the Office of the CEO (demonstrating strong commitment to talent development from the top of the organization, and facilitating strong links with the Corporate Strategy Group). This centralized global team focuses primarily on high-level High Potentials and Top Talents, offering programs such as:

1. Senior Top Talent Summits: groups of executive-level High Potentials work in virtual teams to address strategic business issues and then meet face-to-face for several days. The Summits include external speakers and internal thought leaders, and provide a forum where participants interact with Board members and senior executives to help shape SAP's strategy.
2. Monthly CEO breakfasts: Each month CEO Henning Kagermann meets with a small group of international High Potentials for an informal two-hour discussion at the company headquarters in Germany. In addition, Kagermann often asks the Global Top Talent Management Team to arrange meetings with High Potentials in other countries when he is traveling to their locations.
3. Fellowships: High Potentials can apply for one of the more than 40 six-month Fellowship positions that provide stretch assignments outside their current role – for example, a software developer may take a role in the marketing organization, or a sales executive might move to a role in Service and Support. In addition, the Fellow typically relocates to another country for this assignment. The intent is to broaden the perspective of High Potentials and give them a chance to work on a key project or initiative in a different field. After six months, the Fellow returns to his or her previous job.

4. Top Talent Marketplace: High Potentials can opt to enter a profile and resume in an internal database. Any key global job openings are entered in the database, and the system flags any High Potentials who look like a possible candidate for the open roles. HR employees assigned as "Talent Brokers" contact the High Potentials and ask if they would like to be considered as a candidate for the role. The Talent Marketplace exists in addition to the regular job posting system, which is open to all employees, and gives High Potentials additional visibility.
5. One-on-one coaching for selected High Potentials: Members of the Global Top Talent Management team serve as personal coaches to selected High Potentials. Coaching support focuses on identifying an individual's strengths, weaknesses, and development needs; brainstorming possible development activities; discussing career options; and creating a professional development action plan. The Global Top Talent Management team can also help an individual find external or internal coaches and mentors to address specific development needs.
6. Developmental Assessment and Coaching Process: This option is offered to all high potentials and top talents. Participants complete an on-line assessment, receive a written report, and take part in a one hour debriefing/coaching call with a Caliper Corporation coach. The participant gains valuable insight into his or her strengths and weaknesses relative to a series of attributes in addition to guidance on how to focus professional development action planning. Participants have the option of an additional hour-long coaching call with their direct manager and the Caliper coach; this allows the manager to gain insight into the High Potential's talents and development needs and become a partner in the individual's development.
7. Cascading Strategy Forums: The Global Top Talent Management Team partners with the Corporate Strategy Group to offer one-day workshops where high potential participants discuss elements of SAP's corporate strategy, identify barriers to success, and propose solutions. The two-way interaction ensures that the participants deeply understand SAP's strategy, and provides powerful feedback and "real-world" data to the Corporate Strategy Group.

In addition to the global talent development initiatives, there are talent development programs designed and offered for regional and line of business teams: high potentials in the Latin America business unit participate in strategy formulation project teams to shape the business in that region while the global software development group offers a variety of talent development initiatives for their top talent and High Potential population.

SAP's initiatives are designed to be close to the business, content rich, and delivered primarily by internal senior staff and executives. This ensures maximum relevance, best value for time and money, and a balanced input-output relation. SAP's strategy execution is aligned to these initiatives, and the initiatives aim to build a pool of well-rounded managers.

## MEASURING SUCCESS

Seven years into the journey that began with the Global Leadership Development program, SAP is seeing tangible results. A Board-level Key Performance Indicator was established to measure the percentage of key job openings that are filled with candidates from the High Potential and Top Talent pool. Since the measure was established two years ago, the percentage has steadily increased, already doubling the first quarter's results – "what you can measure, you can improve" at its best.

An assessment of the 2005 High Potential pool showed that one year after their nomination, sixty percent of the population stated that they were in "larger jobs" with additional responsibility, either through promotion or through assignment of greater responsibilities in the same role. Furthermore, the 2006 global employee survey shows that on average, the High Potential population ranked higher on every measure when compared to the non-high potential population – they had higher engagement levels and were more satisfied with development opportunities, degree of empowerment, working relationships, and their direct management.

Success factors that have been a foundation of SAP's approach include:

- Alignment with the strategic goals of the organization
- Clear definition of the talent development responsibilities of the individual, the individual's manager, the HR organization, the lines of business, and the global talent development organizations
- Increased resources and budget dedicated to talent development
- Active support and involvement of the CEO and Board
- Recognition that talent development is key to the strategic success of the organization
- Awareness that management excellence and high-quality talent management represents a shift in corporate culture, requiring constant effort and reinforcement

While there has been great progress over the past few years, there is still much to be done. Continuous efforts are underway to "up-skill" managers in their essential roles of recognizing, engaging, and developing talent. There is room to improve the integration of the assorted processes for recruiting, onboarding, engaging, developing, appraising, and identifying potential. All aspects of the initiative need to be assessed and continuously improved.

The ultimate measure of the success of a talent management initiative is what happens with the talent and what happens with the business. Turnover rates of the SAP talent pool are even lower than the already-low company-wide turnover rate; our key open positions are increasingly filled with internal top talent, and we are successfully hiring top talent from the outside; our customer satisfaction rates arc reaching new highs; and our business is growing dramatically. Talent management produces results!

# ENDNOTES

1.  Charles Fishman, "The War for Talent," Fast Company, July 1998.
2.  Ed Michaels, Helen Handfield-Jones, and Beth Axelrod, The War for Talent, Harvard Business School Press, 2001.
3.  "The Future of HR in Europe – Key challenges through 2015," a Boston Consulting Group/European Association for Personnel Management report, June 2007.
4.  Lynne Morton, "Integrated and Integrative Talent Management: A Strategic HR Framework," The Conference Board, January 2004.
5.  Bradford D. Smart and Geoffrey H. Smart, "Topgrading the Organization," Directors and Boards, Spring 1997.
6.  "The War for Talent," by Charles Fishman, Fast Company, Issue 16, July 1998, Page 104: An interview with War for Talent co-author Ed Michaels.
7.  Internal strategy document, SAP AG, 2007.
8.  Entry for "Talent Management," Wikipedia, June 13, 2007.
9.  Brian Amble, "Talent Management Strategies are Stuck in the Past," Management Issues, November 7, 2003. (http://www.management-issues.com).
10. http://www.talentmgt.com, June 14, 2007.
11. Marcus Buckingham and Curt Coffman, First Break All the Rules, Simon & Schuster: New York, 1999.
12. Bryant Ott, "Investors, Take Note: Engagement Boosts Earnings," Gallup Management Journal, June 14, 2007. (http://gmj.gallup.com/content/27799/Investors-Take-Note-Engagement-Boosts-Earnings.aspx).
13. "Talent Development: Our Managers & Employees Have a Responsibility," SAP World, March 2006.

# IMPROVING KNOWLEDGE WORKER PERFORMANCE

*Tom H. Davenport, President's Chair in Information Technology and Management, Babson College*

Today, between one-fourth and one-third of all workers in advanced economies are knowledge workers. Knowledge workers create the innovations and devise the strategies that keep their firms competitive. They are the key to organizational growth, yet few companies have explicitly addressed the productivity and performance of their knowledge workers, and most continue to manage this new breed of employee with techniques designed for the Industrial Age. As this critical sector of the workforce continues to grow in size and importance, failing to address knowledge worker performance is a mistake that could cost companies their future.

In this chapter, I will explore what a knowledge worker is, the four major categories of knowledge workers, and how these workers differ from traditional employees. Then I will outline the metrics, processes, and technologies that can enhance their productivity and performance. I will also discuss how to develop knowledge workers' capabilities, invest in knowledge networks, and create the conditions that will motivate them to excel. Lastly, I will explain how to change the managerial mindset to match today's knowledge worker environment.

# WHAT IS A KNOWLEDGE WORKER, ANYWAY?

Almost half a century ago, Peter Drucker coined the term "knowledge worker" in his breakthrough 1959 book, *Landmarks of Tomorrow*.[1] By the next decade, he was declaring that improving the productivity of knowledge workers would be the greatest management challenge of the 20th century. By the end of that century, he was predicting that the productivity of knowledge workers was going to define competitive advantage in the decades to come. Why did Drucker – and why should we – believe that knowledge workers and their productivity would be so important? There are three key reasons:

- *First, knowledge workers are a large and growing category of workers.* If we can't figure out how to make a quarter to a third of the labor force more productive, we're going to have problems with our economy overall.
- *Second, knowledge workers are the most expensive type of worker that companies employ*, so it's doubly shameful if they're not as productive as they could be.
- *Third, knowledge workers are essential to the growth of many economies.* Agricultural and manufacturing work is moving to countries with low labor costs, such as China, which means that the jobs that remain in knowledge-based economies (including the United States and Canada, Western Europe, and Japan) are particularly critical to these countries' survival.

Despite the importance of knowledge workers, they are still being managed with methods that were developed in the Industrial Age, when workers did jobs that could easily be observed and measured, when their work processes were highly structured, and when roles were clearly defined. Workers worked – usually making something – and managers managed – usually with an overall corporate interest in mind.

However, as every manager is rapidly learning today, that model doesn't work in the world of knowledge workers, and yet, nothing has come along to take the place of traditional management theories and functions. That leaves a huge vacuum in many corporations, because knowledge workers today are responsible for sparking innovation and growth, for inventing new products, designing marketing programs, even creating strategy.

In fact, the firms with the highest degree and best quality of knowledge workers are the fastest-growing companies – and the most profitable ones, too. Microsoft, for example, is one of the most profitable companies in history. Yet even that very successful firm focuses all of its attention on knowledge workers during the hiring process, and doesn't have any formal approach to improving their productivity and effectiveness after they are hired. I call this the HSPALTA approach – "hire smart people and leave them alone." We can do better.

But what exactly is a *knowledge worker*? When Drucker introduced the term, he defined a knowledge worker as "someone who knows more about his or her job than anyone else in the organization." Drucker was right that knowledge workers often understand their jobs better than others. However, this definition implies that there is only one knowledge worker per job category, which is neither true nor helpful. It also doesn't really address jobs with high knowledge content. For example, it would include taxi drivers, movie theater ticket takers, and ditch diggers. True, they might know more about their jobs than anyone else, but thinking is only a small part of what they do and is not its essence.

I employ the following definition instead: "Knowledge workers have high degrees of expertise, education, or experience, and the primary purpose of their jobs involves the creation, distribution, or application of knowledge." In short, *they think for a living*.

The fact that knowledge workers demand a new management style arises from the fact that they are different from traditional workers in a number of important ways. Let's consider several of these differences. First of all, it's obvious that *knowledge work is far less structured than production work*. You can't tell a knowledge worker to show up at 9 a.m., be creative for exactly eight hours, and then punch out. Further, the work process for knowledge work may be highly variable. Many knowledge workers will argue that there is no process to their work.

Because of the flexible and unpredictable nature of knowledge work, *knowledge workers don't like to be told what to do*. Since they think for a living, they also think for themselves. They have historically enjoyed a high degree of autonomy, and they don't want to give that up.

In addition, since there's no way of knowing what they're thinking, *it's impossible to tell if they're working or not*. Only when there is a tangible result in the end can you measure or value what's been done. So if a computer programmer says he's most productive from 8 p.m. to 4 a.m., an enlightened manager will make sure he is allowed to work those hours. Managers must remember that unlike workers of old, *knowledge workers own their means of production* – their brains – which they can take to another company.

However, just because knowledge workers prefer autonomy doesn't mean they should always be given the maximum amount of it. As we'll see, some efforts to improve performance may involve removing some discretion from the knowledge worker. Even so, it must be done with a light touch and a good, clear reason. Knowledge workers don't like to be told what to do, but *they like to be told what's going on.*

Another attribute of knowledge workers is that *they don't respond well to micro-management of their work process.* Specifying the detailed steps and flow of knowledge-intensive processes is less valuable, and more difficult, for these kinds of workers. You can't reduce their jobs to a series of boxes and arrows on a flow chart.

In most cases, *knowledge workers usually have good reason for doing what they do.* Ordinary process reengineering approaches to knowledge workers are likely to fail without very deep and serious study of what a knowledge worker is doing and how he or she is doing it. Unless the output of a knowledge worker is seriously deficient, the best approach is to assume that his or her processes are the right ones and to tinker with them only with great care.

Another major difference between knowledge workers and traditional workers is that employees could make a widget in a factory even if they hated their jobs, were uninspired, or just didn't care. This isn't the case for knowledge work: *commitment matters.* This has significant ramifications. For one thing, knowledge workers need some say in what they work on and how they do it. This is the idea behind the famous decision at 3M to give researchers 15 percent of their time to work independently on something they think is important. Google goes even further, giving engineers 20 percent of their time to pursue ideas they believe are important.

The last salient feature of knowledge workers is that *they value their knowledge and don't share it easily.* Knowledge is the source of their power and their value. It is the tool of their trade and their means of production. If they give it away, they could be giving away their jobs, too. This doesn't mean that you can't design an organization so that knowledge will flow where it's needed, but without rewards and guarantees, workers will be reluctant to share their knowledge.

The implication of all of these attributes is that knowledge workers simply can't be managed in the traditional sense. They can be led by visionary leaders who have the ability to inspire. Even when visionary leaders are in short supply, as we'll see, there are other ways to intervene and improve productivity. Now let's take a look at the different types of knowledge workers.

## How Knowledge Workers Differ from Each Other

Despite the traits they have in common, knowledge workers aren't all alike. For example, a computer programmer and a physician are both knowledge workers, but they have very different educational backgrounds, working conditions, business processes, and measures of success. Therefore, it's essential to classify knowledge workers so you can determine the best ways to manage, measure, and improve their productivity. Because you can't improve all knowledge workers at once, you need to segment them so you can target the highest-priority workers first.

Two ways to differentiate knowledge work are by the complexity of the work, and by the level of interdependence it involves:

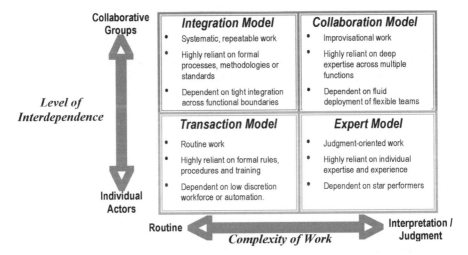

*Figure 1: Four Models of Knowledge Work*

The *complexity* of the work can range from routine jobs to those relying on interpretation and judgment. The *interdependence* can vary from jobs done alone to those requiring collaborative groups. The degree of collaboration often drives the degree of structure and computer mediation that is possible in a particular job. Likewise, the level of complexity of the work can dictate how much knowledge is required to perform successfully. By plotting these two dimensions on a simple matrix, we can identify four basic types of knowledge work:

1. *Transaction workers* have jobs that are low in complexity and interdependence. They do routine work using formal rules, procedures, and training, and they frequently work alone. People who work in call centers fit into this category.
2. *Integration workers* have jobs that are low in complexity but high in interdependence. They do systematic, repeatable work, and they rely on formal processes or standards. However, they depend on

integration across functional boundaries, so they need a greater
degree of collaboration. An example would be a low-level computer
programmer, whose programs must fit into a broader context of I/T
development work.

3. *Expert workers* have highly complex jobs that require little
   interdependence. They perform judgment-oriented work that relies
   on their individual expertise and experience. This kind of work is
   typified by a primary-care physician.

4. *Collaboration workers* have jobs that are high in complexity and
   interdependence. They perform improvisational tasks that rely on
   deep expertise across functions. Such a worker might be found
   in an investment bank, where fluid deployment of flexible teams
   is essential to the job. Examples might be investment bankers,
   consultants, or attorneys working on large teams.

Obviously, knowledge workers in these four categories respond
differently to attempts to increase productivity. For example, it might be
reasonable (albeit not very creative) to create a script for a transaction
worker to read to customers in a call center. However, work requiring more
judgment and collaboration would not benefit from such a script; you can't
script the legal and financial transactions of merger or acquisition work that
is performed by lawyers and investment bankers.

Integration work is often relatively structured, so it is sometimes possible
to capture and reuse knowledge assets. For example, some companies doing
software development will have programmers store their code in libraries
for others to use in future programs. However, this approach would not work
as well for experts or collaborative workers who don't deal with explicit
knowledge to that degree.

Because expert work is largely done by individuals, it is sometimes
possible to use a computer to mediate the work process and inject
organizational knowledge into it. Partners HealthCare System, for example,
has reduced drug errors by 55 percent by embedding knowledge about drugs
into a physician order entry system.[2] Even so, experts can be particularly
difficult subjects when it comes to using someone else's knowledge. For
examples, some physicians at hospitals other than Partners have refused to
use a knowledge-based order entry system.

Collaboration work is possibly the most difficult to improve in any
structured way because of its improvisational nature. This work is often
done by highly educated professionals who are very well-paid, so it is
particularly difficult to get them to do things in a new way that someone else

has prescribed. The typical types of interventions with these workers involve putting together teams, co-locating workers, or making more knowledge available to them in the form of repositories for voluntary use.

There are many other ways to distinguish among knowledge workers, including these five approaches:

1. *Segmenting by knowledge activity* – whether a group of knowledge workers find knowledge, create it, package it, distribute it, or apply it;
2. *Segmenting by the types of ideas with which they deal* – either big ideas for new products, business models, and strategic directions, or small ideas for minor improvements in what companies produce or how they work;
3. *Segmenting by cost and scale* –according to the amount of resources invested in the knowledge workers' compensation and the number of those workers within the organization;
4. *Segmenting by how critical the knowledge workers are to the business* – because some jobs are more important to the bottom line and to the execution of key strategies than others; and
5. *Segmenting by mobility* – according to whether knowledge workers stay in one place, or move around a lot. This approach is popular with technology-oriented companies such as Intel.

Once you've chosen the right segmentation strategy for your organization, you can decide which knowledge work jobs are most important to the company's strategy, and give them the highest priority for your efforts to improve their productivity. At Partners HealthCare, for example, the most important knowledge work process was judged to be patient care, and the most important workers for knowledge-based interventions were judged to be physicians.

## INTERVENTIONS, MEASURES, AND EXPERIMENTS

Peter Drucker once pointed out that we don't really consider productivity when it comes to what used to be called "white collar" workers, which we now call knowledge workers. He also called their work "grotesquely unproductive."[3] If that's true, anyone who can increase knowledge worker productivity will realize a substantial competitive advantage.

Companies are often well aware that some groups of knowledge workers are vastly more productive than others. For example, in one semiconductor company that I researched, a particular development group had a much higher rate of new product development while the products they developed were unusually successful. Unfortunately, the company didn't know why this group was so successful and haven't really attempted to identify the attributes or practices that might be used to spur the less productive groups.

Typically, groups of knowledge workers have been given a high degree of latitude and plenty of autonomy, largely because managers don't really know how workers do what they do or how to measure it. Consequently, managers can't come up with ideas for improving productivity. Moreover, the importance of knowledge workers in the company often shields them from interference.

Nevertheless, companies can't continue to take the productivity of knowledge work for granted, for it has become the key to success – not only for individual companies, but for entire economies. Just as agriculture and manufacturing jobs have moved around the globe to the countries with the lowest costs, so too will knowledge work; those who can do it best and cheapest will get the jobs. To stay ahead of that curve, managers must intervene, even where it is not traditional to do so.

What is needed, then, are powerful approaches to improving the performance of knowledge workers. Managers need to assess both the number and quality of the outputs produced. They need not only to accelerate knowledge work, but also to allow for the reflection and creative thinking that knowledge workers require to be effective. They need not only to improve the processes knowledge workers employ today, but to design entirely new ones that take advantage of technologies that didn't exist a decade ago.

Unlike the conventional notion of productivity, which typically involves the quantity of outputs divided by inputs, knowledge work has a distinct component of quality. *More* is not necessarily better. *Better* is better – in a strategic plan, a marketing campaign, or a new product design – and people pay more for it. Economists judge the value of outputs by how much the market will pay for them, but it's usually not enough to measure how much people will pay; too many different factors are involved. In addition, it is difficult to pin down exactly what defines output when it comes to knowledge work. Is a strategic plan an output? Is the idea for a merger an output?

The same problem of definition applies to inputs to knowledge work. A manager may receive the same salary whether he makes workers happy or miserable, but the results the company gets from the two will be quite different.

Therefore, perhaps a term such as "performance" or "results" would be more appropriate than "productivity" when it comes to knowledge workers. The key then is to develop some way of measuring performance and results. For example, asking a relevant peer group what they think of the work is traditional in science and is also used in evaluating professors for promotion and tenure. Problems of subjectivity in such evaluations are made up for by the number of responses. Even though this is not a precise measurement, it is the best tool available at this time. For an organization assessing the quality of an individual knowledge worker's contributions, it is important to solicit opinions from a wide variety of people and try to remove any sources of bias. For that reason, knowledge workers should maintain a network of people who know and respect the quality of their work.

## KNOWLEDGE WORK PROCESSES

A time-honored way of improving any form of work is to treat it as a process and then impose a formal structure on it, defining the steps and improving them, but knowledge workers often resist such attempts. They demand a more tailored approach, dictated by the demands of the matrix described earlier.

Each of the four types of knowledge workers will require a different approach to process improvement:

- *Transaction workers* need to understand the flow of their work and the knowledge needed to perform it, but they rarely have time to consult external guidelines or knowledge sources. Fortunately, it is often relatively easy to embed a process flow into some form of computer-based application, typically involving structured workflows or scripts. Such systems usually bring the world – and all information required to perform it – to the worker while measuring the process and worker productivity.
- *Integration workers* often use processes that can be articulated in documents, and workers typically have enough time and discretion to consult the documents. Medical technicians, for example, often follow health care protocols in administering tests and treatments.
- *Expert workers* are very autonomous, but some organizations have applied technology to key aspects of their work process, such as hospitals managing and measuring doctors as they order medications and tests. Instead of specifying the details of work flow,

the intervention should provide templates, sample outputs, and high-level guidelines.

- *Collaboration workers* represent the most difficult challenge in terms of process improvement. As with experts, a light touch is preferable. Specifying and measuring outputs, instilling a customer orientation, and fostering a sense of urgency are more likely to be successful than issuing flow charts.

No matter which approach you are taking, it is important to bear in mind that there is always a difference between *the process*, which is the plan or design for how the work is to be done, and *the practice*, which is the way the work is actually done.[4] Analyzing the process means focusing on the design, which is an abstraction from the actual work. In contrast, analyzing the practice is more like organizational anthropology or ethnography, because it describes *what people actually do* and requires detailed observation over long periods of time.

Focusing on the desired process alone is unlikely to succeed. To successfully change knowledge work, you need a delicate interplay of process and practice. Here are six guidelines for getting that done:

- *First, involve the knowledge workers in the design of the new process.* Ask them what they would like to see changed, and what is stopping them from being more effective and efficient.
- *Second, watch them do their work.* It often takes a few weeks to understand the flow, rationale, and variations in the actual practice.
- *Third, talk to knowledge workers about why they do the things they do.* Don't assume you know a better way before detailed investigation – and even then, be conservative about recommendations.
- *Fourth, enlist analysts who have actually done the work.* If you are trying to design new health care processes, use doctors and nurses to design them.
- *Fifth, treat experienced workers as the experts they are.* Assure them that your goal is to make their lives better.
- *Sixth, use the Golden Rule.* Ask yourself if you would want to have your job analyzed and redesigned in the way you are doing so for someone else.

In an ideal situation, knowledge work processes can create a climate in which participative approaches to innovation and discipline co-exist. Let us take a look at how information technologies can help make this a reality.

# ORGANIZATIONAL TECHNOLOGY FOR KNOWLEDGE WORKERS

As anyone who has used technology knows that it is always a double-edged sword. Does technology improve performance, or create more work? Sometimes it is hard to tell. However, from an organizational standpoint, technologies can be used to enhance knowledge work if applied judiciously while considering the different requirements across the matrix.

For example, technologies can automate structured transactions.[5] A call center system that brings calls, along with the relevant information, to a worker is a logical use of technology. Another example lies in product development: engineers may have their work structured by a product lifecycle management (PLM) system that keeps track of designs, components, and approvals. Furthermore, their productivity can be improved with systems for capturing and reusing knowledge, such as design drawings. Even with such technologies, successful reuse isn't likely to happen without clear leadership, visibility of available content assets, and maintenance of high asset quality.

Decision automation is another kind of technology suited for work with middle levels of structure and expertise, such as insurance underwriting and bank credit extension. With jobs that are completely expert, the goal is to find some way of having a computer mediate the work, not fully control it in order to take advantage of both the technology and the expert knowledge. Embedding knowledge in the flow of work and using data mining and decision analysis is an example.

For collaboration workers, the only types of tools that typically work for such complex, inter-related jobs are knowledge repositories and various types of collaboration aids, which are used voluntarily.

The most vexing part of employing any of these technologies is that success is determined not by how good any given technology is, but by how people use it and how it fits the requirements of the job. For example, under the banner of "knowledge management," many organizations have created knowledge repositories, but few workers have the time needed to browse and learn from them. Likewise, embedding knowledge into the flow of the job is a very good idea but extremely difficult to implement well.

In short, organizations need to strike a balance with new technologies for knowledge workers. Organizations must experiment to uncover the potential of each tool for enhancing performance and assess each tool for concrete business results. What's the value? How should improved performance be measured? Is the payoff equal to the cost, not just in hardware and software but in the time it takes to learn, tinker with, and fix the technology? Knowledge worker technology has sometimes gotten a free pass with regard to its value and return, but just because the value is difficult to measure it should still be assessed. Learning and using new technologies is labor-intensive: understanding their value and performance payoff is even more so.

# TECHNOLOGY FOR INDIVIDUAL KNOWLEDGE WORKERS

The problems – and benefits – of technology become even more complex when applied at the individual level. Workers may have many devices and software tools at their disposal, but are they using them efficiently? Are workers getting the most out of these tools? The answer is no, in most cases. There is vast room for improvement in how knowledge workers use their personal technology. The first problem is: How do you find out what employees are really doing so you can help them improve?

To find answers to this question, the Information Work Productivity Council (now called the Institute for Innovation and Information Productivity) funded a number of research projects on personal information and knowledge management in 2003.[6] The Council is a consortium of technology and I/T services vendors whose researchers realized that knowledge workers were spending larger and larger amounts of their time messaging, creating documents, searching for knowledge, and performing other information-intensive activities. In addition, employees had been doing this work without any advice or help from the organization for the most part. Although employees were working with PCs, laptops, cell phones, PDAs, and Blackberries, few knew how to use them effectively. These personal information issues are now coming to the fore, and companies are seeing that they need to take a hand in improving the way their knowledge workers use technology.

Cisco Systems, for example, has begun a program for employees in which it recommends a set of technologies, trains people to use them, and also recommends various changes to help people use the technologies more effectively.

My own IWPC-sponsored research on this subject found some surprising trends.[7] The average user spent three hours and 14 minutes a day using technologies to process work-related information, about 40 percent of a regular workday. Two hours were devoted to e-mail, or 20 percent of the workday, which involved sending 17 e-mails and receiving 44 each day.

Telephone and voice mail took up another 47 minutes. If anything, things have gotten worse since 2003 in this regard.

In short, companies are paying a lot of money to employees to use these technologies. Yet 41 percent of those surveyed said they received little or no help from their organizations with personal information management. Only 3 percent felt their company had mastered the problem. Roughly a quarter of respondents felt overwhelmed by the amount of information they dealt with at work.

To find out how those people who had mastered the personal information environment did it, I conducted a separate survey of 12 leading individual users and found 10 common attributes:

1. *They avoid gadgets.* They find a few key tools and stick with them. They tend to be very conservative in adopting new tools.
2. *They limit the number of devices they use.* One individual does everything on his laptop, another uses Treo –a cell phone and PDA combination.
3. *They invest effort in organizing information.* For example, they devote a couple of hours a week to prioritize a "to do" list, or to organize files and folders.
4. *They aren't missionaries.* They don't advertise their skills or try to convert others to information management. They just do it.
5. *They get help.* They read manuals, call support people, and search the Internet to make the best use of their tools.
6. *They use assistants–but also stay involved.* Most people interviewed have secretaries, and they let them do some of the work: scheduling meetings, confirming, making travel arrangements, and taking care of some communications.
7. *They haven't gone fully electronic.* Most of them still use paper calendars, or print out paper copies of electronic calendars.
8. *They decide what information is most important to them and organize it well.* A professor, for example, has on-line folders for every article or book he's written. A venture capitalist had spreadsheets that summarized the financial situations of all the companies he is involved in. Each individual works on what matters most.
9. *They use lists.* They keep lists of appointments, things to do, contacts, books to read, and so on.
10. *They adapt the use of tools and approaches to the work situation.* One respondent didn't like instant messages and didn't use them.

When she was posted to Prague, however, IM became an integral part of her information management strategy.

The area of personal information management is obviously a new one that will remain in transition for some time to come. There are great opportunities here for unleashing unheard-of performance from knowledge workers who are true masters of individually-focused tools and applications. Companies that get it and help those workers will reap huge competitive advantages.

## INVESTING IN KNOWLEDGE WORKER EDUCATION AND NETWORKS

Technological interventions into knowledge work can be useful, but high-performing knowledge workers say they get most of their valuable information from other people in their social networks. In fact, based on a study I conducted with Rob Cross of the University of Virginia and Sue Cantrell of Accenture, high performers across the four firms we studied have stronger and more diverse networks of relationships than others.[8] High performers are more likely to have ties to distant locations of the organization, reaching up into the hierarchy, as well as having ties to employees with more tenure. They are keenly aware of where the expertise around them lies and can quickly reach out and tap into it when new opportunities or problems arise. In turn, others are aware of the skills of these high performers.

High performers also maintain extensive networks outside the organization. They are more likely to maintain and leverage more relationships than average, reaching both outside their own departments and outside the company itself. Finally, high performers invest more time in developing and maintaining these relationships. While maintaining a level of expertise and utilizing technical resources does improve the performance of knowledge workers, the distinguishing features for the highest performers are those larger and more diversified networks, which allow them to move into action swiftly.

High performers did not necessarily have better education than others, nor are they smarter. Instead, they are effective experiential learners. They tend to learn a more diverse range of skills and get more out of a given experience. They are, in short, *learning all the time.*

High performers tend to have unusual and sometime illogical career paths. However, these different jobs provide them with unique perspectives on problems. Those lateral jobs, in turn, help build the diverse networks that can be leveraged as needed.

Ultimately, these personal networks serve to distinguish high performers most of all. These workers are rarely political networkers or career climbers, rather, they find that by connecting well with others, they get the work done, which is sufficient for advancement. The relationships are important to business, but there is an added element – something in common, whether it be family, background, hobbies, or experiences – that enhances all the contacts with that person. The high performers often said that they had strong friendship networks that overlapped with their business networks.

Almost all high performers are very quick to respond to requests from others. They believe that follow-through is very important. They are people whom others can rely on, and they keep their word. They don't just use other people; they offer help in return or even volunteer information proactively.

Obviously, managers who can facilitate and support these networks and the flow of information through them are likely to see higher levels of productivity from their knowledge workers. By advocating experiential learning, managers can increase a knowledge worker's palette of skills.

Carefully chosen information technology can enhance both networks and the flow of information in them, but clearly, more resources need to be directed toward investment in practices that nurture social networks and human capital.

## THE KNOWLEDGE WORKPLACE

Another factor that affects knowledge worker performance is the physical environment in which the work is performed. Unfortunately, not much is known about the subject. To fill this vacuum, a number of researchers have begun to come up with some hard findings to counter various fads in office design.[9] While far from comprehensive, they provide a tantalizing glimpse of what might be learned through systematic research into the topic. Here are some of the most recent findings:

- *Knowledge workers prefer closed offices but seem to communicate better in open ones.* In other words, when people need focused concentration to get their jobs done, a closed office is preferable. When communication and interaction are critical, an open-plan office works better.

- *Knowledge workers congregate in particular geographical areas.* For example, people involved with information technology gravitate toward living and working in places like Silicon Valley, Boston, and Austin. As a result, they are more productive because they are around other likeminded knowledge workers.
- *Knowledge workers move around in the course of their work.* They spend a lot of time out of the office. That means that companies need to equip and train them for being productive while mobile.
- *Knowledge workers collaborate.* The best office environments include a variety of spaces, technologies, and facilitation approaches for an array of collaborative purposes.
- *Knowledge workers concentrate.* In other words, in addition to collaborative spaces, they need private space as well. A completely open office structure leaves out half of the productivity equation.
- *Knowledge workers work in the office.* Despite the hype about telecommuting, 95 percent of knowledge workers – and even higher percentages outside the U.S. – do their serious work in the office. They recognize the need to be present to share information, absorb tacit knowledge, and to build social capital. Allowing workers to work at home is fine, but it should be occasional, and workers must feel at home at the office as well.
- *Knowledge workers communicate with people who are close by.* In one study, knowledge workers whose desks were more than 30 meters apart had zero communication. Knowledge workers who need to communicate need to be positioned close to each other.
- *Knowledge workers don't care about perks in facilities.* Features like foosball, cappuccino bars, conversation pits, and nap rooms have no measurable influence on knowledge worker performance. In fact, many workers will shun them for fear of not seeming serious about the job.

Managers should know a lot more about the impact of the work space on knowledge workers, but they don't. There are numerous experiments under way, however, that might shed some light on this subject. At SEI Investments, for example, all dividers were torn down to create a big open room and encourage people to communicate more freely. Monsanto also attempted to do away with private offices to reduce hierarchy and increase communication. But what real effect are these efforts having? To gain the true benefit of these experiments, they need to be conducted more rigorously, if not scientifically. They need to include measures, controls, hypotheses, and documentation of lessons learned.

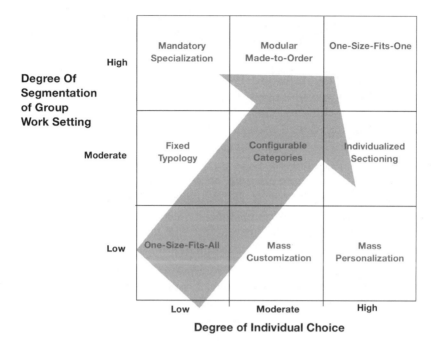

Degree Of
Segmentation
of Group
Work Setting

**Figure 2:** *Designing Knowledge Workspaces*

One of the factors holding back this kind of learning is that workspace changes often require many other kinds of changes as well, making it difficult to isolate cause and effect. The most effective implementations include changes in management and culture, information technology, and physical workspace. Cisco Systems, for example, formed a cross-functional task force to develop an integrated workspace strategy. Once the task force had identified common goals, representatives from each function made presentations to the group. The facilities unit described how Cisco's knowledge workers were already using the existing office space. An I/T staff member previewed the technologies expected to be available in the near future while an HR representative described the characteristics of Cisco's workforce. Gradually, the task force developed a unified vision of the future work environment the firm needed to create. That sort of directed analysis can go a long way toward improving the synergy between environment and productivity.

In considering workspace changes, it is important to take into consideration the degree of segmentation in the group work setting, as well as the degree of individual choice granted to knowledge workers to tailor that setting to their own needs: *transaction workers*, such as those in call centers, need work environments in which they can focus on their transactions; *integration workers* need an ability to communicate easily with co-workers; *expert workers* need the ability to concentrate. These different knowledge work activities would dictate different work environments.

As either the degree of segmentation increases or the degree of fit between worker and work setting increases, the number and variety of work settings within an organization will increase. The most traditional arrangement is seen in firms with a *low degree of segmentation* which provide one standard work setting for all employees.

Firms with a *moderate degree of segmentation* fit employees into a limited number of categories with a predefined setting for each. For example, firms may segment employees by status, geography, or job role, taking into account mobility, amount of teamwork required, number of projects undertaken at one time, or the amount of communication needed. For example, Merrill Lynch segments knowledge workers by job role, such as portfolio managers, traders, and I/T professionals, providing each a different type of workspace. One telecommunications firm employs three different types of engineers: "parachutists," who drop into projects for a short time; "ambassadors," who represent the company to the outside world; and those who perform heads-down, concentrated work on one project at a time. Each type of engineer works in a different type of work environment.

Firms with a *high degree of segmentation* face a more challenging problem. Fidelity Investments, for example, has external consultants who approach each group independently, analyze the work patterns and processes, and then create custom-tailored solutions specific to that group. This approach is obviously ideal if done well, but it is also expensive.

Cost is also a factor in how much choice employees are given about their work environment. Along this axis, there are also three levels: low-choice, medium-choice, and high-choice. Some organizations allow their employees *little or no choice* about changing or designing the work environment. The one-size-fits-all theory is the least expensive – if not the most inspiring – approach. For example, Hewlett-Packard has developed what it calls "a common operating environment" to minimize purchase and support costs.

Other firms offer a *medium level of choice* through a predefined set of solutions. Sun Microsystems, for example, provides its knowledge workers with a menu of physical work environments, such as private offices, shared team rooms, satellite centers, and home offices.

At the opposite end of the scale, some firms allow workers a *high degree of choice* to determine their own work settings. The design firm IDEO, for example, is famous for its radical office design and allows workers to bring in objects with interesting designs from surfboards to their own pets.

Whatever a company's particular decision turns out to be in terms of environment, there is no doubt that many knowledge workspace decisions will continue to be based on less-than-rigorous criteria and that cost will remain a very important factor. However, there is evidence that the physical workspace matters to knowledge worker performance, and managers need to do a better job of housing their most important and expensive personnel.

## MANAGING KNOWLEDGE WORKERS

How should knowledge workers be managed in order to extract the highest possible level of performance and results? Does management even have a role in knowledge work? The idea of managing the work of others was appropriate for the Industrial Age, but some individuals would suggest that it is no longer necessary in an era of self-motivated knowledge workers.

However, there is an important role for managers in overseeing knowledge work and workers. It is a different role than managers performed in the past, so management itself will have to change, in some cases dramatically. Because knowledge is an invisible asset that resides largely in the minds of human beings, management can no longer closely observe and monitor the progress of work. Because knowledge work is done by managers as well as workers, strict separation between them is no longer possible. Because knowledge work has become the key to growth and differentiation in today's economy, the differential in cost and value between knowledge work and management has decreased.

Given these important background factors, managers in the future will have to adapt their activities to the new world they will face by changing in at least eight ways:

1. from overseeing work to *doing work*,
2. from organizing hierarchies to *organizing communities*,
3. from hiring and firing employees to *recruiting and retaining workers*,
4. from building manual skills to *building knowledge skills*,
5. from evaluating visible job performance to *assessing invisible knowledge achievements*,
6. from ignoring culture to *building a knowledge-friendly culture*,
7. from supporting the bureaucracy to *fending off the bureaucracy*, and
8. from relying on internal personnel to *considering a variety of sources*.

These are the new priorities of management. Achieving them will demand a new breed of manager, one who can manage not only the knowledge workers but the conflicts involved in balancing creativity and autonomy with bureaucracy. Such managers, who must also be knowledge workers themselves, will likely rise through the ranks and form their own new culture of knowledge work management, they will have the ability to keep knowledge workers informed of the big picture, and they will be able to manage and learn from dissent while orchestrating group decisions.

Knowledge workers are sophisticated and want to do a good job. The new breed of manager will be able to harness that good intent and make it work to align projects with corporation direction. These managers will be comfortable with a new kind of corporate geography, in which knowledge workers can span traditional boundaries – both physical and organizational – to feed their insatiable curiosity and experiential learning. Finally, these managers will be great facilitators of the social networks that characterize the best performers.

In short, as knowledge work becomes the primary work of the organization, management and managers will continue to exist, if not necessarily in recognizable form. The old model of the manager who sits in an office staring down at the toiling workers is officially obsolete. The new managers appear suspiciously like the knowledge workers themselves: they work like knowledge workers, but they also find and recruit them, create a positive communal environment for them, and remove obstacles to their creative and productive activity.

In the meantime, companies must measure and learn from experiments in the domains of management, technology, physical workspace, and other factors that influence knowledge work performance. Improving knowledge worker performance promises to be the most important factor in global competitive advantage going forward. Countries whose knowledge workers are not highly productive will lose jobs to other parts of the world, where knowledge workers are paid less to do more.

Peter Drucker wasn't exaggerating when he said that the fate of advanced economies depends on making knowledge workers more productive. There is no business or economic issue that is more important to every company's long-term competitiveness and to the standard of living of every economy.

# ENDNOTES

1    Drucker, Peter. *Landmarks of tomorrow.* Harper: 1959.
2    Bates, David W. Computerized physician order entry and medication errors: finding a balance. *Journal of Biomedical Informatics. 2005 Aug;38(4):259-61.*

3   Drucker, Peter quoted in Brent Schlender, Peter Drucker Sets Us Straight, *Fortune*, Dec. 29, 2003.

4   Seely Brown, John and Paul Duguid, *The social life of information*. Harvard Business School Press: 2000.

5   Davenport, Thomas H. and Jeanne G. Harris. Automated decision-making comes of age. *MIT Sloan Management Review*, Summer 2005, 46:4, 83-89.

6   Davenport, Thomas H. Decoding information worker productivity. *Optimize*, April 2004. Online at http://www.optimizemag.com/article/showArticle.jhtml?articleId=1 8600441.

7   Davenport, Thomas H. *Thinking for a living*. Harvard Business School Press: 2005.

8   Davenport, Thomas H., Cross, R., and Cantrell, S. The social side of performance. *MIT Sloan Management Review*, Fall 2003.

9   Becker, Frank and Sims, W. *Offices that work: balancing cost, flexibility, and communication*. Cornell University International Workplace Studies Program (IWSP): 2000.

# 3.3

# PROTECTING CORPORATE REPUTATION IN AN ERA OF INSTANT TRANSPARENCY

**Herbert Heitmann,** *SVP, SAP Global Communications,*
**Brian Lott,** *Managing Director, Burson-Marsteller*

## WHAT IS CORPORATE REPUTATION AND WHY IS IT IMPORTANT?

Your company's reputation can be a valuable asset in facing some of its greatest business challenges: a good reputation on Wall Street and in the global markets can buffer a stock decline in the face of a soft quarter; a good reputation among customers can grow business in lean times; and a good reputation among employees can help you attract and retain the best talent in the industry.

Similar to any tangible asset, it is important to strengthen your corporate reputation and protect it from a competitor's attack, unforeseen crises, or even slow erosion due to neglect.

Communications professionals have been developing the practice of reputation management for decades; however, in the last five to 10 years, protecting corporate reputation has become far more complex with the increase of communications platforms that allow news of a company's foibles or shortfalls to spread instantly around the globe. The invisible wall that once guarded your company's information from media, investors, partners, employees, and customers has become far more permeable, making your organization's reputation more vulnerable and difficult to protect.

## Who Defines Corporate Reputation?

Many groups help to define your company's reputation, but the process begins with the company itself. As a leader of an organization, at some point you must literally take the initiative to define and describe your company, whether on a website, in collateral materials, in speeches, or in presentations.

In addition, many other groups contribute to perceptions of your company's reputation, including industry peers, employees, customers, and those whose job it is to "judge" the company, such as journalists, analysts, regulators, and public officials. Each of these groups forms impressions based on the advertising and corporate materials they digest as well as outside opinions and their own experiences of interacting with your organization. For decades, the most influential filter of public perception has been the media, and the media continue to heavily influence what people think of companies today.

One of the interesting challenges of corporate reputation management is that each constituency has its own set of standards by which it measures your company. Some individuals might base their impressions of the company on profitability and the predictability of growth. Others will evaluate the company by its level of corporate social responsibility or its level of integrity, transparency, and immediacy in communications. Thus, the complexity of managing reputation grows as you take into account each of the publics the organization faces.

When engaging in a discussion about corporation reputation, it is important to examine how those publics form their impressions. Companies that can identify *where* individuals are getting information and *how* they are influencing others have greater insight – and thus considerable leverage – in strengthening and protecting reputation.

## The Value of Reputation to Your Business

A good deal of research has been conducted on corporation reputation and how it impacts a company's success. The World Economic Forum has reported that 59 percent of "influentials" – CEOs, senior executives, financial analysts, business media, and government officials in 65 countries – believe that a company's market capitalization is represented by reputation.

A study by Burson-Marsteller also found that consumers and business influentials alike are more likely to support a company with a good reputation.[1] In fact, companies with a good reputation are:

- Seven times more likely to have customers buy their products or services at a premium price

- Five times more likely to have their stock recommended
- Four times more likely to be recommended as a good place to work
- Three times more likely to be recommended as a good joint venture partner
- 1.5 times more likely to receive the benefit of the doubt

## Role of the CEO in Corporate Reputation

A key contributor to overall corporate reputation is the CEO. Through its "Building CEO Capital™" study, researchers at Burson-Marsteller have measured the degree to which CEO reputation affects corporate reputation. According to the firm's fifth study on this topic, nearly 50 percent of corporate reputation is linked to the CEO, and credibility is the number one driver of CEO reputation.[2] Stories of CEO departures and corporate malfeasance are headline-making news worldwide. Thus, with the spotlight on CEOs shining more intensely each quarter, CEOs need to better understand the inextricable link between their reputations and company reputations.

## Global Communications as Strategic Reputation Gatekeeper

Four out of the five biggest influencers of corporate reputation are derived from perceptions of the corporate brand, underscoring the importance of communications and perception management in protecting corporate reputation. The factors with the biggest impact on corporate reputation are:

- Competitive financial performance
- Reputation of CEO and C-suite
- Quality of products and services, reputation for innovation
- Employee alignment
- Responsibility to community/environment

With such a heavy emphasis on brand perception, the bulk of corporate reputation management falls to the global communications team, which much be versed in a number of practices to successfully keep a corporation's reputation intact.

This is especially true in the midst of a crisis. Handled poorly, a crisis can devastate a company's reputation in terms of its profitability, credibility, competitive position, and ability to retain and attract top performers. On the flip side, a communications team that handles a crisis well has the opportunity to strengthen its company's trust with the public. The recent JetBlue crisis is a good example.

## JetBlue Airlines Strands Thousands

On February 14, 2007, JetBlue Airways experienced one of the largest weather delays in the history of the airline industry. Icy conditions at John F. Kennedy International Airport, combined with internal communications mishaps at the airline, led to the mass cancellation of 1,096 flights and stranded thousands of customers at airports, terminals, and for some, in the planes themselves.

Four months later, public opinion was almost completely restored in the airline, a significant turnaround after the massive public outcry. Crisis experts and corporate reputation specialists almost universally credit JetBlue CEO David Neeleman for essentially saving the airline's name and business future. Neeleman's first step as events worsened was to step up – literally. Where other executives and CEOs have shied away or actually hidden from the media during crisis, Neeleman recognized and embraced his unique and influential position to win back the public's trust.

On the morning of Tuesday, February 20, 2007 alone – six days after the crisis itself – Neelman appeared on CNN's American Morning, CBS's Today, Fox & Friends and CNBC's Squawk Box. That same week he was interviewed by David Letterman and had a customer Bill of Rights up and running on the JetBlue website, which pledged to customers that in the future, their voices would be heard and concerns addressed by the airline itself, outside of any action forced or recommended by federal regulators.

While the numerous errors of the 14th were hard to excuse, Neelman made himself a household name within days by appearing open, honest, and, perhaps most importantly, apologetic about JetBlue's actions and service.

The role of global communications is to be constantly sensitive to where a company's reputation resides within public opinion; the team's ability to do this has to develop dramatically, as it keeps its finger on that pulse not yearly or monthly but in some cases hourly. With the advent of new communications tools, people are not only making snap judgments about your company and its brand but telling it to anyone who will listen. A proficient global communications team must have the right talent and tools to measure corporate reputation and sense how actions may influence reactions to the company and its brand.

# THE ERA OF GLOBAL TRANSPARENCY

## From Print to Digital to "instant" Information

Fifty years ago, companies had to worry less about the immediacy of their communication, which consisted largely of typewritten letters and memos that had to be mailed or, in the case of emergency, couriered to their recipients. In fact, as of 50 years ago, the nature of written communications had not changed too dramatically since the days of John and Abigail Adams, who corresponded on personal and political matters alike during the infancy of the United States.

## The Adams' Early Correspondence and Communications

John and Abigail Adams have a legacy as the most iconic couple during the early years of the United States, marked by their loving union of passion, friendship, and a profound mutual respect. The enterprising lawyer and the minister's daughter wed in 1764, and though Abigail Adams was never formally educated, she was well read; John Adams considered her his intellectual equal, so much that he counted on her sage advice to guide him in the creation of the United States of America.

John Adams's position as a lawyer, member of the Continental Congress, diplomat, and eventually president of the United States frequently called him away from his home with Abigail and their children in the Massachusetts countryside. In the years between 1778 and 1784, for example, the couple spent only three months together, and so throughout their 54-year marriage they relied heavily on correspondence to maintain their close relationship. As John Adams traveled, first throughout New England and later Europe, the two wrote a combined 1,100 letters back and forth discussing everything from the health of their children to what should be included in the Constitution. Letters could often take weeks or months to reach their destination, occasionally arriving together or after Adams had moved on to another city or even country, as was the case when he traveled throughout Europe.

Though the days, weeks, and often months between letters were tedious, it did make their writing all the more rich and descriptive, as events culminated much faster than the early postal service operated. The letters, which have been compiled into numerous books and anthologies, are widely read for an intimate portrait of the early United States, and are an excellent example of how communications have changed in the more than 200 years since the final letters were written. Today, handwriting and paper have been replaced by typed characters on a computer screen, and in the space of moments rather than months today's news can be conveyed.

The story of the Adams family is in stark contrast to today's environment. In the absence of lag time, communicators are now often stuck in a never-ending spiral of reaction to the day's latest news, feeling the pull to respond immediately in a fashion that often lacks the kind of thoughtfulness, insight and wisdom that marked the correspondence of the past.

## The Clock Never Stops, Anywhere in the World

To see how modern communications differs from even 25 years ago, we can use a PR crisis as an example. Let's examine the role of senior communications executives of a food and beverage company with manufacturing and distribution facilities around the globe. One morning, at 7:52 a.m. in Mumbai, a worker dispute breaks out. If the dispute happened 20 years ago, executives from the company's headquarters in Boston (11:22 p.m. local time) would have already nodded off to sleep.

The next morning, they would awaken to find a fax from an executive in Mumbai, requesting direction on how to handle the situation. As they received calls from the media, which also received faxes from reporting affiliates in India, the executives would make known their intention to issue a formal press statement at 11:00 a.m. followed by a question-and-answer opportunity. The morning would be spent in preparation. At the press conference, the management would outline the situation as well as intended next steps and reporters would write and file stories in time for the evening news or the morning papers.

In today's world, if a worker walkout happened at 7:52 a.m. in Mumbai, at 7:53 a.m. in Mumbai a reporter could pick up the news and post his story by 8:30 a.m., which would be 2:00 a.m. in Boston and 11:00 p.m. on the West Coast. Overnight, reporters from Europe would pick up the thread and then post their stories. If the communications executives did not receive calls from reporters overnight, they would awaken the next morning to a rude surprise: substantial coverage from dozens of news organizations, using only the workers' account of the incident.

Knowing that a lack of response would likely be interpreted as insensitive or a sign of incompetence, they would spend the early morning hours placing calls and sifting through e-mails to determine what actually happened in Mumbai and then contacting news organizations to correct stories that had been posted overnight.

In today's scenario, it wouldn't be unheard of to receive a phone call from a reporter asking questions about an incident that senior management is not aware of, much less armed with information with which to respond.

There are few companies these days that don't have a stake in some part of the world in which their corporate behavior can impact their reputation. So, given the fact that online media is accessible everywhere in the world in an instant, you now face a much more significant threat level to your reputation than ever before.

## Blogs, Networks, Message Boards, and Chat Rooms

As if the need for immediate response were not enough, today's companies are faced with the need to monitor a rapidly proliferating number of communications platforms. Twenty years ago, one had to keep tabs on 10 to 15 news outlets. Today, while companies are busy monitoring the *Wall Street Journal,* CNN, and the BBC, hundreds of messages may be flying around on blogs, chat rooms, and message boards saying who knows what about an organization and the worker dispute in Mumbai.

At first glance you might seek some comfort in the thought that well, that's just someone's blog – readership is miniscule compared to the millions who read *the Financial Times.* Yet even this is changing, as blogs increasingly source news stories.

## The Impact of Blogs on Journalism

Blogs emerged in the late 1990s as web journals where anyone, from a well respected journalist to the average citizen with an internet connection, could post anything of choice. The number of bloggers has exploded since those early days, from 50 known blogs in 1999 to more than 100,000 known blogs today. As the number of blogs has increased, the influence of blogs and bloggers has become profoundly greater.

Since bloggers don't have an editor to answer to – or fact checkers to ensure the legitimacy of their comments – their views can be posted in real time. Robert Niles, editor of the *Online Journalism Review* has remarked that the Web basically cuts the middleman out of the picture and allows anyone to get their story out to a global audience immediately. Later, journalists can follow up on the initial blogs or find first-person witnesses to draw out more details, allowing the whole newsgathering process to evolve much more quickly.

Perhaps feeling the pressure, many journalists turn to blogs for story ideas that they can magnify to a larger audience. In a study conducted by Colombia University and Euro RSCG Magnet, 51 percent of journalists were found to use blogs regularly, compared to 11 percent of the general population. Twenty-eight percent of journalists say they use blogs in day-to-day reporting.

Recently, SAP encountered a situation in which a journalist inaccurately reported an executive's comments to a lunch gathering. Before the afternoon was over, the inaccurate coverage had spread throughout the blogosphere. Fortunately, a member of the communications staff had taped the executive's comments and posted the entire speech as a podcast to set the record straight. This started a new wave of discussion – which included posts on the executive's blog – that evolved into a dialogue between the executive, journalists, and bloggers. What started as a potential threat to SAP's reputation turned into an opportunity to open up a discussion on an important topic.

## How Communications Stakeholders Have Changed

As with blogs, new technologies and communications channels are emerging daily, and it is becoming increasingly difficult to locate where stakeholders such as investors, customers, partners, and employees are receiving their information on products and the brand. This has presented an enormous learning curve for communications professionals, who must move beyond traditional media and investor relations tools to understand and evaluate new sources of influence on corporation reputation.

# THE CHANGING ROLE OF COMMUNICATIONS

## From the Annex to the Executive Suite

Years ago the role of the communications department was very discrete. When a product division or an executive needed a press release or a speech written, they would contact the communications department. In some cases the "communications department" would simply *be* a speechwriter plus an additional colleague who communicated to the financial markets.

Over the past several years, the role of the communications professional has evolved as executive management has begun to recognize the importance of corporate reputation as one of its most important assets. In today's companies you will often find communications executives report adjacent to, if not directly to, the CEO. Communications is no longer a small, isolated task within the company but hard-wired into the C-suite.

SAP has had a history of including communications counsel at the executive level, a strategy that paid off during its transition of CEOs in 2003.

## CEO Transition – a Smooth Succession Repositions Leadership

Founded in 1972 in Walldorf, Germany, SAP is the world's largest inter-enterprise software company, and the third-largest independent software supplier. Beginning in 1998, SAP co-founder Hasso Plattner shared the

CEO role with Henning Kagermann with plans for a transition to a single CEO (Kagermann) in 2004.

In the early years of his tenure as co-CEO, Henning Kagermann was characterized as a "cerebral" leader and SAP's management team remained relatively unknown. The SAP Global Communications Team recognized that in order to preserve SAP's reputation and competitive stance, it would need to raise Kagermann's profile significantly and reassure global audiences that Plattner's departure from day-to-day operations would not throw SAP off course when the transition came to fruition. At a time in which CEOs were being scrutinized because of corporate scandals and a major overhaul of German corporate governance regulations and U.S. SEC laws was taking place, the communications team realized a smooth CEO transition was critical.

SAP engaged with its partner Burson-Marsteller to ensure a smooth transition from two CEOs to one by raising Kagermann's visibility globally while maintaining Plattner's legacy. The goal was to demonstrate the stability and depth of the entire top management team and establish Kagermann's leadership agenda and vision for SAP during his critical first 100 days as sole CEO.

The Burson-Marsteller team conducted and leveraged extensive research on the role of the CEO and the impact of CEO transition on corporate reputation to understand the impacts and outcomes of both successful and unsuccessful efforts.

SAP and Burson-Marsteller then developed a strategy which included:

- Creating comprehensive communications plans tailored to the specifics of SAP's CEO transition, and creating a fact-based timeline for change
- Leveraging Burson-Marsteller research results to position plans and thought leadership platforms, and obtaining buy-in and support from both co-CEOs and SAP's top management team
- Developing CEO Kagermann's critical "100 Day" plan
- Establishing metrics for success

After initial outreach, SAP continued to focus on Kagermann's strong leadership for over 12 months, placing profiles for maximum effect and carefully repositioning Kagermann as the lead on key announcements and at major customer and employee events. Consistent messages and ongoing activities demonstrated stability in SAP's leadership.

The transition came one year before originally anticipated, but the work SAP Global Communications had done to build Kagermann's reputation in the community paid off. The detailed advance planning by the SAP/Burson-Marsteller team made it possible to readily accommodate the accelerated transition.

During the transition, the company's financial performance and stock price remained steady, and key performance metrics increased as follows:

- SAP's global market share increased to over 51 percent;
- The company's market share is now more than that of its next five largest competitors combined;
- The fourth quarter of 2002 saw SAP achieve the best earnings in its 30-year history;
- Results of SAP surveys indicate increased customer satisfaction – especially in the U.S. SAP's more than 10 percent increase in market share from 2001 to 2002 bears this out.
- The German business magazine, *Focus Money,* honored SAP with its 2002 Company of the Year award – with top grades for "Strong Income."

Despite premature speculation about Plattner's retirement, the actual news of his departure had no negative impact on the business, and key audiences were comfortable with the transition. Media coverage reflected messages about Plattner's legacy and the positive reaction to Kagermann, while analysts agreed that Kagermann was the right person to lead SAP. Profiles of Kagermann appeared months ahead of the transition in *The Economist, The Financial Times, The Financial Times Deutschland,* and in other media in Germany, China, and wherever he traveled. Kagermann's speaking engagements doubled, including top global/technology events such as the World Economic Forum and PC Forum.[3]

Within weeks of his transition, Kagermann was recognized as a leading technology CEO in *The Economist* technology review, which observed that "the tone in the industry may no longer be set by people such as [Oracle CEO] Mr. Ellison, but by more prudent and cerebral chief executives, such as SAP's Henning Kagermann.[4]" Kagermann was also named "one of the most highly regarded CEOs," in a survey of fund managers by *Institutional Investor.[5]*

One of the great accomplishments of the CEO transition was the fact that SAP Global Communications started early, aligning with the executive board and the Supervisory Board and identifying that Henning Kagermann was the most likely candidate to succeed Hasso Plattner. This gave the team time to develop a plan to position Kagermann as not just the co-CEO but someone who was ready to fully take the reigns and the responsibility of the position.

In 2002, SAP Global Communications began its evolution from a fragmented communications organization that focused largely on product public relations and media relations to a more integrated team that focused on a broader range of constituencies with a more strategic and proactive approach. At this point, the organization also began to globalize its communications activities and integrated several of its country-specific communications teams into a global unit, allowing for seamless communication globally of the CEO transition.

## Incoming Versus Outgoing Communications

Proactive planning around events such as SAP's CEO transition is becoming more challenging due to the changing ratio between incoming and outgoing communication. The balance is shifting from largely outgoing communications – pitches, speeches, and press announcements that you could plan and through which you could "control" messages about your company – to incoming communications from customers, partners, media, and analysts on anything from print publications to television and the Internet. The news sources used to be large and simple; a company had the opportunity to build a relationship over time with the reporters who were assigned the beat concerning that company's product or marketplace.

This new media group has been a force for public relations to reckon with. Instead of anticipating the reactions to a planned execution of a news story, communications professionals must respond to bloggers and alternative media sources that are likely to speak up without any nudging. This is not necessarily a positive thing – the feedback gets a company's name on the public's lips, but a bad review or angry rant can turn opinion quickly, despite the potentially questionable credentials of the source.

No communications team can garner the energy to track every mention of its company or client in the news, let alone every mention in the ever expanding blogosphere – particularly if the company is a large enterprise with a global reach. That's why it is essential to prioritize which stakeholders are most important, which outlets are most important, and what actions have the most impact on your corporate reputation. From there, a certain portion of resources can be dedicated to monitoring and dealing with those forces to allow for flexibility.

SAP quickly recognized the growing power of bloggers and wanted to be sure to develop a strong relationship with this community, so it selected SAPPHIRE 2006, its annual user conference, to reach out to the blogosphere by establishing a "Blogger's Corner" as a special venue within the larger conference.

The objective of Blogger's Corner was to establish a dialogue with the top bloggers in the technology industry about SAP and its business strategy. SAP began strengthening relations in the blogosphere with the participation of an SAP employee who was also a respected blogger. His reputation and blog helped to establish a presence for SAP in the blogosphere while also solidifying relationships with prominent bloggers interested in enterprise software. Awareness of the importance of the blogosphere was also raised within the ranks at SAP through the addition of blog coverage beginning in March 2007 to the *Early Bird*, the company's daily internal news digest that provides highlighted coverage from around the globe.

SAP had traditionally invited members of the press and industry analysts to its SAPPHIRE news program and hosted a separate program for financial analysts, and the decision to invite bloggers to the conference was a step in a new direction. The team did not necessarily select the bloggers whose postings received the most traffic. Although they considered this aspect, SAP primarily picked bloggers based on their knowledge of enterprise software, their ability to be engaged in multi-faceted debate, and their diverse backgrounds. The invited bloggers received the same access and resources given to reporters and were told that they could write anything as long as they were willing to let SAP respond to their comments.

As a result of its efforts, SAP saw more than 50 blog posts written about SAPPHIRE; and that number continued to grow as the invited bloggers cited information learned and interviews held at SAPPHIRE in their entries. SAP executives who had previously been skeptical about the credibility of bloggers were impressed by the professionalism and industry knowledge the bloggers demonstrated at SAPPHIRE. Additionally, executives – who prior to SAPPHIRE had schedules "too full" to meet with bloggers – cleared time on their own initiative to meet with them. SAP also caught the attention of other bloggers and received praise for being ahead of the pack regarding social media strategies in comparison to other large companies.

The bloggers made a collective effort to come away with as much information as possible from the event. Unlike the press who typically compete for exclusive stories, the bloggers worked together to attend keynotes and interviews and together formulated ideas about SAP which they then collectively posted for the public. In turn, the in-person experience solidified a relationship among the bloggers that has continued well after SAPPHIRE. They have dubbed themselves the "Irregulars" and have regularly collaborated using multiple communication channels in which they roundtable topics about the enterprise market. The "Irregulars" currently have a Crispynews site that allows them to contribute links to articles and then comment and rate them on the site, much like the news site Digg.com.

The group also has held email debates which the members have posted on their respective blogs, has jointly published articles, holds conference calls, and is looking into podcasts. It has expanded to include bloggers not at SAPPHIRE and has caught the attention of other bloggers and journalists, spawning conversation, debate, and multiple blog postings about enterprise software. Consequently, a virtual community of trusted, credible bloggers has been created around SAP.

Noted blogger and industry expert Ross Mayfield noted of the event, "Attending SAPPHIRE as a credentialed blogger was not only a wonderful personal experience, but perhaps a watershed moment for how enterprises engage in social media."

## The Increasing Importance of Corporate Content

We've all read several stories about the proliferation of user-generated communities, such as MySpace or YouTube. However, what most people don't realize is that, while millions watch YouTube, only a handful actually post content, which means there is a demand for interesting content and an opportunity for companies that can think beyond traditional forms of advertising such as the radio commercial or newspaper ad to create clever and relevant content that supports their corporate reputation and that people *want* to see.

## Mentos and Diet Coke Experiment on YouTube

In June of 2006, some pranksters revived the long-standing curiosity that dropping Mentos mints into a liter of Diet Coke will produce a bubbling explosion, spewing the soda heavenward in an oddly beautiful arced geyser. However, the urban myth was not relegated to a simple backyard; it was videotaped and posted on YouTube, garnering millions of views and thousands of copycat postings.

As the weeks passed, so did the intensity of the demonstrations. Perfectly choreographed experiments drew more and more viewers, and the snack companies experienced a spike in sales, if only for scientific purposes. How did Mentos and Diet Coke react?

Mentos, owned by Italy's Perfetti Van Melle, is a small company when compared to the giant that is the Coca-Cola Corporation. Mentos estimated that $15.8 million worth of free publicity came from the experiments, and embraced the movement by holding competitions for the best performance. Diet Coke, in its own right, has released this statement: "We would hope people want to drink Diet Coke more than try to experiment with it." The result: Hitwise.com, an online marketing website, reported that in the weeks of June 11$^{th}$ and June 18$^{th}$, 2006, searches for the word "Mentos" increased by 142 percent, with Diet Coke up by 34 percent. Futhermore, Mentos enjoyed a 15 percent sales spike during the height of the experiment popularity. Figures were not available for Coke.

# THE NEW COMMUNICATORS

## Communication "knowledge workers"

If you think of the communicator of 1947, you would envision a person with very good media relations understanding and very good writing skills. In 2007, the picture is a bit different. Although media relations and writing skills continue to be important, the communication "knowledge worker" of the 21$^{st}$ century must understand new terms and technology as well as how different audiences are using these tools to form opinions about corporate brands and reputation.

Today you must know the difference between an RSS feed and a blog and know how to respond when a journalist calls and says, "Hey, I just noticed that your site has been tagged on Digg and that its ranking is far below where it was a week ago." You must be able to, to some degree, respond to all of these different communications needs and tools in a way that is entirely new. Fifty years ago, you could assume that people were reading the paper or watching television. Today's communications knowledge worker must understand a larger universe of communications vehicles.

Today's communicators must also appreciate the dynamic of how a reputation can evaporate quickly in the event of a crisis, and they must possess the ability to guide the company in a 24/7 environment. They must be prepared to answer the phone, for instance, at 2:00 in the morning and speak on behalf of a corporation and perhaps its 50,000 employees at a moment's notice. That's a very different mindset than it was 50 years ago, when you had the luxury of a "tomorrow" deadline.

The communications landscape has also changed by becoming more "global." A truly global communications department or function has to be able to operate in sync to maintain a constant reputation perception barometer and to respond with a consistent message in order to retain the credibility of the organization. To do this, a communications professional in Tokyo must understand the impact of his or her activities on colleagues in New York, in addition to possessing the ability to impact the communications process in his local culture, language, and region.

The world is not homogenous and neither should the communications team be. Effective communication requires different sensitivities based on the countries in which your company is located or conducts business. Thus, a skilled global communicator must be able to take very sophisticated communications processes and make them relevant to the audience that they are serving, whether it is a local country or a specific audience. The most effective communications teams will include many with international experience: people who have lived and worked in foreign countries, ideally having learned or at least operated in different languages. These experiences provide people with a unique perspective and help them to better recognize sensitivities and understand what is relevant in different cultures.

## Growing Importance of Internal Communications

Harold Burson is quick to point out that as the dynamic of corporate reputation has become more viral, so has the importance of internal and employee communications. Each individual employee becomes a representative of the company's brand and must be able to articulate its brand promise. In other words: How does Employee X describe the company to neighbors or friends?

In general, people look more to their peers than to paid advertising when seeking a credible reputation about a brand. Companies are thus under greater obligation, as communication has become more "democratized," to ensure the regular employee can give the "elevator speech" and concisely discuss the brand – as well as behave according to the brand's principles.

## Leveraging Technology Globally

One of the more surprising findings of market research conducted by Burson-Marsteller is that only 5 percent of senior executives believe that updating their website can be an effective tool in their crisis management and corporate reputation turnaround strategy.[6]

Just as technology can help you monitor incoming communications, it can also help you proactively build and strengthen your company's reputation. In fact, web-based communications give senior leaders the most immediate channel for delivering messages of vital importance to key internal and external audiences.

The Mentos/Diet Coke experiment is a good example of how a new communications platform such as YouTube can help a company's reputation and, in this case, even its sales. SAP has been doing some experimentation of its own, including using resources such as the NewsMarket – a relatively new service that uses the latest Web technology to facilitate easy and efficient transfers of broadcast-standard digital video and other multimedia content from providers to journalists – to make photos and video of the company immediately and easily accessible to the media. Five years ago, you would need to film a segment, beam it up to a satellite, and then issue a satellite news release or call every TV station all over the world and ask them to set their dishes at the appropriate time and location to download the video. Following this complicated process, they would have to edit the video or maybe not even use it.

Now, you can upload video to content repositories such as the NewsMarket immediately. There, journalists can download the video whether they want to stream it on a station as video, add it to any respective online media they are working with, or simply watch the video to quote the executive in a print publication.

Communications has become more intense and immediate, but this can work *for* your organization and corporate reputation as well as against it.

One good example of how SAP has leveraged technology to its advantage is the Early Bird alert system, which notifies executives and communications professionals immediately of threats to corporate reputation.

## The Early Bird Catches the News

The SAP Early Bird internal newsletter is an early alert system developed and managed by teams in the U.S. and Germany as a service to SAP Executive Board members, SAP Executives, and the Global PR Network. Originally designed as an alert to any overnight developments in the global market, the Early Bird has also become what a SAP VP of Communications described as a "wonderfully informative platform of communication." The Early Bird sets the agenda for the VP's daily editorial calls with the heads of all global communications teams – such as Investor Relations, Government Relations, Products and Industry – and is often the springboard for action items.

The Early Bird includes an overview of SAP press releases; top news stories about SAP; competitive press releases and news stories; industry analyst quotes from the news; a financial roundup and excerpts from financial analysts, provided by SAP Investor Relations; as well as relevant news from public affairs/government relations and other industry news that impacts SAP business. The newsletter comes in three formats: a Word version with interactive links to stories and press releases, a PDF version for easy international printing, and an abbreviated Blackberry version.

Unlike other SAP media monitoring and news digests, the Early Bird reports like a newspaper or magazine, not repeating news unless it moves the story along. The Early Bird News bureau follows the sun, gathering news as it develops around the world with the help of correspondents based in every region to help monitor, collect, and translate local news. It is this international flavor that is especially appealing to busy SAP executives who can boast that "they see everything" as one executive replied when a Latin American colleague questioned how the executive could possibly have seen remarks he made in a Spanish-speaking publication.

The Early Bird was designed as an objective snapshot of the news rather than a tool that could be manipulated or censored to promote internal objectives or points of view. It does however help the communications group do its job better by alerting team members to market developments around the globe so that they can prepare for questions from customers, reporters, analysts, or others about SAP-relevant news items. On numerous occasions, the Early Bird has enabled the SAP global communications team to respond quickly to reporters to squelch potentially negative misrepresentation or quickly correct information in areas of the world far removed from headquarters.

The SAP Early Bird has become essential daily reading for a subscriber base that has quickly grown from 300 subscribers to more than several thousand, and which continues to increase every day.

## Reputation 2010

It is telling that we are naming this section "reputation 2010" instead of "reputation 2020." Years ago, we may have had the nerve to do a 50-year outlook on the road ahead. However, if the past five years is any indicator, the rate of change will only accelerate, leaving us all to wonder what the communications landscape will look like in just three years. In late 2004, SAP partnered with the Economist Intelligence Unit (EIU) to answer this question, researching how companies are engaging in communications and business today and how they will do so in the future.

The EIU designed and fielded a survey to elicit the views of business leaders on business models, strategy, innovation, competition, and information technology and how they might be impacted by the high-paced, ever-changing business world over the next five years. A total of 4,018 executives from 23 countries across Europe participated in the survey, with at least 50 percent of respondents at the C-level or equivalent. The general key message elicited from the survey was a revelation: in 2010, survival in a fiercely competitive global economy will depend more on adapting new business models, or the *way* an organization operates, rather than *what* it does. The survey noted that organizations would have to confront challenges like commoditization, business model innovation, and new business ecosystems to retain a competitive status. Furthermore, the survey concluded that companies must abandon reactive communications and drive the business dialogue.

Burson-Marsteller and SAP put these findings to the test, turning the results of the study into a driver for a proactive communications campaign designed to elevate SAP's thought leadership stature in the business arena and to help SAP executives connect with the broader business community.

The team created a Business 2010 Communications Pack to be distributed throughout regional and local markets to ensure each area's PR team was operating under the same set of information and principles. Burson-Marsteller communications trainers then led workshops in regional PR meetings across Europe to approximately 50 SAP executives. Once communications executives felt confident that the findings from the survey were well understood across spokespeople in the European market, the team made preparations to present the results to the general public.

On February 24, 2005, the team held a media day and featured Henning Kagermann, SAP CEO and executive board member, along with board members Léo Apotheker and Shai Agassi. Regional CEOs from Asia and Latin America also attended to gather insights to share with their markets. The event gathered 30 local market business media, which resulted in press stories in such publications as the *The Financial Times, The Guardian, The Times, The Financial Times Deutschland, Il Sore 24ore, Finanz and Wirtschaft,* and *Vremya.*

In the weeks to follow, SAP leveraged the messaging at customer, partner, and media activities at SAPPHIRE events in the U.S., Europe, and Asia and conducted a local rollout in China, Singapore, India, Japan, and Russia. Teams customized presentations for each country, taking into account the specific markets, economies, and communications methods as it related to the research. Discussions ensued with top business leaders in every area, broadening the perspective of business and messaging challenges that can be expected and conquered in the near, and distant, future.

As a result of the entire proactive communications campaign, the global business media has written approximately 100 articles on SAP and the EIU study. In addition, the campaign provided an opportunity for SAP executives to engage with key business reporters and open the door to further discussions about SAP's business model, product roap map and technology innovations.

## A Game That Never Ends

As we look into 2010 and beyond, one thing we have come to trust is that the game of managing corporate reputation never really ends. Endurance, patience, and an ability to think long-term in a reactive world is necessary in order to navigate the communications landscape of today and tomorrow. We found this to be true for SAP when, following a few years of stable growth and a solid reputation, SAP Global Communications had to manage an unexpected development: the departure of executive board member Shai Agassi.

Shai Agassi, an Israeli entrepreneur and technology genius, founded TopTier Software in 1992 and ran the company until SAP acquired it in 2001. Still very involved in his company's software aims and goals, he was appointed to the SAP board in 2002 and quickly acquired a reputation in Silicon Valley as the young, fresh face of the company. Members of the press liked the personable, knowledgeable Agassi and often interviewed him and featured his opinions on SAP and the ERP landscape in their articles. So when Agassi decided in March of 2007 to leave SAP in order to pursue personal goals in the fields of alternative energy and climate change, the immediate perception was that the company might suffer.

SAP could not avoid the press coverage that the departure would receive, so the communications team detailed a strategy to address the issue. At 5:00 p.m. Central European Time (CET) on the day of Shai's announcement, the supervisory board met in Walldorf, Germany to determine their next steps. By 6:00 p.m., Burson-Marsteller had gathered its global teams, which began a worldwide coverage sweep starting with the initial *Wall Street Journal* story and subsequent coverage as more sources picked up the news. The Burson-Marsteller and SAP communications team also created a protocol that governed how to treat all incoming and outgoing messages. In addition, the team quickly designated spokespeople to simplify the inundation of press inquiries and scheduled a conference call for media at 9:00 pm CET, 3:00 pm Eastern time in the United States.

One hour before the conference call, the team distributed a press release globally and began one-on-one interviews with key publications and analysts. At 9:00 p.m. CET, Hasso Plattner and Henning Kagermann welcomed everyone to the press and analyst briefing, expressing the company's disappointment in Agassi's departure but outlining a plan for the board and company in his absence. Plattner and Kagermann fielded questions from journalists together.

With Agassi's full cooperation and the openness of the SAP executives to discuss the issue, the coverage regarding Agassi was dominated by positive quotes from Kagermann and Plattner. Influential blogger Joshua Greenbaum of ZDNet reflected, "In the end, all companies go through this kind of management shift. SAP has, for better or worse, initiated a major shift at one of the more critical inflection points in its history...While the line of succession looks strong, we'll all have to wait until late April for SAPPHIRE, SAP's big annual user conference, to get the full details on what the new SAP will look and act like." SAPPHIRE brought with it a new lineup of executives well-received by the media and analysts, and new communications challenges for the company and its public relations partner.

Looking ahead, we can anticipate a further dynamism in the communications landscape for global companies, as "instant transparency" brings with it a never-ending news cycle and ramifications on the brand and those who evaluate it on a constant basis.

# ENDNOTES

1	Burson-Marsteller/ Wirthlin Worldwide, *Maximizing Corporate Reputation*, 1998.
2	Burson-Marsteller, *Building CEO Capital* survey, 2005.
3	Anonymous. "Face Value: The software professor, Henning Kagermann, Boss of SAP." *The Economist.* 8 August, 2002. http://www.economist.com/business/displaystory.cfm?story_id=E1_TNSDGDP.
	Benoit, Bertrand. "New Face to Raise Profile." *Financial Times, Financial Times Deutschland.* 15 March, 2003. http://search.ft.com/iab?queryText=Henning%20Kagermann&aje=true&id=030317001049&page=11&location=http%3A%2F%2Fsearch.ft.com%2FftArticle%3FqueryText%3DHenning+Kagermann%26aje%3Dtrue%26id%3D030317001049%26page%3D11&referer=http%3A%2F%2Fsearch.ft.com%2Fsearch%3FqueryText%3DHenning+Kagermann.
	Kagermann, Henning. "An Open Source Model for Creating Value." Contributor. World Economic Forum. Davos, Switzerland. 24 January, 2004.
	Kagermann, Henning. "Panelist." PC Forum. Scottsdale, Arizona. 27 March, 2002.
4	Anonymous. "At Your Service: Despite Early Failures, computing will eventually become a utility." *The Economist.* 8 May, 2003. http://www.economist.com/surveys/displaystory.cfm?story_id=E1_TSQSPVN.
5	Anonymous. "Europe's Best CEOs." *Institutional Investor.* 1 July, 2003. http://www.iimagazine.com/article.aspx?articleID=1026850.
6	Burson-Marsteller, *Building CEO Capital Survey*, 2005.

# SECTION 4:

---

# BUSINESS-LED
# INFORMATION
# TECHNOLOGY

## 4.1

# FOUR VECTORS OF BUSINESS MODEL INNOVATION: VALUE CAPTURE IN A NETWORK ERA

*N Venkatraman,* Professor of Management, Boston
University School of Management
*John C. Henderson,* Professor of Management, Boston
University School of Management

**Acknowledgements**

We thank Douglas Henderson for his research assistance in assembling the data to support the cases and for providing comments and suggestions on an earlier draft. We thank SAP for providing research support.

## INTRODUCTION: A DIFFERENT KIND OF INNOVATION

The first decade of the 21st century is marked by profound shifts: companies find themselves in a global marketplace with fierce competition for resources, talent, technologies, and customers. The logic of winning that worked well in the last decades of the 20th century seem ill-tuned to the requirements of the 21st century. Managers, analysts, venture capitalists, and others are looking for principles likely to guide and govern business successes in the 21st century. While there are many rules based on how companies innovated during the last century, those rules and approaches do not appear to give confidence to guide enterprises into the uncharted territories of today. The future is not an extrapolation of the past. Success in the past is no longer adequate to guarantee success in the future. Very few companies have consistently been on the Fortune 100 list over the last decade and the composition of the Dow Jones 30 (and NASDAQ 100) keeps changing.

Bill Ford of Ford Motor Company, on the occasion of seeking a leader from outside to head up Ford, observed in an internal memo to employees that: "The business model that sustained us for decades is no longer sufficient to sustain profitability... We must change to a new business model that requires greater bottom-line contributions from cars and crossovers, continued leadership in pickups in North America, healthier profits from all other business units, growth in Asia, greater integration of our global operations, and an evaluation of strategic alliances."

Bill Ford is not alone as senior leaders in many sectors realize the need to adapt their business models that worked well in the industrial age to business logics that are likely to prove successful in the post-industrial, global market place. In many cases senior managers may find that they need to jettison their old business models and invent new ones as they face up to the opportunities and challenges in the early 21$^{st}$ century. One thing that is clear however, is that it is no longer adequate to innovate in narrow domains – products, processes and services. Because of the fundamental shifts from industrial age to post-industrial age, we need to innovate more holistically – namely: the entire business model (which encompasses customer value proposition, operating model, management processes, and roles and responsibilities of multiple partners with shared incentives and decision rights). The focus is now on how to achieve continuous growth and profitability simultaneously. Profitability is a necessary (but not sufficient) requirement and the operative phrase is *profitable growth* through innovations in contrast to *profitless growth* that characterized the dotcom boom in the late 1990s. While the capability to execute has been refined by many enterprises, the requisite capability to simultaneously manage top-line growth and bottom-line profits is lacking. The new leadership mandate is to develop sustained business model innovations and value capture.

## OUR VIEW ON BUSINESS MODEL INNOVATION

Over the last five years, we have seen a steady increase in the call for attention to innovation in different areas of management. You have no doubt seen the rapid increase in management books devoted to the subject. You cannot peruse issues of business periodicals or listen to CEO interviews without reference to innovations or stumbling upon rules and guidelines for innovators.[1] These discussions mostly focus on *generic* requirements of innovations – structure, climate, culture, resource allocation processes, autonomy, incentives, and different yardsticks for performance measurement. In this chapter, we lay out our view on business model innovations before we discuss the framework and supporting case evidence. We urge you to look at business model innovation using three criteria.

**One:** The new strategic mantra is "business model innovation."

Much attention is focused on innovations in specific domains such as product (e.g., product line extensions, product portfolio rationalization, and new product introductions), process (e.g., quality enhancements, global supply chain, and ERP systems), and service (e.g., superior customer service, different modes of customer-interactions and channels of service delivery). These innovations are functionally driven without a more complete, system-wide view of the drivers of value creation and capture. In our research, we found that the term "business model innovation" is overused with no coherent understanding of what it stands for among different managers within the same company. Is it new product introduction? Is it new process improvements? Is it new management practices such as outsourcing and partnering? Is it setting up a new incubator? Our feeling is that we need to look at a more holistic view of innovations – "innovations-in-the-large" or "wholesale change" as different managers put it – that focus on a radically different future state rather than incremental innovations that fine-tune today's practices. We concur with Bruce Nussbaum of Business Week, who remarked: "Even though Ford has some great technology, it isn't enough if the business model isn't right." Innovations have been piecemeal and disconnected across different functions and locations without overarching logic for corporate-wide innovations. Best practices exist for localized, incremental innovations, but there is a clear lack of management frameworks for business model innovations that create new rules of competition.

**Two:** It is time to place information technology squarely at the center of business model innovation and implementation.

The discussions on innovation have mostly failed to recognize adequately the central role and potential impact of information technology – especially the developments in hardware, software, and telecommunication – which offer new sources of opportunities while threatening outmoded ways of working. Software has played a significant role in enhancing the productivity of individual knowledge workers. It has also contributed significantly to enhance the efficiency of many of the core processes of enterprises. Telecommunications are changing the geography of work and the locus of value creation with India and China emerging as global back-offices and factories respectively.

The role of I/T in impacting operating efficiency is clearly understood, thanks to the last decade of reengineering efforts. However, we have not demonstrated the role of I/T in creating robust business models. The *skeptics* point to the failed dotcom revolution to argue that information technology has been over-hyped. On the other hand, the *realists* recognize the promise of I/T but do not have good frameworks to think about business model innovations. They see the possibilities of new opportunities as traditional industries blur; they also see the commoditization of their current product-service delivery model and the need to add value through digitization, information, and expertise. Many managers see isolated examples of companies experimenting with new business models driven by new I/T functionality, but they do not have a coherent way to go from those examples to actionable plans in their own settings.

**Three:** Business model innovation is to be framed in network-centric (rather than firm-centric) terms with greater recognition of co-creation of value.

We believe that business model innovations should be seen as involving a set of external partners and relationships. Our belief is that there is a profound shift underway in the shape of corporations. We urge you to think about innovations of your business models as being co-created with a set of partners including, in some cases, the end-customers. In a global, networked world, a corporation is not an isolated entity but is embedded in a network of relationships tied through joint ventures, cooperative R&D, marketing agreements, patent licensing, equity investments, and inter-locked memberships on boards. Business ecosystems play an important part in creating new models of value creation as well as in implementing those strategies to maximize value to the constituent entities.

Taken together, the core thesis of this chapter emerges: Business model innovation specifies the logic of how a firm delivers sustained superior value to end customers on a powerful information technology infrastructure involving a set of business relationships for complementary capabilities. We elaborate on this thesis using a framework, supported by a set of cases. Our framework is aimed at senior business and technology managers in their joint pursuit of developing robust business models and value capture.

# OUR FRAMEWORK: FOUR VECTORS OF BUSINESS MODEL INNOVATIONS

Look at Figure 1. We use two axes to map four different vectors of business model innovations. The two axes are: (1) value creation approach – either deliberate or emergent; and (2) scope of relationships in the network – either exclusive or inclusive. This mapping scheme allows us to depict four stylized vectors of business model innovation approaches. We use a set of examples to highlight the strengths and limitations of each and derive key implications for each. However, before we begin discussing those examples, let's take a moment to delve deeper into our two axes.

As we noted above, we argue that the axis (1) value creation approach can be either deliberate or emergent. The key questions you as the senior manager must ask yourself are how do you differentiate the two approaches? And, once you understand the differences, how do you recognize where the different parts of your organization fall along the axis? By giving you a description of how we differentiate and identify the two approaches to value creation – supported later in the chapter with case examples – we hope to help you answer these two questions simultaneously.

A deliberate approach to value creation is a well coordinated and focused process that is understood and accepted throughout the organization. The process is tightly connected to the company's business model and follows a clear organizational strategy. Generally, the process is developed at the highest levels of the company with the input of key managers and decision makers, before being disseminated down through the levels of the firm. For example, a deliberate approach to innovation could entail coordinating the development and release of a new product with well defined economic targets and pre-determined deadlines. The roles and responsibilities for the project would be clearly outlined and leadership would be held accountable for its success or failure. This process will be very familiar to managers schooled over the past 30 years in US and international universities. It is a tried and true approach to value creation and one that is commonly adopted still today with great success.

On the other end of the continuum lies an emergent approach to value creation. This approach lacks the tight control that is the hallmark of a deliberate approach to innovation, and rather embraces fast changing shifts in the industry with quick modifications and alterations to the organization's business model. Inspirations that lead to innovations are not necessarily top-down in nature but are dispersed through every level of the company where outside-the-box-thinking and practices are more common. Employees are encouraged to assess opportunities outside the organization and to put themselves in situations to identify new ideas. Finally partners – and even sometimes competitors – are viewed as potential sources for innovation and value creation, and these business partnerships are leveraged in order to develop new sources of revenue.

Axis (2), scope of relationships in the network, is on a continuum from exclusive to inclusive. Again, it is important to ask the same questions about the differences of the two and how they apply to your organization in order to gain a better understanding of where your company falls within our framework.

Exclusive relationships in the network are generally tight knit, centrally controlled partnerships or alliances, with clear and well defined boundaries. The stylized model of a supply chain that is oftcn used for strategy implementation serves to explain this position. At each point in the chain lies a vital link that aims to move a product from the supplier to the customer. Each link has a defined purpose, and the movement of goods is well coordinated from beginning to end. Exclusive relationships help organizations control the level of complexity by reducing the number of partners involved in the process while at the same time recognizing the value of intangible concepts inherent in partnerships, such as trust and shared knowledge that are developed over time. Intellectual property is also more easily managed as contracts tend to be clearly defined and closely followed.

Inclusive relationships in the network on the other hand broaden the process to incorporate many different partnerships and alliances in a more loosely controlled and organized manner. A good example could be the open source movement. Open source projects allow a wide array of developers to be included in the design and production of a final product or good. The process occurs organically and collaboratively, with each participant sharing in the final creation. Inclusive relationships enable organizations to leverage active user communities, tapping into the collective creativity of the group while leveraging their diversity of skills and perspectives in order to help promote innovation. The wide range of companies using Application Programming Interfaces (APIs) including Yahoo, Amazon, and Google are good candidates at this end of the spectrum. At the same time, it reduces the need for centrally controlled processes and increases opportunities for cooperation. Of course if the process is left unchecked, it can result in chaos.

Our belief is that you can use these vectors collectively as different avenues for thinking through ways to can create powerful business models. We fully recognize that we cannot (and should not) reduce the complex challenge of strategy creation into simple frameworks, rules, and workbooks. Our hope is that this new perspective will stimulate conversations within

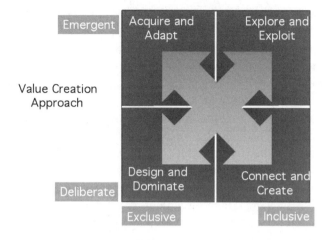

**Figure 1:** *Four Vectors of Business Model Innovations*

your management team to work through the different requirements of crafting winning business models.

## Vector 1: Design and Dominate

What is common between Nike and Apple beyond their jointly introduced Nike + offering (a version of Apple iPod linked to a specific model of Nike shoes)? For the last two decades, Nike has often been touted as a company that understood the power of orchestrating a network of supply relationships2 while embracing principles of virtual organizing.[3] You may have seen discussions of Nike's outsourcing of advertising (through its longstanding relationship with Wieden+Kennedy and signing of top-tier athletes in every sports category), production (three-tiers of Asian suppliers), as well as distribution involving a combination of retail outlets (Footlocker) supported by flagship Niketown showrooms.

Nike – in our opinion – is an example of continuous business model adaptation without ever losing sight of the core design of its product (and supporting brand image). Nike is a powerful illustration of a company that dominated a category with superior design over a period of time. It is also one of the finest examples of business model innovation from a network-centric point of view using information technology for efficient and effective coordination with its array of partners. Their manufacturing and supply network has been refined over time with an emphasis on process innovation (do it different), continuous improvement (do it better), and execution discipline (do it right). What's not discussed much in the literature is that Nike never lost sight of the importance of design over time.

Nike is taking advantage of powerful information technology developments to create personalization of shoes and apparel for individuals (e.g., Nikeid and Mylocker) but also for teams (teamlocker). Nike is also adapting its business model to recognize the growing importance of the community of end-customers by creating communities of Nike users in specific domains such as football (Nike Football), basketball (jointly with the NBA), and running (with Apple to create Nike +). In addition, Nike joined with Google to create a community of soccer fans for the 2006 World Cup (www.joga.com).

Today, Nike is a marketer of athletic footwear and apparel with a distinctive competence in design, supported by a core, longstanding network of complementary firms in different functional domains with a marked commitment to involving end customers in shaping future design.

Furthermore, Apple, like Nike, is to be seen through its use of design as the basis for adapting its business model over the last three decades from Apple Computers (1977) to Apple Inc. (2007). When you open a product from Apple and look for the obligatory "Made in....." sign, you are more likely to see the phrase: "Designed in California and Made in.... (China)." That expression captures the spirit of Apple as an innovator in the network era. It highlights that design is the differentiator; design is where Apple sees the distinct value.

Apple innovated with the personal computer by creating a distinct design with features that have been embraced widely within the industry (e.g., mouse, graphical user interface, etc.) The transformation from being a computer company (Apple Computer in 1997) to being an enterprise with a broader scope and bigger ambition (Apple Inc. in 2007) is clearly rooted in Steve Jobs' focus on distinctive, elegant design. Apple has consistently won awards and accolades for its design – beginning with the Macintosh, then with iPod and now with the impending launch of iPhone. And while patents did not protect the early designs of the Macintosh line of computers, Apple has of late filed and received patents that underlie many of the distinctive design features that it has incorporated in iPod and iPhone.

Apple has also relied on an exclusive tight-knit set of partners to execute on its business model. Apple has historically relied on a set of partners to produce its products and, over time, has innovated its supply chain process as well. Indeed, in a recent survey by AMR Research, Apple was considered #2 in supply chain management – ahead of Wal-Mart and just behind Nokia – reinforcing Apple's attention to the product supply chain's importance in translating design dominance to business profitability.

| Dominant Product | Macintosh Computer | iPod & iTunes | iPhone |
|---|---|---|---|
| Design | Mac OS, Graphical User Interface | iPod (click-wheel) and Video iPod | Mac OS, Safari browser, Multi-touch screen |
| Customer Network | Niche market segments (media & hobbyists) | Network of consumers using Windows and Macintosh | Network of consumers using Windows and Macintosh |
| Complementor Network | IBM PowerPC and later Intel | Network of music content labels and podcasters | Launch partner with AT&T; Google and Yahoo search |
| Time period | 1984—till date | 2001—till date | 2007—till date |

*Figure 2:* Evolution of Apple's Business Model Innovations

The role of tight-knit partners is also seen as Apple expanded its business scope from computers to include media and entertainment through iPod (supported by iTunes software and the iTunes store). While design is central to both the hardware (iPod with its trademark click-wheel) and the iTunes store (especially, the ease of use), it is not enough. Apple orchestrated a network of partners involving music labels (Warner Music, EMI, and others) – who saw iTunes as a way to combat illegal piracy of legitimate content. To make iPod integration easy in automobiles and airlines, Apple has partnered with leading automakers and airlines. Going beyond music into videos, Apple also created close working relationships with Disney (joint board interlocks with Steve Jobs) and other content owners to distribute free unpaid podcasts and other subscription-based content. The business model innovation has also involved exploring multiple ways to monetize content through digital rights management (DRM)-enforced pricing (99 cents per music track) as well as DRM-free pricing (with a premium).

The recognition of the network-era is also evident with Apple's decision (after being known for its closed architecture with Macintosh computers) to selectively open iPod and iTunes to work with the Windows operating systems, thereby potentially appealing to a larger customer base (direct network effects) and consequently attracting more content providers to the iTunes platform (indirect network effects). The virtuous cycle of direct and indirect network effects reinforcing each other is an important requirement for successful business models in the network era.

Beyond music, Apple's design-and-dominate model has extended to the television space with video iPod and Apple TV. Following the enthusiastic response to downloading TV episodes on video iPods, Apple created Apple TV – elegant in design and simple to use in contrast to clunky set top boxes that come bundled with cable and satellite services. Interestingly, Apple has partnered with YouTube (part of Google) to make YouTube content accessible through Apple TV. Looking at these moves in a holistic way, we are persuaded to conclude that Apple's metamorphosis from a computer company to a broader media and entertainment company is far from complete. Nevertheless, we see that this transformation is based on superior design supported by the ability of close-knit partners and alliances to execute on operational efficiency while Apple is continuously shaping and adapting its market positioning in the media and entertainment landscape. Figure 2 is a schematic representation of design-and-dominate as an innovation vector as it applies to Apple over time.

## Vector 2: Acquire and Adapt

What is the connection between GE and Cisco? Those of you interested in corporate trivia may have noticed that Cisco briefly (for a day in early 2000 during the height of the dotcom boom) overtook GE as the largest company in terms of market capitalization. Beyond that tangential note, do you see anything that connects GE and Cisco?

GE has been on the Dow Dozen since Charles Dow created the index in 1896 to capture the strength of US industrial economy. It is still on the Dow Jones 30, but, at its core, GE is no longer an industrial company. GE's transformation to a service company occurred through major acquisitions and divestments over the last century. Corporate diversification as a strategy has been widely practiced by many leading companies over the last four decades and continues to hold the interest of top managers even today (witness the record levels of mergers and acquisitions in 2006).

There are some companies that have developed the capability to effectively integrate acquisitions and derive value from the potential synergy that initially motivated the deals; GE is an acknowledged leader of this group. Specifically, GE Capital is seen as a role model for integrating a wide range of acquisitions and is credited with GE Finance's success over the last two decades. While GE is a leader in adapting its business portfolio, Cisco is seen as a leader in scanning for and identifying potential acquisitions through a wide range of early stage investments. John Chambers and his team have refined the approach to business model adaptation by mastering the art of placing bets (investments and venture capital) in a wide range of companies tinkering with emerging technologies. For more than 20 years, Cisco has successfully made over a hundred acquisitions – including Linksys ($ 500 million) and Scientific Atlanta ($6.9 billion) – in order to systematically adapt its business model.

What makes Cisco's acquire-and-adapt strategy different from others pursuing a similar strategy? Several distinct points are worth noting. One: in addition to a sound business case (matching visions, enhanced shareholder value, and superior advantage to different stakeholders), Cisco focuses on people-chemistry since part of the new competencies lie in human capital. This is particularly true when acquiring and assimilating an early-stage, high-tech, knowledge-intensive company. Cisco has created a buddy system whereby an acquired employee is matched with a Cisco employee to streamline the integration process. Two: Cisco executives sit on Boards of early start-up companies as conduits to understand how emerging technologies could be harnessed by Cisco. Three: when operating business managers identify a promising technology and no start-up company exists, they create a spin-in company – a sponsored start-up funded by Cisco to motivate managers to pursue the technology to a logical stage of commercial viability. Four: Cisco also leverages the power of a close-knit Silicon Valley venture capital community to identify promising companies for acquisitions. The early-stage involvement in start-ups has proved fruitful to Cisco as it ends up acquiring about 25% of those companies that it invests in during the early stage.

Cisco's acquire-and-adapt business model is a good illustration of the logic of the Strategic Options Navigator that involves four interconnected stages reflecting a real-options perspective to navigating an uncertain business and technology landscape.[4] From an emergent approach to value creation and capture, the four steps are: 1. **Assess opportunities** by thinking about the "possible" and not simply the "probable" future outcomes. Cisco explores a wide range of possible options by recognizing a larger range of potentially important technologies. 2. **Acquire options** by making investments that provide flexibility to make future strategic moves that can be conditioned by future outcomes. The use of minority equity investments is a classic textbook case of acquiring options and specifying trigger conditions for changing the governance approach.[3] **Nurture options** by continually re-assessing and taking needed actions to keep the options alive. By having Cisco employees actively involved in the start-up companies, they are able to gain first-hand direct information about the state of developments and the potential role of those technologies on Cisco's business model. 4. **Harness value** by exercising the options in a timely manner. Cisco's track record of acquiring 25% of the companies that it makes some investment in is a

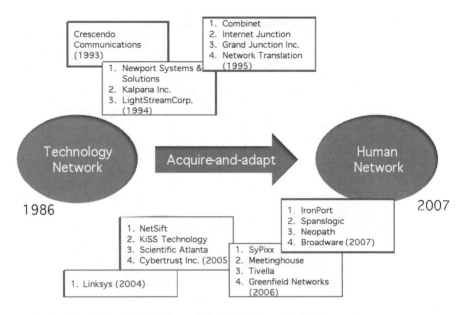

*Figure 3: Evolution of Cisco's Business Model Innovations*

testimony to their active application of the real-options perspective.[5] Thus, the emergent nature of value creation through investments and acquisitions is managed through the discipline of real-options thinking. Figure 3 is a schematic representation of the acquire-and-adapt vector of business model innovation as it applies to Cisco.

## Vector 3: Connect and Create

Is there a connection between Procter and Gamble and Microsoft? At a first blush, they do not seem to have much in common except that they both have products that are household names. However, they both – in their own ways – have been embracing the view that strategy should be framed beyond firm-centric thinking to include partners and customers. While the value creation approach may be deliberate, the scope of external partners could be more inclusive than the two previous vectors discussed before. Unlike Nike, Apple, GE, and Cisco, which explicitly circumscribed the scope of potential partners, P&G and Microsoft rely on a vibrant and dynamic ecosystem of partners to adapt and evolve their business models.

In 2000, P&G faced the situation that its internal R&D could not sustain the expected 4-6% annual growth. Overall R&D productivity had decreased and innovation success rates, which measure the percentage of new products that come to market and meet financial objectives, had stagnated at 35%.[6] P&G's CEO Alan Lafley charged the company with reinventing its innovation approach with the goal that 50% of all new P&G innovations would have outside elements contained in the final product. This challenge resulted in a new product innovation model called *Connect and Develop*. Essentially, P&G would open its R&D process to the external world – outside companies, institutions, and individuals who could directly contribute ideas and products. P&G looked for products that had shown some initial promise but could benefit from P&G's massive global resources, including R&D, manufacturing, purchasing, and marketing. This model is a success: By 2006, 35% of all new P&G products had outside elements contained within them, R&D productivity had increased 60%, the innovation success rate had doubled, and R&D investment as a percentage of sales had decreased from 4.8% in 2000 to 3.4% in 2006. In addition, the company's share price had performed better than the market.

While P&G leveraged a broad base of external entities to accelerate its new products, Microsoft's case is one of leveraging third-party developers to produce complementary products and services to support the market acceptance of its products. Software is a classic case of system-based competition where the value of any software is a function of its interoperability with certain hardware and other software programs and applications. So, Microsoft's business model success and adaptation has historically hinged on complementors.[7]

Microsoft's evolution from being a supplier of software to IBM personal computers to dominating the computer industry (in the late 1990s) is largely based on its organizational ability to reach out to many independent developers and complementary hardware providers and system integrators to ensure that its software is well positioned as part of the I/T architecture of many different vertical industries. This approach has led many to observe that Microsoft enjoys high *application barriers to entry* – referring to the advantage that it has by virtue of the commitment and loyalty of an extended community of developers. Microsoft's move beyond personal computers (Windows and Office platforms) into music (Play-for-Sure and Zune), videogames (Xbox), automotive telematics (launch of Sync with Ford Motor Company), and online advertising (Live) all rely on its ability to invite a broad set of partners into its fold.

The connect-and-create approach is clearly seen in the case of interlinking third-party developers of Windows and Xbox platforms. Historically, the networks of third-party developers of game consoles and personal computers were distinct and unconnected. However, increased computer power (thanks to Moore's Law) has brought these segments together and

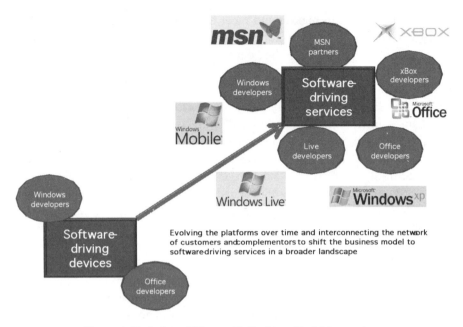

***Figure 4:*** *Evolution of Microsoft's Business Model Innovations*

Microsoft has used the XNA middleware software tool to interconnect game developers across Windows XP and Vista. This move has allowed Microsoft to marshal a larger base of developers in ways that its competitors (Nintendo and Sony) are unable to do because of their narrow business scope. While computers and videogames may have appeared somewhat unrelated when Microsoft first launched Xbox, the business model innovation is aligning technology trends (faster and cheaper computing power) with the business practice of leveraging complementary competencies of partners (third-party development programs). The same approach seems to be working as Microsoft tries to become dominant in operating systems for mobile phones with Windows Mobile competing against Palm and Symbian.

Analyzing Microsoft allows us to develop an important lesson in business model innovation from a network-point of view. When looking at the business model innovations of your competitors, do not simply evaluate the intrinsic merits and distinctive features of their product-service offering; look underneath for how the company could leverage its network of complementary relationships to further evolve and refine the offering to win. A logical corollary is to then look at how you can marshal a broader set of extended partners to leverage their complementary competencies better than your competitors are able to do. In other words: the intensity of competition shifts from "firm-to-firm" to "ecosystem-to-ecosystem." Figure 4 is a schematic representation of the connect-and-create vector of business model innovation as it applies to Microsoft.

## Vector 4: Explore and Exploit

Google and Microsoft are considered fierce competitors. Why? At first glance, it may appear that Microsoft is in software, while Google is a search engine; they should be partners and coordinate their products and services rather than compete against each other. As *Fortune* noted in an April 18, 2003 article: "It was December 2003. He (Bill Gates) was poking around on the Google company website and came across a help-wanted page with descriptions of all the open jobs at Google. Why, he wondered, were the qualifications for so many of them identical to Microsoft job specs? Google was a web search business, yet here on the screen were postings for engineers with backgrounds that had nothing to do with search and everything to do with Microsoft's core business – people trained in things like  operating-system design, compiler optimization, and distributed-systems architecture. Gates wondered whether Microsoft might be facing much more than a war in search. An e-mail he sent to a handful of execs that day said, in effect – we have to watch these guys. It looks like they are building something to compete with us."

Indeed, as we have seen over the last two years, the competitive rivalry has only intensified. While Microsoft emerged as the leader during the shift from a hardware-centric world to a software-centric world, Google seems to be the current leader during the shift to an era of software-enabled services. The Google business model seeks to commoditize software functionality (or at least minimize its value) while establishing different revenue models based on a consumers use of the services (for searching, transacting, connecting etc.) enabled by the software. The Google-Microsoft comparative analysis brings to sharp relief the complex challenges of business model innovation in the network era shaped by a powerful information technology infrastructure. A major challenge for you as a manager is to recognize the blurring boundaries between companies that could have easily – but incorrectly – indicated distinct industries with minimal competitive threat.

Look at our positioning of this vector on the original mapping scheme of business model innovations (Figure 1). This vector intersects the emergent approach to value creation by including a wide range of partners (in the true sense of dynamic business networks). Strategic evolution is less deliberate (no lofty business visions that become quickly obsolete), and there is a tendency to invite a large following of complementors. This may look like an invitation to chaos for many of you schooled in rational, calendar-driven strategic planning and resource allocation and rigid controls. Left unchecked, this could be chaotic except when supported by core principles of *managing on the edge*[8] that is required under fast-changing conditions.

Google – despite its relative infancy – serves as the best example to illustrate this vector. Google's business scope defies easy categorization and its approach to innovation – continuous and organizationally diffused – is distinctive as it rapidly adapts its business model (but perhaps not its core values) to fierce competition from a wide ranging set of companies while seeking to work in a cooperative way with many of them.

Look at Google's advertising services through AdWords and AdSense. Placed on the side of Google's webpage (including Google Maps and GMail), AdWords displaying the results of a search are becoming as ubiquitous as advertisements placed on newspapers and magazines. Moreover, AdSense delivers advertisements related to search and content on a wide range of other sites including blogs as well. "Ads by Google" on web pages is becoming the network-era equivalent of "Intel Inside" in the personal computer era. This complementary service expands the scope of advertisements beyond Google-owned sites and envelops a large cross-section of web search activities. AdWords and AdSense combined generate over 95% of Google's revenue and profits. In addition, many observers believe that we are in the early stages of targeted advertising that combines on-line and off-line activities.

Focusing on Google Labs best shows how Google embraces an emergent approach to value-creation. By allowing every employee freedom (20% of time allocated to refine and extend core search and 10% of time to areas unrelated to current business operations), Google strives to overcome the rigidity of business practices and competency traps that impact most successful companies. Google Labs and associated blogs provide a peek into the innovation playground where new business ideas take shape by leveraging the power of information technologies. These labs and services in beta versions also allow Google to get early feedback and suggestions from their active community of users (eager beta testers). Thus, communities of users are included in the early phases of value creation.

If you have not done so, take a look at Google Labs and see how these initiatives could change and impact broader industries and product-service offerings. Also take a close look at the graduates of Google Labs and how they could evolve in the future. For example, Google News: this service aggregates news stories from over 4,500 global sources using computer algorithms – and bypassing human editors – and provides updates every fifteen minutes. Delivery of *relevant* news based on individual search could

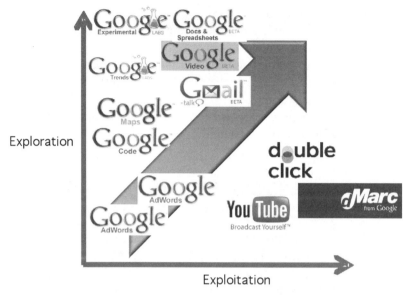

**Figure 5:** *Evolution of Google's Business Model Innovations*

radically alter the newspaper business in the coming years. Furthermore, look at Google Maps and examine how mash-ups and applets using the maps could deliver superior, differentiated services to consumers.

Google's acquisition of YouTube has caused some uproar in the media industry since it has legitimized the role of user-generated content. Media companies such as BBC, NBC, CBS, and ABC/Disney are scrambling to evaluate how their media should be distributed on the web. Advertising companies such as WPP are wondering what Google might do in the advertising world beyond just rendering relevant ads at the point of search. As Google's business model spans multiple different industries, you are best advised to track the key moves by Google to see how they might intersect with your operations. Connecting the dots of Google's various moves is an important requirement for uncovering potential impacts and likely trajectories of intersection with Google.

One of the perennial challenges in management is to optimize today's operations (profitability; efficiency) while investing for tomorrow's opportunities (growth; effectiveness). In essence, successful companies fail not because they under-leverage or under-invest in their core competencies but because they continue to believe that today's successful routines will guarantee them success tomorrow. In other words, they fall into their own competency traps. Success breeds rigidity whereby new ideas and innovations are rejected. A new breed of companies approach value creation in a more emergent way and are quick to seize on multiple streams of innovations in the broader network. They see opportunities and possibilities in a less constrained way. The entrepreneurial spirit with a greater willingness to explore new modes of seeking and capturing value is reflected in this vector of business model innovation.[9]

Figure 5 is a schematic representation of the explore-and-exploit vector of business model innovation as it applies to Google.

# BUSINESS MODEL INNOVATIONS: IMPLICATIONS FOR ACTION

We are in the midst of profound shifts from the industrial age to the network era on a powerful global information-technology enabled infrastructure. Thus, innovations are not likely to be static and well defined. They are more likely to be fluid, dynamic and evolving. The logic of value creation and the scope of complementary partners create important choices for companies as they shift their frame of strategic thinking and actions from being individual firm-centric to network-centric. In this chapter, we developed four vectors with supporting case evidence to illustrate different contexts for business model innovations. We chose the term vectors rather than types because they are not clearly demarcated archetypes of business model innovations. Our hope is that you will use this framework to guide and orchestrate conversations about (1) the need for business model innovation; and (2) systematically thinking through the best way to challenge and adapt your business models in a proactive way.

## 1. Recognition of the "Burning Platform"

The case for change begins with the recognition of the proverbial "burning platform." Leaders have often communicated the urgency by showing how maintaining the status-quo is not an option and that doing nothing (inaction) will only make things worse. Some leaders realize that their main responsibility is to show that the signals are evident and create the condition for change. Business model innovations of the kind that we have described here call for widespread recognition of the burning platform: the shift from the vertically integrated, firm-centric approach to strategy towards network-centric logic is real and imminent. The industrial age is giving way to a global, interconnected information technology infrastructure that changes the geography of work. We extend Tom Friedman's description of the "World is Flat" to say that the "Business World is Networked." Now, we ask you to think about what this could mean for your business model.

The key challenge is to identify a key issue that can be used to rally the organization around business model innovations. It is easier if the organization is in crisis, but the leadership challenge is to energize the organization to innovate under normal operating conditions. The hallmark of a leader is to proactively innovate and adapt the business models before the signs are obvious to everyone involved. Two sets of memos from Bill Gates (in 1995 and 2006) show how he created the burning platform to adapt the business models of Microsoft. The 1995 memo extolled Microsoft's managers to embrace the Internet and the 2006 memo called attention to software-enabled services and the recognition of new competitors in the form of Google and Yahoo. Focus on the critical triggers in order to galvanize these innovations – in some case, triggers could be internal performance levels (e.g., IBM and Sony) while in other settings they could be exciting new opportunities and possibilities to establish new leadership positions (e.g., Apple and Cisco). *So, what's your burning platform for business model innovation? Do you see it? Can you galvanize your organization to act?*

## 2. Map Your Ecosystems and Business Networks

In the industrial age, innovations occurred at the level of a single enterprise. The classic examples of business innovations in the industrial age were: Ford Model T (streamlined production process for standardization and efficiency), Kodak camera (photolithography), Xerox (xerography), Sony (Color TVs and Walkman), GE (light bulbs), Bell Telephone (telephone), IBM (mainframe computer), Atari (videogames), and so on. Enterprises succeeded through fundamental innovations that they mastered and often patented.

Successful business model innovations in the network era require vibrant dynamic ecosystems because these innovations straddle multiple companies and involve the coordination of the capabilities of different companies in order to succeed. A videogame console from Sony or Microsoft succeeds not just because of its superior design and development; it succeeds because of the availability of complementary software that runs on those consoles – and many of these games are developed by third-party independent developers. State-of-the art videogame consoles are useless unless they have complementary videogames that make use of the power and functionality of the hardware consoles. The current battle in videogames goes beyond the functionality of the dominant consoles (Sony's PlayStation vs. Microsoft Xbox vs. Nintendo Wii). The ecosystem also involves key technology relationships (IBM, Intel, and Toshiba), licensing of content (Disney, Warner Brothers), game design and development (Electronic Arts, Sega, Konami), retail distribution, and online portals (Yahoo, MSN). Success involves effective coordination of this dynamic ecosystem.

This notion of complementary hardware-software-services ecosystems is central to succeeding in the network era. Let us go back to the fast changing music and entertainment ecosystem. Digital players capable of playing music on MP3 format existed before Apple introduced its iPod. What made Apple different is its orchestration of an entire ecosystem: changes in the content creation processes (e.g., some music available digitally on iTunes only, creation of podcasts), delivery of content online and over cellular networks, streamlined pricing logic, and the sharing of music within customer communities – but under protected digital rights management. Consumer electronics companies who introduced digital music players focused on narrow domains of product innovation while Apple connected the relevant parts of the innovation ecosystem. In this transformation, the traditional music labels find themselves playing supporting roles to the central orchestrators such as Apple, Microsoft (Zune), and Yahoo with their alliances and partnerships.

Increasingly, more business models will shift from being firm-centric to network-centric. Success is not just based on the core competencies of independent firms but on the collective competencies of ecosystems. So, this shift is not just in a few industries such as computers or music or media. Nearly every business sector is evolving into ecosystem-based competition on a global basis. Software may emerge as the critical glue that defines the shape and structure of the ecosystem and the relative power and value contribution of the different entities within. *So, do you see yourself in an advantageous position within your ecosystems or do you see potential threats?*

## 3. Energize Your Organization to Continually Innovate

Despite the need to recognize the broader innovation ecosystem, the central locus of business model innovation is still within the internal organization. Much has been written on the management challenges of adaptation of business models and the leadership requirements of mobilizing the organization to embrace change. But some points are worth highlighting in the context of the business model innovation propelled by technology.

Within the technology sector, there are many cases of companies that failed to innovate their business models to respond to external changes. These include Digital Equipment, Wang, Data General, Fujitsu, Atari, NCR, and others. At the same time, there are few stellar examples of technology companies that have embarked on business model innovations. We highlighted four in this chapter that have clearly shown some best characteristics of business model innovations in progress.

Apple's Steve Jobs, Microsoft's Bill Gates (and Steve Ballmer), Cisco's John Chambers, and Google's Eric Schmidt are in a different league from other leaders. When the history of the technology sector is written decades from now, they will be considered amongst the elite in the Hall of Fame. Why? They led and adapted their organizations through a tumultuous period of shifts in business models and overcame fierce competitive battles. *So, do you have the intrinsic capability to marshal the collective energy of the organization to continually adapt business models to win in global networks?*

## 4. Anticipate and Prepare for the Inevitable Bumpy Ride

Successful companies recognize that business models are not static but evolve to reflect changing external and internal conditions. Motorola has evolved from its origins in pagers, car radios, and Walkie-talkies for soldiers to now becoming a major leader in a portfolio of communication devices that allow for seamless mobility – a transparent and connected experience as people move between environments and switch their activities among devices and networks. Ed Zander, Chairman and CEO of Motorola described his two years at Motorola in the following way: "All I've done since I got here is focus on one word: *innovation*." It is because without innovation, technology companies face the real possibility of commoditization.

Innovation is not just for high-technology companies. Jeff Immelt at GE observed that: "Constant reinvention is the central necessity at GE. We're all just a moment away from commodity hell." So, he challenged the organization that he inherited from Jack Welch to come up with "imagination breakthroughs" that could generate at least $100 million in new revenue within three years. Under Welch, GE focused on growth through acquisition while Immelt's directive is on innovations from within – representing a different set of principles for innovation. And, Michael Dell has taken over the reins at Dell Computer to shepherd the organization to a new business model just as Bill Ford brought in a new CEO to do the same at Ford Motor Company. *Do you recognize leadership talent in your company that can guide the organization to recognize weak signals and avoid competency traps?*

# CONCLUSIONS

The early years of the post-industrial age offer profound opportunities for some companies and hint at serious challenges for others. Our belief is that successful companies will be differentiated by their ability to understand the technological forces and exploit them to create powerful business models. These business models will be characterized by dynamic adaptation that will allow companies to take advantage of technological developments. Successful business models will emerge from organizations that have leaders who understand the need to craft business strategies that put technology squarely at the center rather than at the periphery. These organizations will also be characterized by mutual recognition and respect for business and I/T competencies and will align their goals and priorities to maximize profitability in the short term while striving for growth in the long term.

# ENDNOTES

1   Vijay Govindarajan and Chris Trimble, *Ten Rules for Strategic Innovators: From Idea to Execution*. Boston, MA: Harvard Business School Press, 2005.

2   James Brian Quinn, *Intelligent Enterprise: A Knowledge and Service Based Paradigm for Industry*. New York, NY: Free Press, 1992.

3   N. Venkatraman and John C. Henderson, "Real Strategies for Virtual Organizing," *Sloan Management Review*, 1998.

4   Nalin Kulatilaka and N. Venkatraman, "Strategic Options in the Digital Era," *Business Strategy Review*, 2001.

5   Martha Amram and Nalin Kulatilaka, *Real Options: Managing Strategic Investments in an Uncertain World*. Boston, MA: Harvard Business School Press, 1998.

6   L. Houston and N. Sakkab, "Connect and Develop: Inside Procter & Gamble's New Model for Innovation," *Harvard Business Review*, March 2006.

7   Annabelle Gawer and Michael Cusumano, *Platform Leadership: How Intel, Microsoft, and Cisco Drive Industry Innovation*. Boston, MA: Harvard Business School Press, 2002.

8   Shona Brown and Kathleen M. Eisenhardt, *Competing on Edge: Strategy as Structured Chaos*. Boston, MA: Harvard Business School Press, 1998.

9   N. Venkatraman, "Lesson's From Google's Playbook," *Leading Edge Forum Journal*, 2006. (http://lef.csc.com).

## 4.2

# ADAPTIVE I/T ARCHITECTURES: THE RISE OF BUSINESS PLATFORMS

**Peter M. Heinckiens,** *Toyota Motor Europe*

## ABSTRACT

Business innovation forces organizations to continuously adapt themselves: they need to support new products, new business processes, and even totally new business models. Doing so successfully requires an organizational capability that is geared towards supporting business innovation. This capability must be engrained in the business and I/T architecture. The agility of the architecture will define how easily an organization can adapt to new business opportunities, and will directly influence the competitiveness of the organization. An adaptive architecture will be a competitive asset, while a non-adaptive architecture may pose a threat for the future success of the company.

This chapter will describe some of the key elements of such an adaptive architecture, and will examine the role of business platforms in creating such an architecture. It will show how business platforms can be built using a mix of ERP systems and in-house developed systems. It will also show how such an architecture requires a new view on software systems.

# A WORLD OF CONSTANT CHANGE

As was extensively discussed in other chapters in this book, the business environment of the 21$^{st}$ century poses important challenges to organizations, among which globalization, innovation, and compliance take a prominent place.

1. Globalization deals with the challenges with which organizations needs to cope in order to move to world-wide operations. This needs to deal with mergers and acquisitions, with aligning different organizational units to act as one single organization, with creating a capability for fast roll out in new markets, with standardizing operations, etc.
2. The innovation challenge is centred around the creation of customer value through the improvement or creation of new products, processes, and business models. In these cases, the time to market and the flexibility with which the organization can produce the value proposition are critical success factors.
3. On the compliance domain, organizations have struggled – and are still struggling – heavily on implementing a set of regulations such as SOX. These regulations require the organization to prove structural compliance to a set of rules.

For most organizations, the above challenges have created a heavy strain and workload on the organization and its I/T department. Furthermore, these challenges often result in conflicting forces.

Indeed, often a marketing department identifies an opportunity, and the I/T organization needs to create an ad-hoc solution as a race against the clock. The result is a working, but point-to-point solution, which poorly integrates with the rest of the organization's activities (and I/T systems). Moreover, since typically a large number of such value propositions need to be created and maintained, such initiatives can result in extensive operational efforts and costs. The silos created by these ad-hoc solutions often counteract the standardization efforts that are being executed by other business departments.

Furthermore, this is not a challenge that must be executed one single time. The current business climate requires continual change and execution. It is hardly surprising that most organizations find that their I/T capabilities limit – rather than create – new business opportunities.[1] These limitations come mainly from the large amount of systems within these companies that were designed in a silo-ed manner as a response to specific business needs rather than from a global, company-wide perspective.

In order to avoid such a situation, we need to create a structural agility in the organization and its I/T systems to guide globalization and enable business innovation. We will show how we can do so by introducing a structural alignment between the organizational strategy and its I/T systems, so that those I/T systems are easily adapted to the changing business environments.

# THE INTEGRATION AND STANDARDIZATION CHALLENGE

The operation model developed by Ross et al.[2] can be used to position the impact of globalization and business innovation. Organizations will need to decide on the level of process standardization they need, and on the degree of business integration they want to pursue (see Figure 1).

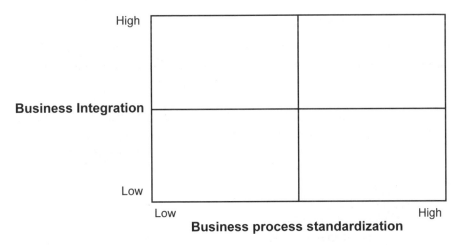

**Figure 1:** *Operating Model  © MIT CISR*

## Standardization

On the one hand, as organizations increase their global operations, there is a drive towards business process standardization. There are a number of reasons for this standardization:

- Improving quality: standardized processes have a well-defined and predictable outcome, and, as such, allow implementing best practices and continuously improving on these.
- Cost-effectiveness: the standardized processes allow the organization to make use of scale-effects – for example, to consolidate certain processes in shared services centers, etc.
- Time to market: having standardized processes allows the organization to roll-out much faster – it can go to a certain new market (country) and roll out its standardized set of processes.
- Responsiveness: creating organizational consistency through standardized processes allows introducing higher responsiveness in the organization.

With regard to the standardization dimension, trade-offs must be made that balance the standardization of business processes to allow your company to operate as a global entity, while still maintaining enough flexibility to cope with local market conditions.

## Business Integration

Integration has to do with improving the information visibility and information flow between the different business processes and different partners in the supply chain. This takes two main forms:

1. **Data integration:** Many organizations feel the need to break the silos and improve the visibility and consistency of key data. This effort could occur within the organization itself, or between the organization and its other partners in the supply chain. We will give an example of each:

   - Within the organization: consider a bank that merges with another bank; it may be advantageous to have a single view on key data, such as customer data. This data can then be consistently used within different departments and by different I/T systems.
   - Between partners in the supply chain: here an example could be sharing customer data, product availability, or sales data between supply chain partners. Sharing data poses many challenges: on the I/T level it requires integration between I/T systems from many different companies, on the business level there may be conflicts as to who owns the customer data. Many organizations are not willing to share this valuable data. Furthermore, maintaining

consistency between all these different databases poses a significant challenge.

2. **Process integration:** Apart from the logical reason of supply-chain responsiveness, organizations are viewing process integration as an important element for value creation and differentiation. The most sophisticated organizations are able to create fully personalized supply-chains that are deeply integrated with their customer's business processes and with those of other trading partners.[3] These organizations see competition more and more in terms of competition between supply chains instead of competition between individual organizations. As such, an organization's competitiveness depends on its ability to create such virtual supply chains and/or easily integrate with those created by other trading partners.

# CASE: LARGE CAR MANUFACTURER

To make our discussions as concrete as possible, we illustrate them using a simple case, which is based on the European expansion of a large car manufacturer.[4] This manufacturer had historically grown its European operations by installing distributors in most European countries. These distributors were introduced over a time period of more than 20 years, and they operated fully independently. In order to meet aggressive growth targets, and to further implement its vision of making the customer central to all processes, the organization needed to start acting as one European company.

## Standardization

The organization started to standardize many of its core processes. As a result, the role of the distributor was revised to focus on marketing and sales for its specific country, taking into account the local market conditions. Many of the logistic processes, on the other hand, were standardized and, in certain cases, also centralized. Examples are the creation of central parts warehouses and central vehicle hubs. Apart from the cost reduction, this synergy also allowed the company to further optimize the supply chain: the shared warehouses allowed for much better parts lead time and became an important component in reducing dealer stock.

This standardization process – which took place for all of the organization's back-end processes – took many years: new warehouses and vehicle hubs needed to be built, others needed to be closed, formerly independent distributors needed to adopt certain standards, etc. The result of standardization, however, had an important impact on the organization.

Apart from harmonizing its current operations, the standardized set of processes (and I/T applications) allowed the organization to enable its growth by being able to accelerate the set up of operations in newly developing markets.

## Innovative and Integrated Processes

The organization also wanted to standardize many of its customer-touching processes in order to ensure a consistent, high-quality customer experience. It furthermore wanted to make those processes end-to-end, thus offering the customer a fully integrated view on the organization and enabling an optimal integration of the demand and supply chain.

As an example, the manufacturer decided to provide the customer with better visibility into the car maintenance process through a number of new offerings. This enhanced the customer experience overall by providing the customer with better up-front knowledge of the cost of maintenance interventions.

*Figure 2: End-to-end Process*

Figure 2 shows how such an integrated process might work. It allows the customer to book a maintenance service – knowing upfront what this maintenance includes and what it will cost. Upon acceptance of this quote, a slot is automatically booked with the repairer, and a work card is created for the technician, detailing the needed service. The end-to-end integration further improves the responsiveness of the supply chain by enabling automatic ordering of the needed parts (using just-in-time principles, and thus reducing dealer stock).

# ARCHITECTURAL CHALLENGES

This case is characteristic of the challenges of organizations that are trying to move to the upper right quadrant in the operating model (see Figure 3):

they want to standardize the business processes to implement best practices, offer a standard experience to the customer, and improve global ability to execute. They also want to increase business process integration from retailer to manufacturer in order to implement customer-centric processes and increase the responsiveness of the supply chain.

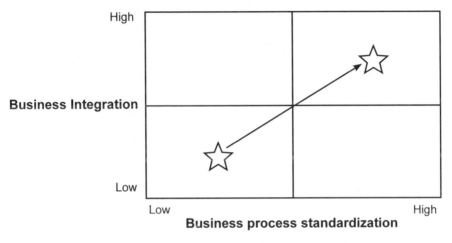

*Figure 3: Desired Operating Model Migration Path*

Making this move proves challenging in two ways:

1. *Challenges of today*: Many organizations have an important legacy environment, thus how can they make this migration within an acceptable time and budget?
2. *Challenges of tomorrow*: How to create an environment that can stand the test of time, in other words, which gives the organization the needed flexibility to adapt to rapidly changing business environments and to implement the necessary changes to support its product and business model innovations.

An adaptive architecture will be needed to address both of these challenges. The first challenge requires adaptability in order to guide the change from the existing business environment to the new environment; the second challenge requires adaptability to implement future strategic initiatives.

The complexity of the existing environment, the required organizational change management, and the amount of legacy systems involved, can soon make even the simple example of the car-maintenance process look like an insurmountable challenge (see Figure 4).

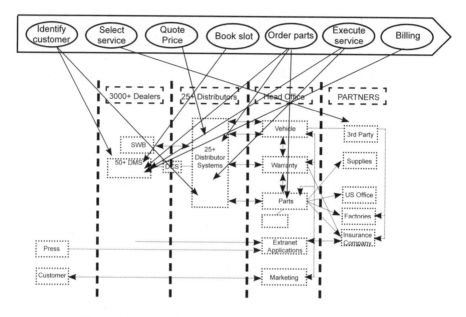

*Figure 4: Integrated Process Mapped onto Legacy Environment*

The first obvious issue is the large number of interactions between the integrated process and various business partners and different I/T systems. For example, the workshop booking step needs to exchange data with the dealer management system (the organization has over 50 different systems in Europe, most of them developed & distributed by third parties), the price quote is done by the distributor system (with over 25 distributors in Europe, and each with its own system), and other process steps are implemented in different systems (some through a head office system, others are outsourced to business partners).

Apart from the system-integration problems, there are also a number of less visible, but equally lethal business problems:

1. Policy issues: for example, the legislation in certain European countries does not allow sharing customer data. How can we safeguard the organization from breaking policy rules (and facing the resulting legal claims)?
2. Data ownership: for commercial reasons, certain business partners (distributors, dealers) may be hesitant to give away "their" customer data.
3. Quality issues: how do we ensure that the data is of the right quality (completeness, correctness)? Furthermore, since this process is

relying on so many different systems, what happens if one of these systems goes offline? How do we ensure quality of service?

4. Cross-business unit view: definitions are not necessarily the same for the different business units. In our example, the definition of a "spare part" could for a dealer include all parts available on the market, while for the head office it only includes parts supplied by this manufacturer.

5. Roll out issues: this integrated process may depend on systems that are not yet fully rolled out. In our example: the "order part" step needs to use the central ordering system. For certain countries this business model is already available, while for other countries this business model will take some years to be implemented, and thus the "old" ordering process must be used. How can we deal with this gradual roll out and how can we adapt the system with minimal changes when the future business model is rolled out for a particular country?

We thus see that instead of just being able to focus on implementing the business system, the project team has to solve a wide range of other organizational concerns. These concerns are often far beyond their scope of influence to solve, and thus often resulting in stagnation of the project.

# IS IMPLEMENTING AN ERP THE ANSWER?

In the past, many organizations tried to move to the upper-right quadrant in Figure 3 through the implementation of an ERP.

This approach to solving the standardization / integration challenge worked relatively well in cases where this organizational change was top-down and implemented by a strong CEO and highly empowered CIO. This strong empowerment and support from the executive board was needed because the choice for an ERP impacts the entire organization and needs a good trade-off between buy and build. An organization gets the maximum benefit from an ERP if it can adapt its business processes fully to those implemented in the ERP – hence the need for good organizational change management and for a strong commitment to move to standardized processes. If, regardless of this empowerment, customizations to the processes are still needed, it often results in expensive customization and maintenance costs.

In order to see how such ERP implementations hold up in the light of globalization and innovation challenges, let us go back to our example.

Imagine that the large car manufacturer already implemented its back-end processes for parts ordering and warehousing using an ERP. We might now decide to extend this ERP system with the following business processes (see Figure 5):

1. The processes to be standardized on distributor and dealer level (such as pricing and billing).
2. The customer-touching vehicle-maintenance process (the integrated end-to-end process).

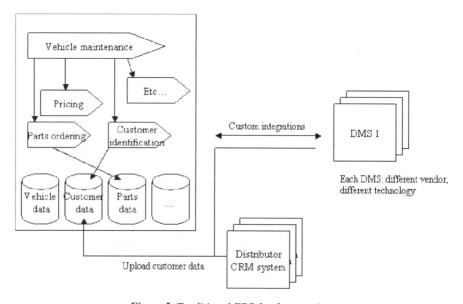

*Figure 5: Traditional ERP Implementation*

## Evaluation of the architecture

### *Standardization versus local flexibility*
By implementing the business processes of the different value-chain partners (head office, distributor, dealer) in the same ERP system, we get a good integration between those partners, but we also limit the local flexibility. The ERP system makes the fundamental assumption that the implemented business processes are (and will remain) standard for all distributors. Furthermore, the above architecture hard-wires those standardization decisions into the integrated end-to-end business processes. This reduces the flexibility of future decisions with regard to the supporting business processes (such as outsourcing or customizing processes).

*Integrated end-to-end process*

The end-to-end process relies on functionality and data that is not implemented in the ERP system (and belongs to other parties). Since traditional ERP implementations require all data to be in the ERP system, we need to create an interface between the ERP and the systems that contain the customer database in order to upload the necessary data (and we thus first need to solve the related data-ownership issues).

We then also need to interface the ERP with the dealer management system (DMS)– or replace the dealer management system with a new system owned by the manufacturer – in order to integrate the workshop bookings.

The costs associated with interfacing different systems account for a large part of the total ERP cost. Furthermore, since such interfacing is largely point-to-point, it provides little structural guarantee for policy enforcement and correct data ownership responsibilities.

*Time to value*

The system – and its architecture as presented above – is implemented as a total offering, and thus assumes an all-or-nothing approach. This means that one either uses the system – and all of its consequences – or doesn't. Because of the complexity of implementing such a system, as well as the organizational change management that it requires, the time-to-value of such implementations may take several years.

As a result, the different business partners (the distributors in our example) may request an improved time-to-value by gradually introducing the new business model in line with that business partner's own organizational change. The introduction of such a partial implementation typically takes on two forms:

1. Some organizations want to start using the advantages of the integrated end-to-end process while still being able to use their legacy implementations of some of the supporting processes (such as the parts ordering). This results in expensive and difficult-to-maintain customizations to the ERP (Figure 6a).
2. Other organizations may not be ready to implement the end-to-end process, but may want to use several of the standardized processes that the ERP implemented, such as the just-in-time parts ordering, or the standardized pricing. This results in expensive ad-hoc integrations (Figure 6b).

The monolithic approach of the system architecture makes both requests expensive and difficult to answer. Furthermore, the heavy customization to the ERP takes away several of its original advantages (having a standard package) and results in extensive difficulties and costs with regard to upgrades to future releases of the ERP.

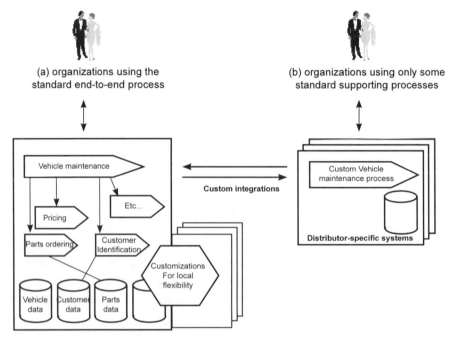

*Figure 6: Impact of Partial Roll-out*

## The Old Assumptions no Longer Hold True

If we investigate more closely the problems with the previous architecture, we find that that there is a major difference with today's business models and the ones implemented by traditional ERP roll-outs. Such traditional ERP implementations made a number of important assumptions about the business processes they implemented:

1. The processes could be highly standardized
2. There is only slow evolution in process changes
3. The end-to-end processes and all of their sub-processes are fully under the control of the organization implementing the ERP.

Today, these assumptions no longer hold:

1. Although many of the processes can still be standardized, organizations want the possibility to differentiate through organization-specific processes. Furthermore globalization requirements oblige us to be able to quickly shift between standardization and localization decisions.
2. Product, process, and business model innovation require must faster process changes
3. Organizations create customer value by implementing end-to-end processes that span the entire value chain, and thus span multiple business partners. Hence, we can no longer assume that these end-to-end processes are under the control of a single organization.

Figure 7 illustrates the new situation created by the end-to-end processes. It distinguishes two types of processes: the end-to-end processes and the business-unit-level processes.

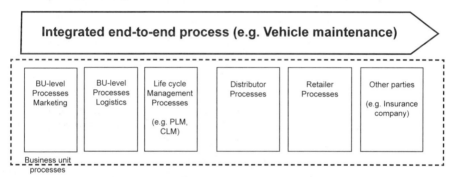

*Figure 7: Cross-organization Processes*

Fundamental about the BU-level process is that it has clear ownership: its implementation is under full control of the business unit that is responsible for it. Examples are: parts ordering (belongs to the parts business unit), workshop booking (belongs to the dealer), etc.

The end-to-end processes, on the other hand, do not belong to any single business unit, not even any single organization. Since the end-to-end process becomes a value proposition in itself, and is often customized to certain customer types, we could argue that this process belongs to the customer. Furthermore, since these are a value proposition in themselves, they need strong flexibility to change.

When looking back at the basic assumptions for implementing ERP's, we see that these may still hold for the internals of the different boxes in

Figure 7, but not for the integrated process. Hence, while an ERP system can be used to implement each of the individual business-unit (or business partner) processes, it is not suited to implement the cross-value-chain processes.

In summary, traditional ERP implementations are suitable as long as they remain within one single organizational unit. In this context, such an organizational unit means a unit in which all decisions on standardization are within the same ownership, have similar needs towards local flexibility (none), and all processes have similar time dynamics. If business processes from multiple organizational units are combined within one integrated ERP implementation, the processes are hard-coupled and have thus no freedom towards local flexibility.

# TOWARDS AN ADAPTIVE ARCHITECTURE

Notice that, although the problem of the non-adaptive architecture described in the previous section was manifested on the I/T level, at its root this is a business problem:

- This entire project was focused on creating a solution for a fixed defined problem, rather than creating a set of business capabilities with which a large set of business problems can be addressed (and then assembling these into a solution).
- The architecture implemented processes that are positioned on multiple levels of ownership: it contained the processes that are centralized at the head office (the parts logistics), but also process implementation at other business partners (such as pricing process at the distributors). We need to ask ourselves if we really want to do this, because this may further increase time-to-market (do all countries buy into this standardized pricing process) and will certainly limit future agility: if market conditions in a certain country demand a different pricing approach, this will be difficult and costly to implement.
- Referring back to the operating model, we tried to move along the two axes within the same implementation. It is important to realize that these axes have totally different dynamics. Standardization is typically a long process: it requires thorough understanding of the current processes and strong evaluation and consensus building on the future processes. As we already explained before, the implementation of this standardization can also result in significant

organizational changes, and thus may take a long time to implement. The integration axis, on the other hand, is largely dictated by process-innovation. Since these projects have an important competitive value positioning, they require fast roll-out times.

Hard-wiring the two types of axes on the same project results in a time-to-market that is defined by the slowest of the two above dynamics. To improve time-to-market of the system, and the agility of the organization, it is thus important to be able to implement both dynamics independently of each other.

An adaptive architecture can be built by explicitly specifying in the architecture what the organization implicitly does: integrating a number of processes to create larger processes.

In order to do so, we must focus on identifying the basic building blocks – the business capabilities – that an organization needs in order to construct its value propositions. Such building blocks could be either data-related (such as an integrated customer-view, and integrated product-view), or process-related (such as a pricing process, an ordering process, a billing process, etc.). Furthermore, these building blocks should be closely aligned with organizational structure and policies.

Table 1 shows some of the building blocks for our case study:

| Building block (enterprise service) | Owner | Remarks |
| --- | --- | --- |
| Ordering | Head office | Part of multi-year roll-out plan |
| Billing | Retailer | |
| Pricing | Distributor | Standardization of pricing rules under discussion |
| Customer management | Distributor | In certain countries: owner is the retailer |
| Workshop booking | Retailer | |
| Service definitions | Head office | Maintenance outsourced to 3rd party |

*Table 1: Enterprise Business Service Definitions*

Once the building blocks are identified and aligned with organizational structure and policies, the organization can focus on *using* these building blocks – we will call them enterprise business services – to construct a value offering. Figure 8 illustrates this for our vehicle-maintenance process. Such an end-to-end process could consist of the organization's own business services, but could also rely on services offered by other business partners (e.g. insurance company, outsourced processes, etc.). Many small and medium enterprises (SMEs) are today specializing in one or more enterprise business services and offering these as an outsourced process to other companies.

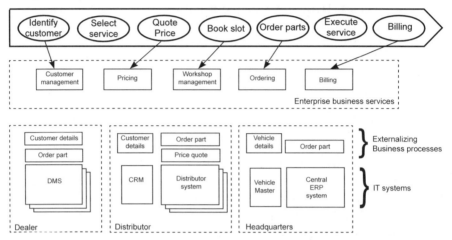

*Figure 8: Orchestrating the End-to-end Business Process*

# BUSINESS PLATFORMS

In the previous section we showed how to take the discussion away from merely building applications to creating and leveraging business capabilities. Technological evolutions, such as service-oriented architectures (SOA) have helped us to set an important step in reflecting the above discussions in the way that I/T systems are developed. They do so by offering a standard technology in which such services can be made available in a standard, platform-independent, and location-transparent way.

Recent evolutions in ERP technology have now leveraged SOA to move the ERP's from traditional monolithic business applications to flexible business platforms. Such a business platform consists of two main elements:

1. A catalogue of (standard) business services that can be individually addressed, and which have the required governance processes in place (to ensure ownership, compliance, etc).
2. An environment to create innovative value offerings by orchestrating the business services into end-to-end processes.

Such a business platform thus allows us to create a structural alignment between the organizational change-process and the I/T systems that support this organization.

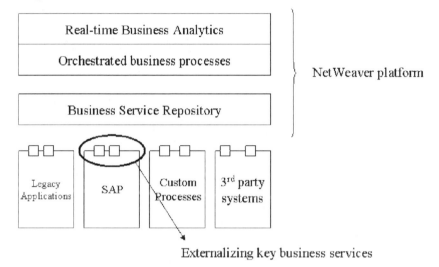

Externalizing key business services

*Figure 9: Business Platform*

SAP, for example, has made the development of such a business platform the cornerstone of its strategy (Figure 9). It has fully embraced the SOA concept by opening up (externalizing) its business processes as enterprise services, and by offering a dedicated platform (NetWeaver) to orchestrate these. As such SAP has taken an important step towards becoming a real business platform that can be the core engine for creating a highly adaptive architecture that is able to support business innovation.

SAP currently has a wide variety of business services available. This allows organizations to combine the better of two worlds: for those business processes that are standard, they can leverage on the out-of-the box functionality and the well-known advantages of mature ERP systems, while they can use custom development for the processes that cannot be mapped onto the default ERP functionality. As such, organizations avoid hard-wiring customizations within the ERP.

The NetWeaver platform offers an advanced development environment to manage and orchestrate the business services. As such, it allows building highly adaptive and agile systems. Such platforms also collect key metrics on the end-to-end business processes, which then can be used to obtain insight into the business process and continuously optimize the business process. The most advanced applications of this technology actually allow real-time optimization of the business process – for example by adapting the pricing mechanism according to current demand and product availability.

# AGILITY TOWARDS PROCESS AND PRODUCT INNOVATION

The architectural approach described in the previous sections allows decoupling the two axes in the operating model, and thus separating their different dynamics (Figure 10). We will discuss this below.

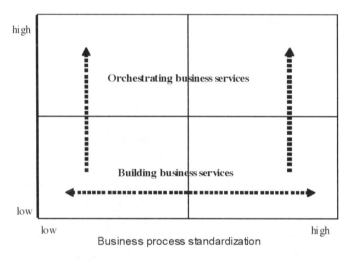

*Figure 10: Decoupling Standardization and Integration*

## Flexibility Between Standardization and Localization

The discussion about building the enterprise business services happens along the standardization axis. After identifying the necessary business capabilities, the organization needs to decide on the optimal level of standardization, and how to implement this standardization (along with roll-out schedule, etc.). The organization also needs to decide whether it will keep this capability in house, or whether it wants the flexibility of outsourcing.

Over time, the answers to the above questions might evolve (e.g. as the organization addresses new markets, or as the result of innovation, new market conditions, merger and acquisitions, etc.). For example, an organization could decide to largely standardize a certain process over its current scope of operations. But then, as it enters a new market in which is has limited ability to execute, outsource the process for that particular market.

The enterprise services architecture offers the organization the needed flexibility to adapt its future business model by separating the "what" from the "how" question:

- The "What" question deals with what we need, and is about externalizing a business service to the rest of the organization. It is about defining what it means when we talk about an order, about a price, and so on. While the implementation of these services may vary from business partner to business partner, on this level we want a clear definition of the service contract: what we enter, and what we get back. By explicitly defining and standardizing such a set of service specifications, we actually construct a common business language to be used between all partners in the supply chain.
- The "How" question deals with the actual implementation of the business service. This implementation could significantly differ depending on factors specific to a certain country or business partner.

Since an enterprise service architecture exposes only the service definitions to the organization while keeping the actual implementation of the service encapsulated within a relatively small unit of work, it becomes possible to flexibly switch between such implementations, or to use different implementations for different countries or business partners.

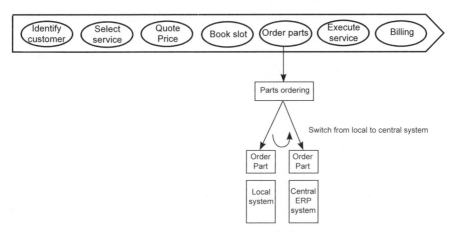

*Figure 11: Flexibility Between Localization and Standardization*

This allows the organization to continuously optimize and improve on its business capabilities without impacting the deployed business systems. For example, the organization can move a new country into the centralized stock model by simply switching that country's parts ordering service from the legacy system towards the ERP (see Figure 11). Vice-versa, one can decide to implement local flexibility by redirecting a standard implementation to a local version for a particular market. An example could be optimizing the pricing process to accommodate the local needs of a certain market. Thanks to the encapsulation offered by the enterprise services, these changes do not impact the often many systems that implement the end-to-end processes.

## Process Agility

The discussion about orchestrating end-to-end processes happens along the integration axis; this is not so much a question of implementing the different process steps, it is much more a matter of orchestrating these steps. Indeed, how the different process steps (e.g. ordering, financing, etc.) are implemented is the responsibility of the different business units, and is addressed within the implementation of the business service. The integration question is about just that: integrating the different individual processes in an end-to-end process to deliver customer value. It is thus a question of assembling the different business capabilities into a larger entity.

As the organization assembles data about the effectiveness of the business processes, these processes can easily be adapted to take into account this new knowledge. It is also relatively easy to adapt the processes to new market conditions (such new customer types, etc.), and to flexibly change or extend the business processes.

In our example, imagine that as part of a continuous quest for quality and customer satisfaction, the marketing department (a different department from the one that implemented the vehicle maintenance process) wants to measure the customer satisfaction each time a customer has a significant interaction with a dealer. This includes extending the business with an additional step.

Figure 12 shows how this is just a matter of including a call to an extra business service in the orchestrated process:

- The team that is responsible for the implementation of the end-to-end process (in this case somebody from the after-sales department) does not have to worry about the workings or internals of this extra step; they just call it.

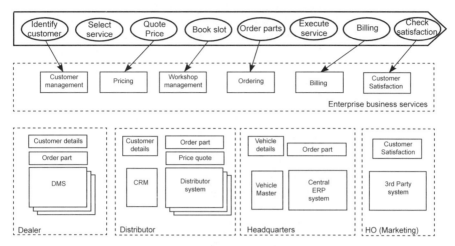

*Figure 12: Extending the End-to-end Process*

- The business unit responsible for this process step (marketing) needs to implement the business service, and decide on issues such as standardization, business process outsourcing, etc.

Thanks to the architectural approach it becomes relatively straightforward to adapt the system to support the process innovation, both on a technical and an organizational level. In traditional architectures, this would have resulted in expensive custom integrations, and also in long discussions between the marketing department and the after-sales department on how to integrate the third party system with "their" system.

## BUSINESS ASPECTS OF SERVICES

The previous sections showed that an adaptive business architecture based on enterprise services goes much further than the choice and usage of a number of technologies. It is in the first place a matter of correctly defining business services, recognizing ownership of these services, complying with rules and regulations, and defining and implementing roles and responsibilities.

One of the most impacting consequences of the SOA paradigm is the cross-business-unit view that it implies. Indeed, where each business unit was previously responsible for and in complete ownership of "their" I/T systems, this is now no longer the case. While business units maintain ownership of the BU-level processes implemented by those systems, they also have an enterprise-wide responsibility for externalizing these BU-level processes and the enterprise data implemented by their systems. Furthermore, business units cannot simply expect to own the customer-touching end-to-end processes.

The example of Figure 12, where we extended the car-maintenance process with the customer-satisfaction follow-up, showed how the end-to-end process crosses business units. Even if the original implementation looked confined to the after-sales business unit, the introduced process change has made this cross-business-unit aspect visible: the integrated process got a step that is owned by the marketing department.

This may pose significant challenge for teams that are used to thinking only about their silo. It will require them to architect their systems to correctly represent the BU-level specific part within a larger context of cross-organizational processes. Furthermore, when implementing the BU-specific processes they need to think about the bigger picture: they can no longer take an application (or a business service) offline whenever they want as it could be used by another business process. In a similar way, business units cannot just change a definition of a data element, as it needs to be positioned in an enterprise view.

As a result, clear governance, including service level agreements (SLA's) are fundamental for the success of such an architecture. Below are some guidelines that can help in positioning projects in an enterprise services architecture.

- Evaluate if the business project contains aspects with different time dynamics (per our discussion about standardization versus integration). If this is the case, you should try to separate these aspects. Otherwise the time-to-value will be determined by the slowest of these dynamics. A good way of doing so is to separate the parts of the business project that have to do with business process integration from the parts that are about business process standardization.
- Since standardization and integration projects have different dynamics, do not mix them. Integration projects should concentrate on the *specification* and integration of business services: identifying the needed services, agreeing on their service contract, and then integrating these into a larger business process. Standardization projects should concentrate on gradual standardization of the *implementation* of such business services.

- To identify the services for a new business project, ask yourself "which elementary business capabilities (business services) do I need in order to implement this new value offering?" In our example this would result in services for ordering, parts availability, pricing, customer information, etc.

  The next question is then, who owns these services. For those services for which the ownership belongs to your own business unit, you will be responsible for implementing them. When doing so, think about whether you may need flexibility for future localization. For services for which the ownership should structurally be with another business unit, a discussion must take place with that business unit on making the needed functionality available. Keep the discussion on the "what" level and avoid discussions about the "how" part.

  This brings with it some important challenges. The most obvious one is funding: who is supposed to pay for this extra effort – both for the initial development and for the maintenance? Should the business unit requesting the service or the business unit that owns the service pay the costs? Multiple options are possible, and require the definition of a clear governance model at the enterprise level.

- If a business system that you are implementing contains processes that can be needed by other actors in the supply chain, you should consider externalizing these processes as enterprise services.

- Do not hardwire business processes that belong to different organizational units (even if these processes are standardized). This would reduce future agility towards process outsourcing, or localization of the process. Integrate the processes through an enterprise business service instead.

- Even if an end-to-end process looks like it is owned by your business unit, in most cases it is not, and may need future extension. Hence, do not hardwire this process with its supporting processes.

In our experience it has proven advantageous to have this discussion facilitated by an enterprise architecture (EA) department. This department is then responsible for helping to translate the original business question into an aggregation of business capabilities, and for helping to identify the business owners for the corresponding business services. This department can also play a central role in helping to standardize these service definitions and giving them an enterprise-wide scope. The EA department will typically also be responsible for maintaining the catalogue of enterprise services.

# CONCLUSION

In today's world of globalization and constant business innovation, adaptive architectures are crucial for the long-term competitiveness of organizations. We showed how a business platform based on an enterprise-service architecture can form the cornerstone of such an adaptive architecture.

It requires organizations to change their view on application development from "building applications" to (1) creating business capabilities embedded in enterprise services, and then (2) using these services to create innovative value propositions. Since these services contain, besides the I/T implementation, also rules about ownership, policy enforcement, and standardization, they allow a structural enforcement of compliance rules and organizational roles and responsibilities.

We showed how modern ERP platforms – such as SAP and its Netweaver platform – leverage such an architecture by offering sets of pre-defined enterprise services and an environment to flexibly integrate these services. As such, modern ERP platforms can form the basis for implementing and integrating a core set of business capabilities. Such a platform also allows organizations to address the buy versus build trade-off: the ERP can be used to implement the standard services, while the organization's differentiating processes can be exposed as custom-built services, and then easily integrated into the ERP platform.

# ENDNOTES

1   Jeanne W. Ross, "Creating a strategic IT alignment competency: learning in stages," *MIT Sloan School of Management Working Paper No 4314-03*, 2003.
2   Jeanne W. Ross, Peter Weill, David Robertson, *Enterprise Architecture as Strategy*, Harvard Business School Press, 2006.
3   See for example: A.F. Farhoomand, P.S.P. Ng, W.L. Conley, "Building a successful e-business: The FedEx Story," *Communications of the ACM*, Vol 46. No4, 2003.
4   This case is for illustrative purposes only. Although it is based on actual experiences of the author, it has been simplified and adapted for this book. Furthermore, the details of the projects presented in this case have been modified and should not be seen as representing or reflecting any real strategy or situation of the car manufacturer on which this case is inspired.

# ABOUT THE CONTRIBUTORS

## Dan Pantaleo

After a career of twenty-five years in higher education as a faculty member, Fulbright Scholar, dean, academic vice president, and provost, Dan Pantaleo spent four years as Vice President for Product Development with an interactive multimedia education and training developer.

Dan left that post to assume the responsibilities of Program Manager for SAP America's University Alliance Program where he has been able to apply his knowledge of higher education and interactive learning to significantly develop the Program into a leading global, corporate higher-education program.

As a Vice President in the Global Communications organization, Dan is presently head of the Corporate Thought Leadership team responsible for the development of corporate thought leadership content in collaboration with external experts in a variety of fields. His responsibilities also include Corporate Social Responsibility, Corporate Content Management, and Executive Communications.

Dan holds a B.S. degree in chemistry from Manhattan College and a Ph.D. in Inorganic Chemistry from Emory University. He served as a Fulbright Scholar in Science Education, held a post-doctoral appointment in the chemistry department at Louisiana State University, and took post-doctoral coursework in astrophysics at Georgia State University.

Dan co-authored the book, The Agile Enterprise, which was published by Springer in 2005.

## Nirmal Pal

Nirmal Pal retired in August, 2005 as the Executive Director of the eBusiness Research Center at The Pennsylvania State University (eBRC), which fosters research in e-business strategy, management, marketing, and other related areas to improve business operations. He assumed this role in February, 2000. Before joining the University, he was Director, IBM Global Services Consulting Group, White Plains, New York. As a part of a distinguished

39-year career at IBM, he directed IBM's e-business consulting practice worldwide and worked closely with Fortune 500 clients on e-business strategies. His IBM network of e-business consultants worldwide entered into many consulting engagements with major organizations to help them with e-business, e-commerce, Intranet/Extranet, and other Internet related activities. He has been a member of IBM Consulting Group's management team since its inception in 1991 and helped grow the business for this unit from zero to over one billion US dollars, and from zero to over 5000 consultants, in just seven years.

Under his leadership, the Penn State eBusiness Research Center (eBRC) is considered a preeminent research center in this country. eRBC, which is now called Center For Digital Transformation, has established a network of world renowned scholars and many of their research papers are available on line at the eBRC web site. Nirmal is sought after by the media for his expert opinion on many e-business and related issues. He has given talks on e-business in many conferences both at national and international levels. eBRC published a book in 2001 called Pushing the Digital Frontier, which was rated by the Choice magazine as one of the two best academic titles of 2001. Nirmal published two more books, the Power of One in 2003, and the Agile Enterprise in 2005. He holds degrees in Electrical Engineering and Computer Science.

## Nenshad Bardoliwalla

Nenshad Bardoliwalla is Vice President, Solution Management for Corporate Performance Management products at SAP. In this role, Nenshad is responsible for defining the vision, strategy, and product definition of Performance Management products @ SAP. In his role as visionary, Nenshad developed the positioning of SAP's business intelligence, analytic applications, and performance management products into the industry's most comprehensive portfolio of products for providing business insight in the context of core business processes. In his role as strategist, Nenshad was the architect behind SAP's dramatic investment in the performance management space, leading to the strategic acquisitions of Pilot Software and OutlookSoft.

Nenshad began his career in Business Analytics at Siebel Systems, Inc., where he was responsible for building the company's first analytic application for customer service using Business Objects and led the company's internal deployment of Siebel Analytics immediately after Siebel's acquisition of nQuire. He spent two years as the premier customer-facing expert on Siebel Analytics as a member of Expert Services, and was the first-call resource of

Siebel's executive team for assisting strategic customers like Cisco, Procter & Gamble, Microsoft, and HP. In his last role at Siebel, he led the platform product management team for Siebel Analytics and oversaw the release of Siebel Analytics 7.8, by which point Siebel Analytics was both the fastest growing and second largest product line at Siebel.

After his stint at Siebel, Nenshad was Senior Manager on Hyperion Solutions' Product Strategy team. In this role, he was responsible for the Product Marketing of the Business Intelligence components of Hyperion System 9, the company's most successful product launch in its history. He was also a key architect of Hyperion's next-generation Business Performance Management Strategy which contributed to Hyperion's move into the Leader's position of the Gartner Magic Quadrant for Corporate Performance Management Suites.

## Lilac Berniker

Lilac Berniker is Manager, Innosight, LLC. Lilac has focused the majority of her work on assisting technology, pharmaceutical, and chemicals clients to leverage disruptive theory to further their businesses.

Prior to joining Innosight, Lilac led competitive and business strategy efforts within IBM's Grid Computing group, one of IBM's emerging business areas. This role required her to work across the layers of information technology, from storage to servers and from hardware to software, each with their own flavor of proprietary and open architectures. Her work at IBM built on her experience as a computer scientist at Argonne National Laboratory, working with the leading grid research effort, The Globus Project, in its early years.

Between her time at Argonne and IBM, Lilac served as a Principal Information Architect at Fidelity Investments, designing online financial planning tools for customer use. She also managed web content at Blue Cross Blue Shield of Massachusetts, leading the HMO's web site redesign project to facilitate customer self-service.

Lilac has an MBA from the MIT Sloan School of Management, as well as a B.S in Computer Science and a B.A. in French, with minors in English Writing and Philosophy from Pacific Lutheran University.

## Ranga Bodla

Ranga Bodla is Director, Solutions Management, SAP Corporate Performance Management. As Director of Solutions Management for SAP Strategy Management, Ranga Bodla is chartered with leading the vision for delivery of innovative strategy management products as part of SAP's broader Corporate Performance Management offerings. Leveraging over 12 years of experience in building products for both large and small high-tech companies, Bodla is responsible for bringing relevant and innovative solutions to improve business performance.

He is a frequent speaker and contributor to the performance management community having written and presented extensively on numerous topics related to Performance Management. Prior to joining SAP, Bodla led marketing for Pilot Software (acquired by SAP) as well as Hyperion and IBM.

## Harald Borner

Harald Borner is SAP's Head of Global Top Talent Management in the office of the CEO. He reports to Henning Kagermann, Chairman of the Executive Board of SAP AG and Chief Executive Officer.

Harald joined SAP in 2003 to help build its global Corporate Strategy Group (CSG) in Walldorf, Germany and Palo Alto, CA. As a member of the CSG senior management team, he focused on the strategy and organization of the field and support services businesses of SAP. In 2005, Borner was appointed to his current role as SVP and global head of SAP's Top Talent Management to build a team that drives cross-line of business activities for the senior top talent population.

For ten years before life at SAP, Borner was at the Boston Consulting Group (BCG) as a Principal in Munich and Paris, concentrating on technology customers' strategy and operations assignments. He also served as recruiting director for Germany and Austria.

Borner's professional career began in international high tech research as a fellow scholar and project leader at CERN, the European laboratory for particle physics in Geneva, where he worked in the Delphi collaboration at the Large Electron-Positron Collider (LEP) Accelerator.

Borner holds both master's and doctorate degrees in physics from Oxford University, as well as a bachelor's degree in economics and operations research, earned in parallel to his doctoral research. He commenced his studies of physics, mathematics, and philosophy in Munich.

## Amit Chatterjee

Amit Chatterjee is senior vice president, commercialization, for SAP's Business User Development group. In this role, Chatterjee is responsible for the business strategy and product road map for key enterprise solutions in the areas of Governance, Risk and Compliance (GRC), Analytics and Corporate Performance Management (CPM), enterprise search, user interface, mobile applications, and Duet (SAP's joint offering with Microsoft), among others.

Prior to this role, Chatterjee was senior vice president and general manager of SAP's GRC business unit, where he was instrumental in the creation, growth and success of the unit and its solutions. Before leading the GRC team, Chatterjee held a number of senior management positions at SAP, where he played an integral role in strategy and product development efforts for important initiatives such as SAP NetWeaver and Enterprise Service-Oriented Architecture (Enterprise SOA).

Prior to SAP, Chatterjee held management roles at McKinsey, Excite@ Home, Luminant Worldwide and Kendara. He attended the University of California, Berkeley and Stanford University.

## Stacy Comes

Stacy Comes is the Director of Corporate Thought Leadership for SAP Global Communications. In this role, Stacy is responsible for developing executive platforms on issues that affect future business growth for the company in conjunction with communications leaders to position senior executives as industry thought leaders. She also has the responsibility to identify thought leaders to provide specialized expertise for collaborative research projects and executive information programs that benefit SAP and SAP customers.

Stacy joined SAP America in 1998 as a project manager in Education Services, responsible for the introduction and marketing of new products. She moved into a product manager role shortly thereafter managing the roll-out and training for new education products in the US market. Prior to joining SAP, she began her career at CIGNA Corporation in Philadelphia, Pennsylvania. At CIGNA, Stacy successfully completed a management development program and held a number of positions in the Human Resources and Financial departments. Upon completion of the program, she managed the Philadelphia-based University Relations department and was responsible for all undergraduate and graduate level recruiting.

Ms. Comes holds an undergraduate degree in Accounting and Business Management from Franklin and Marshall College and an MBA with a concentration in Strategic Management from Temple University. She is an active board member of The Pennsylvania State University Center for Digital Business and the Temple University Institute for Business and Information Technology.

## Thomas H. Davenport

Tom Davenport holds the President's Chair in Information Technology and Management at Babson College. He is a widely published author and acclaimed speaker and consultant on the topics of business analytics, process management, information and knowledge management, reengineering, enterprise systems, and electronic business and markets. He has a Ph.D. from Harvard University in organizational behavior and has taught at the Harvard Business School, the University of Chicago, Dartmouth's Tuck School of Business, and the University of Texas at Austin. He was previously a partner and head of the Accenture Institute for Strategic Change, and also directed research at several other consulting firms, including McKinsey & Company and Ernst & Young.

Tom's most recent book (with Jeanne Harris) is *Competing on Analytics: The New Science of Winning.* Tom wrote, co-authored or edited eleven other books, including the first books on business process reengineering and achieving value from enterprise systems. He has written over 100 articles for such publications as *Harvard Business Review, Sloan Management Review, California Management Review,* the *Financial Times*, and many other publications. Tom has also been a columnist for *CIO, InformationWeek,* and *Darwin* magazines. In 2003 he was named one of the world's "Top 25 Consultants" by *Consulting* magazine. In 2005 he was named one of the top 3 "Business/Technology Analysts" in the world by *Optimize* magazine. In 2007 he was named one of the 100 most influential people in the information technology industry by Ziff-Davis magazines, and was the highest-ranked business academic.

## Peter Heinckiens

Peter M. Heinckiens is Chief Architect and Deputy General Manager I/T Strategy at Toyota Motor Europe, where he is responsible for developing and implementing the strategy for the integration of Toyota's European value chain.

A significant part of Peter's efforts go to transforming traditional business models & supply chains using the potential of new technologies. This includes externalization and redesign of business processes, virtualizing the supply chain and integrating it with the demand chain, and implementing adaptive architectures to enable business innovation. One of the main undertakings he is currently involved in is providing the necessary business agility through the introduction of an SOA-based business architecture over

28 countries and over hundreds of different systems.

Dr. Heinckiens has a wide experience in different industries: he has led strategic projects in an international banking context, in government, in manufacturing, in telecom, and in logistics. He has been working in international and multi-cultural environments (Europe, US, Africa, and Asia) most of his professional life. He especially enjoys the opportunity to combine his business and technological skills with the social and communication skills needed to handle the "people issues" that are crucial for the success of a project.

He is a frequently invited speaker at international conferences, lectures at several universities, and is author of three books.

## Herbert M. Heitmann

Herbert Heitmann is Senior Vice President, Global Communications, Office of the CEO, SAP AG. As senior vice president of Global Communications for SAP AG, Herbert Heitmann leads all communications activities for SAP stakeholders around the globe, including investors, customers, partners, employees, and the general public. He is also responsible for corporate reputation building and management. In his role, Heitmann acts as an advisor to Henning Kagermann, CEO of SAP AG, regarding all aspects of communications strategy.

Heitmann has more than 15 years of experience in corporate and public communications. He has a wide range of past experience in the public and private sector, from research and development at leading corporations including Procter & Gamble (P&G) and Henkel, to a political advisory role in Germany's parliament. Throughout his professional career, Heitmann's main focus has been on driving effective communications among very diverse stakeholders.

Heitmann joined SAP in 1998 as a speechwriter for Hasso Plattner (an SAP co-founder and current chairperson of the SAP Supervisory Board) directly from the German Parliament where he served as a political consultant on technical, educational, and scientific issues. He played a strategic role in several political campaigns and cross-party negotiations, for example, on issues ranging from the future of nuclear power in Germany, to the European Space Station and the creation of Germany's first law on genetic engineering. He also participated in an exchange program with the United States Congress.

Prior to his tenure in the German government, Heitmann worked as a chemical engineer, responsible for paper products design optimization at P&G; the automation of consumer testing at Henkel; and efficiency gains in the gold refinery process at Johannesburg Consolidated Investments.

Heitmann is a member of the *Arthur W. Page Society*, a professional association that aims to strengthen the management policy role of senior communications executives and is also an associate of the European Round Table of Industrialists, where he heads up their communications task force.

Heitmann earned his doctorate in chemical engineering from the University of Dortmund, Germany.

## John C. Henderson

Professor John C. Henderson is the Richard C. Shipley Jr. Professor of Management at Boston University's School of Management. He also serves as the Director of the Boston University Institute for Leading in a Dynamic Economy, BUILDE at the School. He received his Ph.D. from the University of Texas at Austin. He is a noted researcher, consultant and executive educator with published papers appearing in journals such as *Management Science, Sloan Management Review, MIS Quarterly, IBM Systems Journal, European Management Journal*, and many others. He is the co-author of the *Knowledge Engine*, which explores how effective leaders leverage the firm's knowledge assets. He is also a member of the board of Directors for ICEX, and the Digital and Communication Technology Advisory Board for BP.

His co-authored paper with N. Venkatraman on Strategic Alignment of Business and I/T Strategies was selected by the *IBM Systems Journal* as a "turning point" article, one of the most influential papers on Information Technology strategy published by the Journal since 1962. His work on Alliances and Partnerships is widely used by public and private organizations to help executives structure and lead network-based organizations. Professor Henderson's current research focuses on three main areas: wireless networks and the economics of business platforms, managing strategic partnerships, and aligning business and I/T strategies. Prior to joining Boston University, he was a faculty member at the MIT Sloan School of Management.

## Mark Johnson

Mark Johnson is co-founder and chairman of Innosight, an innovation-based consulting and executive training firm focused on helping companies and institutions innovate for new growth and transformation. He co-founded the firm with Harvard Business School professor and best selling author on innovation, Clayton M. Christensen.

Mark has led numerous consulting engagements within Fortune 500 companies in a broad range of industries, including consumer packaged goods, healthcare, commercial enterprise I/T, oil and gas, aerospace/defense, and government labs. Mark has also done work at the country level, having led a large-scale innovation management project for the government of Singapore. Many of the insights from Mark's client work can be found in the award winning article from the 2002 spring issue of Sloan Management Review entitled, "Foundations for Growth: How to Build Disruptive New Businesses," which he co-authored with Clayton Christensen.

Mark's most recent work has focused on business model innovation, helping companies create distinct business models, strategies, and skills to manage new market growth. A Harvard Business Review article describing these concepts is forthcoming.

Mark is a much requested authority and speaker on innovation, transformation, and business model change and has been a featured speaker at several conferences in the defense, automotive, healthcare, financial services, and venture capital industries. In November 2006, Mark was a featured speaker at the Fortune Innovation Forum in New York.

Prior to co-founding Innosight, Mark was a consultant at Booz | Allen | Hamilton where he worked on a variety of assignments for clients involved in managing innovation and comprehensive change programs. Additionally, Mark worked with Harvard Business School professor David Garvin in developing an approach and tools to help clients improve their strategy development process through learning based methods. Prior to joining Booz | Allen | Hamilton, Mark was an officer in the U.S. Navy. He is a veteran of Operation Desert Storm.

Mark received his MBA with second year honors from the Harvard Business School. He received a Master's degree in Civil Engineering and Engineering Mechanics from Columbia University and a Bachelor's degree in Aerospace Engineering from the United States Naval Academy.

## John M. Jordan

John Jordan is Executive Director, Center for Digital Transformation. Dr. Jordan received his Ph.D. in American Studies from the University of Michigan, an MAR from Yale University, and a B.A. in Political Science and History from Duke University. His research focuses on emerging technologies and their impact on business strategy, design, and practice. His Ph.D. dissertation, on the wide use of engineering images and metaphors in American society in early 20th century America, was published by University of North Carolina Press. In addition to placing articles in *American National Biography*, *Technology and Culture*, and other professional publications, he has written a monthly emerging technologies newsletter since 1997 and reviewed books for both *Harvard Review* and *Upside*. Dr. Jordan has also been profiled in the *Wall Street Journal, Fast Company, Investor's Business*

*Daily,* and *The International Herald Tribune.*

Dr. Jordan teaches Information Technology and Innovation and Entrepreneurship in the MBA program. Before coming to Smeal, he combined business and technology research with client responsibilities in the Office of the Chief Technologist at Capgemini, the Center for Business Innovation at Ernst & Young, and the Applied Technology Group at Computer Sciences Corporation. His clients included leaders on four continents in pharmaceuticals, travel and tourism, manufacturing and logistics, financial services, and consumer products and retail. Prior to entering consulting, he won teaching awards at Harvard University and the University of Michigan.

He has served on the advisory boards of the Demo emerging technologies conference, the Gartner G2 industry service, and several startup companies.

## Mathias Kirchmer

Mathias Kirchmer is Chief Innovation and Marketing Officer, IDS Scheer Global, the leading provider of business process excellence solutions. The company's ARIS based solutions offer a complete portfolio for "Business Process Excellence," including the services, software, and methods to address all phases of the business process lifecycle: design, implementation, execution, and continuous improvement.

Dr. Kirchmer, a renowned expert in business process management, is a member of the Senior Management Team of IDS Scheer AG. Located in the USA, he is an affiliated faculty member of the Center for Organizational Dynamics of the University of Pennsylvania, Philadelphia, as well as a faculty member of the Business School of Widener University, Philadelphia.

Dr. Kirchmer has been instrumental in designing and implementing business processes, as well as directing numerous business process improvement initiatives, including multiple process-orientated software implementations, especially in the field of SAP applications. In 1996, Dr. Kirchmer left Germany to serve as Vice President, then as President, and last as CEO of IDS Scheer North America and has since played a pivotal role in building the company's North American operations into a leading center for business process excellence. Since the beginning of 2001 he has also been responsible for the Japanese business of IDS Scheer. At the beginning of 2005 the management responsibility for South America was added to his responsibilities. In 2007 Dr. Kirchmer was appointed Chief Innovation and Marketing Officer for IDS Scheer Global, and thus moved to a corporate position of the IDS Scheer Group.

Dr. Kirchmer graduated from the Karlsruhe Technical University in Germany, with an MA in Computer Science and Business Administration. He also holds an MA in Economics from the Paris-Dauphine University in France. Dr. Kirchmer obtained a Ph.D from the Saarbrucken University in Germany, for his research concerning the business process-orientated implementation of standard software packages.

## Brian Lott

Brian Lott is Managing Director, Burson-Marsteller San Francisco. In addition, he is Burson-Marsteller's Global Client Leader for SAP, the world's leading provider of enterprise software. Based in San Francisco, he also manages the Technology Practice for the U.S. Western Region. Prior to assuming the global client leader role, Lott was the European Client Leader for SAP, working out of B-M's Frankfurt office. He also headed the B-M corporate practice in Germany. Lott began with B-M in Washington, D.C., where he served as the client leader for Securicor/Argenbright, ProcureNet, Greyhound Lines, and the Presidential Task Force on Employment of Adults with Disabilities. He has worked on a number of other significant Burson-Marsteller clients, including Accenture, Cordiem, Orbitz, and American Airlines. Prior to his career at B-M, Lott worked for 14 years on Capitol Hill. As Chief of Staff and Press Secretary to U.S. Rep. Jerry Costello, he served as the congressman's spokesperson, administrator, and legislative counsel for nine years. He also worked for U.S. Rep. Richard J. Durbin.

Lott has extensive experience in campaigning and politics. He served as campaign manager to Costello for Congress for five consecutive winning campaigns from 1990-1998, and worked on the communications staff at the 1988, 1996, and 2000 Democratic National Conventions.

Lott graduated from the University of Iowa with a Bachelor of Arts with Honors in Journalism and Mass Communication. He has also studied at the John F. Kennedy School of Government and City University of London.

## Chris Mark

Chris Mark is a member of the Corporate Strategy Group team in the Office of the CEO at SAP AG, one of the world's largest software companies. Corporate Strategy at SAP has operational responsibility for mid-term strategic planning, acquisitions strategy, and strategic performance management.

Prior to joining SAP in early 2006, Chris was part of the management team for the Operations Practice at The Boston Consulting Group, a leading strategy consulting firm. At BCG, he was responsible for worldwide research, marketing, and communications initiatives, as well as strategic partnerships and academic alliances.

From 1991 through 2000, Chris was an editor and writer for The Wall Street Journal in New York and Hong Kong, ultimately serving as Assistant National News Editor for technology and e-business.

## David Milam

David Milam is vice president, solution management, for SAP's Governance, Risk, and Compliance (GRC) business unit. He is responsible for product strategy and delivery and is regularly invited to speak internationally on the topics of corporate governance and enterprise risk. Previously, he led solution marketing for SAP's High-Tech sector; in this position he oversaw market strategy and positioning and identified opportunities and strategies that helped fuel rapid revenue growth.

Prior to SAP, Milam cofounded supply-chain software provider iMark (acquired by FreeMarkets), and held marketing and business development management positions at several enterprise software startups. He started his career at Procter & Gamble, where he executed new manufacturing and operational compliance initiatives. Milam holds a Bachelor of Engineering degree from the University of Illinois at Urbana-Champaign, and an MBA from Xavier University.

## Ryan Nichols

Ryan Nichols is a member of the Corporate Strategy Group team at SAP. In this role, he helps SAP understand how to best support information workers and drive customer and partner adoption of enterprise SOA. He supported the launch of SAP's internal strategy management process as well as SAP's acquisitions in this area.

Before joining SAP in 2004, Ryan's background spanned the world of software and consulting: client service at a retail-focused analytics software startup, product management at Intuit, and strategy consulting at McKinsey & Company. He is a graduate of Williams College and Stanford's Graduate School of Business, where he graduated as an Arjay Miller Scholar.

## Paul Austin Orleman

Paul is the Director of Top Talent Management, SAP Americas, in the Office of the CEO. He is responsible for accelerating the development of

SAP's high potential pool. Paul recently returned from a five-year expatriate assignment in Paris and Heidelberg, where he served as head of Global Management Development for SAP.

Previous roles at SAP included Director, Organizational Development, for the Americas and Europe/Middle East/Africa regions. Prior to joining SAP in 1998, Paul spent ten years with Rhone-Poulenc Rorer (RPR, now Sanofi-Aventis) in a variety of roles, including Director, Global Training and Development. His tenure with RPR included a four-year expatriate assignment in Paris.

Previous positions involved customer-driven TQM with ARBOR, Inc., Project Management consulting and training with Planalog, and Employee Development with Decision Data Computer Corporation.

Paul has a B.S. from Villanova University and a M.S. in Organizational Dynamics from the University of Pennsylvania. His passions include managing across cultures, global leadership development, intercultural team effectiveness, management excellence, and employee engagement.

### Sanjay Poonen

Sanjay Poonen is Senior VP and GM of Analytics at SAP, responsible for the analytic applications business at SAP, a key area of SAP Board's focus. Prior to SAP, Sanjay served as VP of Line of Business Operations, at Symantec, reporting to the President and Vice-Chairman and playing a key role in the merger integration of VERITAS and Symantec. Prior to the merger, Sanjay was Vice President of Strategic Operations at VERITAS with sales responsibility for $400MM+ of VERITAS' revenue from strategic accounts like Microsoft, IBM, HP, Sun, Dell, and others. Prior to VERITAS, Sanjay was at Informatica, where he served as an executive officer of the company, first as VP and GM of the Analytics Business Unit and then as SVP of Worldwide Marketing, growing Informatica's revenues to $220M and establishing Informatica's leadership in the data integration market. Prior to Informatica, Sanjay was a founder at Alphablox (acquired by IBM), and worked at Apple Computer, Taligent (acquired by IBM), and Regis McKenna Group. Sanjay started his career as a software engineer at Microsoft, working on early forms of Microsoft Exchange.

Sanjay has an MBA from Harvard Business School, where he graduated as a Baker Scholar; a Master's degree in Management Science and Engineering from Stanford University; and a Bachelor's degree in Computer Science & Math/Engineering from Dartmouth College where he graduated summa cum laude and Phi Beta Kappa.

## Josh Suskewicz

Josh Suskewicz is an Associate at Innosight where he has worked on consulting projects and executive education programs for financial services, media, consumer packaged goods, and automotive companies. A focus of Josh's work has been developing and applying the theories of business model innovation in dynamic market contexts.

Previously, Josh served as a research analyst covering emerging technologies in the alternative energy, clean technology, and sustainable development sectors. He has also worked as a researcher/writer for Let's Go Travel Guides and as a research assistant for a think tank focused on Middle Eastern history and politics. Josh holds an honors A.B. in English Literature from Harvard College.

## Adam Thier

Adam Thier is the vice president of development for SAP's corporate performance management products (CPM). Prior to SAP, Mr. Thier designed and ran the development of the other two primary CPM products on the market at both Hyperion and Cognos. With over 5000 organizations using these solutions, Mr. Thier is one of the most experienced and knowledgeable experts in the world on how world-class companies measure and manage their performance.

Prior to his CPM focus, his background was with more traditional financial software systems; VP of Financial Systems Development at Lawson Software, and Director or Product Marketing/Management at Computron. Mr. Thier also spent time as a Sr. Research Analyst at Meta Group, advising organizations on both their ERP systems, and the associated data warehouses and data marts.

## Daniel R. Trotzer

Dan currently serves as V.P. of Business Development with Bhootan, an interactive, out-of-home media company that introduces contemporary entertainment and advertising solutions to public environments via high definition digital television and mobile handsets.

Dan has over 12 years of experience in business development, marketing and strategy development roles for entrepreneurial and innovative companies such as CDNOW and Catavault with particular expertise in new technology commercialization.

Dan received his B.A. in Architecture from the University of Pennsylvania and his MBA from the Penn State Smeal College of Business where he received a graduate Assistantship with the Farrell Center for Corporate Innovation and Entrepreneurship. As a graduate assistant for the Farrell Center, Dan led a research initiative and co-authored a research paper focused on developing new models for the effective transfer of University-developed technology to the marketplace. The paper "Creative Models for University Technology Transfer" is currently under review for publication.

## N. Venkatraman

N. Venkatraman is the David J. McGrath Jr. Professor of Management at the Boston University School of Management. Previously, he taught at MIT Sloan School (1984-1993) and London Business School (1999-2001). He was awarded the 2004 and 2006 IBM Faculty Fellowship for his work focusing on business challenges in the network era. His research and teaching lie at the interface between strategic management and information technology with a particular focus on how companies position to win in a network era.

He has been recently recognized by Thomson Financial/ISI as one of the most cited researchers in strategy and information technology. His 1989 paper in Management Science is considered as one of the highly cited papers over the 50 years of the history of the journal. His research has won awards from *The Academy of Management* (AT Kearney Award for Outstanding Doctoral Research) and *Strategic Management Society* (McKinsey Honorable Mention) and his doctoral students have been awarded prizes for their thesis work.

He writes papers for managerial audience and academic publications. His papers for managers have been published in the *Sloan Management Review* over the last decade. He has also published in *IBM Systems Journal* (1993 Special Issue on Strategic Alignment, the Turning Points issue in 2000), *Business Strategy Review* (London Business School) and *Financial Times*. His academic research has been published in *Management Science, Strategic Management Journal, Information Systems Review, Academy of Management Journal, Academy of Management Review,* and others.

He has consulted and/or lectured for many corporations in the USA, Europe, and South Africa including IBM, Microsoft, CSC, BP, Novartis, Ericsson, Canal+, ABN-AMRO, Zurich Financial, McKinsey & Co., Federal Express and others. He holds a B. Tech degree from IIT, Kharagpur (1976); an MBA from IIM Calcutta (1979); and Ph.D. from University of Pittsburgh (1985). Presently, he is engaged in a variety of projects to understand the challenges of winning.

# INDEX

Printing: Krips bv, Meppel, The Netherlands
Binding: Stürtz, Würzburg, Germany